ENGAGING THE
NEW TESTAMENT

ENGAGING THE

NEW TESTAMENT

A SHORT INTRODUCTION
FOR STUDENTS AND MINISTERS

MIGUEL G. ECHEVARRÍA

Baker Academic
a division of Baker Publishing Group
Grand Rapids, Michigan

© 2024 by Miguel G. Echevarría

Published by Baker Academic
a division of Baker Publishing Group
Grand Rapids, Michigan
www.bakeracademic.com

Printed in the United States of America

Library of Congress Cataloging-in-Publication Data
Names: Echevarría, Miguel G., Jr., author.
Title: Engaging the New Testament : a short introduction for students and ministers / Miguel G.
    Echevarría.
Description: Grand Rapids, Michigan : Baker Academic, a division of Baker Publishing Group,
    [2024] | Includes bibliographical references and index.
Identifiers: LCCN 2023035149 | ISBN 9781540963796 (paperback) | ISBN 9781540967268
    (casebound) | ISBN 9781493444250 (ebook) | ISBN 9781493444267 (pdf)
Subjects: LCSH: Bible. New Testament—Study and teaching.
Classification: LCC BS2535.3 .E25 2024 | DDC 225.6/1076—dc23/eng/20230921
LC record available at https://lccn.loc.gov/2023035149

Baker Publishing Group publications use paper produced from sustainable forestry practices and post-consumer waste whenever possible.

24   25   26   27   28   29   30   7   6   5   4   3   2   1

For Francis,
precious child
(1 Cor. 15:53–55)

CONTENTS

ACKNOWLEDGMENTS

Writing books is not for the faint of heart. The process has many stages, including everything from rough drafts to copyediting to final proofs. Not to mention initial research and writing. There is also rewriting and more rewriting until the work starts to make sense. At least to the author, anyway. Along the way, there is joy and exhilaration but also weariness and frustration. Without help and support, a book will rarely reach the publication stage. That's why it takes a village to raise a book.

Several people directly contributed to the growth and maturity of this one. Bryan Dyer of Baker Academic oversaw the manuscript from its infantile stage as a proposal to its more developed stage as a publishable manuscript. His suggestions were always helpful and insightful. Melisa Blok's editorial care for the manuscript made it fit to be released into the world. Daniel Carroll Rodas is a father to many in our village, especially to those of us who grew up on arroz con frijoles. His advice on life and academics was invaluable for the completion of this project. Southeastern Baptist Theological Seminary doctoral student and academic assistant Hayden Fleming read the initial draft of the manuscript and provided careful feedback. He also assisted with the figures in appendix 1—without him readers would have been left with crooked lines, leading to an entirely new solution to the Synoptic problem. Last but not least, I would like to thank my wife, Hollie, for supporting my work and allowing me extra time in the evenings and on the weekends to bring this book to completion. Your grace has enabled this book to reach a level of maturity that will hopefully result in the spiritual growth of those who read it.

ONE

INTRODUCTION

Those who teach and research in the field of New Testament studies have likely read dozens of New Testament introductions. So they may approach this book with a caricature of the content associated with such volumes, expecting extensive analyses of critical matters such as authorship, dating, and audience, with little discussion of the text of Scripture. Others may be less acquainted with biblical introductions and so have different expectations.

This book is unlike the majority of New Testament introductions. It is not that critical matters are unimportant for a seminary or college curriculum or interested laypeople. It is just that there are already plenty of texts that provide extensive discussions on issues such as form criticism of the Gospels and the authorship of the Pastoral epistles. This introduction focuses more on what is "in" the text of Scripture than on the historical issues that lie "behind" it.

With that in mind, the following sections highlight the distinctives of this book, which distinguish it from standard introductions to the New Testament. These distinctives set the expectations for my approach to the New Testament writings. The chapter closes with an overview of the book's content.

Light on Historical Criticism

Many students and pastors may be unaware of the history of New Testament introductions—that they arose from modernity's quest to understand the origins of ancient texts. This pursuit is better known as "historical criticism."

New Testament introductions have changed relatively little since the 1800s.[1] They still, for instance, take an approach akin to that in Heinrich Holtzmann's two-volume *Introduction to the New Testament* and the similarly titled three-volume work of Theodor Zahn, both written in the late nineteenth century. These works focus on issues such as text criticism, redaction criticism, source criticism, and the authorship and historical setting of each book in the New Testament.[2] Since then, the field has changed little—still bound to the similar set of assumptions that has guided standard works for the last several centuries. One of the most curious aspects of this observation is that even many evangelicals, who claim a high view of Scripture, follow the unspoken rules for biblical introductions set by higher criticism, prioritizing details about how we got our texts over interpreting their final canonical forms.

For the sake of clarification, I am not saying that critical matters are unimportant. That would be taking my observations in a far too *uncritical* direction. Students and pastors should have a firm grasp of the authorship of the disputed Pauline epistles, the Synoptic problem, the authorship of the writings historically attributed to the apostle John, and various other arguments related to the history and composition of the New Testament writings. Too often, however, introductions focus on critical matters, with only cursory discussions of the twenty-seven books of the New Testament. Consequently, what students and laypersons spend most of their time studying is radically different from the concerns of those serving the church, who are generally more interested in interpreting and applying the Scriptures. This volume will be sensitive to this reality, providing streamlined and accessible background discussions related to the New Testament writings while focusing on interpreting the New Testament writings.

Critical discussions normally found at the beginning of introductions, such as discussions of the Synoptic problem, have been placed in appendixes. This is so that readers will not get bogged down by too many historical matters before ever getting to the text. Critical issues normally associated with individual books—such as authorship, dating, and audience—are located at the end of the respective chapters on the canonical books of the New Testament.

---

1. Two of the first New Testament introductions were Richard Simon's *Histoire critique du texte du Nouveau Testament* (Rotterdam: Reinier Leers, 1689) and J. D. Michaelis, *Einleitung in die göttlichen Schriften des Neuen Bundes*, 4th rev. ed., 2 vols. (Göttingen: Vandenhoeck & Ruprecht, 1788).

2. Theodor Zahn's original version was written in German. The faculty at Hartford Theological Seminary made a formal request for the book's translation into English. See Zahn's *Introduction to the New Testament*, 3 vols., trans. Melanchthon Williams Jacobus (Edinburgh: T&T Clark, 1909).

This approach makes essential critical information available in a way that will not distract from the interpretation of the New Testament text.

Focused on the New Testament Books in Their Canonical Contexts

"Canon" is a term we will use throughout the book. So it is important that we know what it means. The word is of Greek origin, referring to a "rule" or "standard."[3] Over time, it came to refer to the official collection of Christian Scriptures, those writings deemed inspired and authoritative for believers. These books are considered "canonical," each contributing their individual voice to the collective message of Scripture.

Chapter 2 will elaborate on what it means to read canonically. For now, we affirm that the Gospels, Acts, the Pauline epistles, the Catholic epistles, and Revelation form the parameters of the New Testament canon and are themselves situated within the whole Bible. The New Testament writings are organized not according to their chronological order of composition but according to their place in the redemptive story of Scripture. The Gospel of John, for instance, concludes with the expectation that the resurrected Jesus will send his Spirit. Acts then narrates the arrival of the promised Spirit, who empowers the apostles to take the gospel of the kingdom to the nations. The sequential organization of John and Acts does not reflect chronology. If their arrangement were based on chronology, then John (written in the AD 80s) would be located after Acts (written in the AD 60s). As it stands, the canonical placement of these writings is determined by their contribution to the biblical story.

This book focuses on interpreting the New Testament books in their canonical contexts. This approach depends on interpreting books not according to their precise dating but according to their contribution to the canon of Scripture.

Sensitive to Ministry-Related Application

Those involved in theological education of some sort, whether in the academy or the local church, know that students of the Bible want to know more than just how to interpret the text. They want to know how to apply it. They want to know how to connect what they are learning to ministry. Since most

3. Roger T. Beckwith, "The Canon of Scripture," in *New Dictionary of Biblical Theology*, ed. T. Desmond Alexander and Brian S. Rosner (Downers Grove, IL: InterVarsity, 2000), 27–34; Bruce M. Metzger, *The Canon of the New Testament: Its Origin, Development, and Significance* (Oxford: Clarendon, 1997), 289–93.

introductions are more concerned about historical-critical matters, they fail to discuss the importance of applying the biblical text. Without taking anything away from critical discussions, New Testament introductions should encourage application to real-life scenarios. This book addresses the application of biblical content through sidebar discussions that encourage readers to think about applying texts to various ministry contexts.

User-Friendly

This book is written with both the student and the teacher in mind. For the student, the book is informed by the latest scholarship, yet the language and terminology are accessible to those with no prior theological education. More difficult terms like "propitiation" and "righteousness" are defined. The book includes discussions on recent scholarship, such as the New Perspective on Paul and John Barclay's *Paul and the Gift*, in sidebar notes. For the teacher, the chapters follow a logical flow that can be used in one-semester survey classes at the college or seminary level.

Content of the Book

The distinctives shape how the book presents the content. Readers should expect that every chapter is (1) light on historical criticism, (2) focused on reading the New Testament books in their canonical contexts, (3) sensitive to ministry-related application, and (4) user-friendly. In keeping with these distinctives, the following is an overview of the book's content.

- Chapter 2 provides the canonical context for reading the New Testament, overviewing the essential thematic elements of the Old Testament canon and discussing the development and order of the New Testament canon.
- Chapter 3 discusses the interpretive approach of the New Testament authors, such as how they use the Old Testament in their writings to show that Jesus fulfills centuries of messianic expectations.
- Chapter 4 commences the study of the New Testament with a discussion of the Gospels and Acts.
- Chapter 5 covers the undisputed and disputed Pauline epistles. Since we are reading canonically, what matters is the Christian community's acceptance of a book's authoritative status. So we give equal importance

to all the Pauline epistles, regardless of concerns about authorship. We apply this principle to all disputed books of the New Testament.

- Chapter 6 covers the Catholic (or General) epistles. Though the Gospels and Paul's letters often receive more attention, the Catholic epistles contain important admonitions about eschatology, holy living, and false teachers in light of Christ's second coming.
- Chapter 7 addresses the book of Revelation, a fitting climax to the New Testament and the entire canon of Scripture.
- The appendixes include critical information about the relationship between the Gospels and about the text of the New Testament. In keeping with the book's distinctives, this material is available at the end of the book so as not to take the focus off the actual text of the New Testament.

I hope the book's focus on the New Testament text will cause readers to grow in their love for God and others. Augustine puts it well: "Whoever, then, thinks that he understands the Holy Scriptures, or any part of them, but puts such an interpretation upon them as does not tend to build up this twofold love of God and our neighbor, does not yet understand them as he ought."[4]

SUGGESTED RESOURCES

Beale, G. K., and Benjamin L. Gladd. *The Story Retold: A Biblical-Theological Introduction to the New Testament*. Downers Grove, IL: IVP Academic, 2020.

Campbell, Constantine R., and Jonathan T. Pennington. *Reading the New Testament as Christian Scripture: A Literary, Canonical, and Theological Survey*. Grand Rapids: Baker Academic, 2020.

Carson, D. A., and Douglas J. Moo. *An Introduction to the New Testament*. 2nd ed. Grand Rapids: Zondervan, 2005.

Köstenberger, Andreas J., L. Scott Kellum, and Charles L. Quarles. *The Cradle, the Cross, and the Crown: An Introduction to the New Testament*. 2nd ed. Nashville: B&H Academic, 2016.

Kruger, Michael J., ed. *A Biblical-Theological Introduction to the New Testament: The Gospel Realized*. Wheaton: Crossway, 2016.

Nienhuis, David R. *A Concise Guide to Reading the New Testament: A Canonical Introduction*. Grand Rapids: Baker Academic, 2018.

---

4. Augustine of Hippo, *On Christian Doctrine* 1.36.40, trans. J. F. Shaw, in *Nicene and Post-Nicene Fathers*, series 1, ed. Philip Schaff (Buffalo: Christian Literature Company, 1887), 2:533.

TWO

THE CANONICAL CONTEXT
FOR THE
NEW TESTAMENT

The Bible is an extraordinary book—some would argue the most extraordinary! The more often we read the Bible from beginning to end, the more we are fascinated by the story that runs through its sixty-six books. The major divisions in which we encounter these books are the Old Testament, which is composed of thirty-nine books, and the New Testament, which is composed of twenty-seven books. Together, each of the sixty-six books contributes to a riveting narrative. The story loses its coherence if we read the books of the Bible as if they tell separate or irreconcilable accounts. We would not do that with the chapters in stories like *Don Quixote* or the Chronicles of Narnia. So why would we do that with the books of the Bible?

The Bible hints about the kind of story it tells in the names of its major divisions, the Old and New Testaments. The word "testament" comes from the Latin word *testamentum*, translated as "covenant." The Bible tells a covenantal story, wherein lie written expectations and consequences between two parties: God and humans. Scripture testifies to God's unwavering covenantal loyalty and humanity's unfaithfulness, which requires the intervention of a faithful God to save his people from the curses they deserve.

Another important matter is the order of the Old and New Testaments. That the Old Testament precedes the New Testament does not mean that the

INTRODUCTORY QUESTIONS

Before we read the remainder of the chapter, let's take a moment to think about the following questions. Have you ever considered reading the Bible as a coherent story? Have you thought about the contribution each book makes to the Bible? Have you considered that the books of the Bible have been arranged so as to facilitate the narrative that runs throughout Scripture? What difference would such considerations make to your interpretation of Scripture?

prior corpus is inferior or obsolete.[1] A helpful way to think about the relationship between the testaments is one of promise and fulfillment.[2] The Old Testament records covenantal promises, which find their fulfillment in the New Testament. The promises are fulfilled in Jesus the Messiah, who initiates a new covenant in his blood (Jer. 31:31–34; Matt. 26:28; Luke 22:20). The testaments therefore exist in a state of shared continuity, the story of which climaxes and coheres in the person and work of Jesus. Moreover, the arrival of Jesus in the New Testament is what allows us to read the Old Testament in view of a forward-pointing trajectory. We see this when we read Scripture "backwards," taking our interpretive framework from the New Testament. In so doing, our eyes are opened to how institutions like the priesthood and figures like Moses find their fulfillment in Jesus the Messiah.[3]

These matters prepare us to familiarize ourselves with the canonical context for reading the New Testament. We will start with the major thematic elements of the Old Testament so that we can then understand how New Testament books fit within the larger context of Scripture. Then we will discuss the development of the New Testament canon and the order of the New Testament books. The latter will be important for our discussion on the canonical function of books, since the order of the twenty-seven New Testament documents is based not on chronology but on the progression of the covenantal story from the Old Testament to its continuation and conclusion in the New Testament.

1. My thoughts here are influenced by Constantine R. Campbell and Jonathan T. Pennington, *Reading the New Testament as Christian Scripture: A Literary, Canonical, and Theological Survey* (Grand Rapids: Baker Academic, 2020), 4–5. Given the pejorative connotations associated with the word "old," Christopher Seitz prefers the term "Elder Testament." *The Elder Testament: Canon, Theology, Trinity* (Waco: Baylor University Press, 2018), 13–14.

2. Craig L. Blomberg follows this pattern in his *A New Testament Theology* (Waco: Baylor University Press, 2018).

3. See Richard B. Hays, *Reading Backwards: Figural Christology and the Fourfold Gospel Witness* (Waco: Baylor University Press, 2014).

▮ Old Testament

The contents of the Old Testament are associated with the old covenant.[4] The Pentateuch and historical books, for instance, establish a link with "the book of the covenant" (e.g., Exod. 24:7; Deut. 29:20; 2 Chron. 34:30).[5] The author of the second-century Jewish writing 1 Maccabees calls an individual book of Scripture "a book of the covenant" (1:57). As a new-covenant Jew, Paul speaks of Israel's Scriptures as "the old covenant" (2 Cor. 3:14).[6] While there is more we can say, such observations show that the Old Testament could just as well be called "the old covenant Scriptures."

The Old Testament is organized along the lines of a tripart division known as the Law, the Prophets, and the Writings.[7] While the Law contains promissory elements, it also stipulates the regulations (Exodus, Leviticus, Deuteronomy) and blessings and curses (Lev. 17–26; Deut. 28) associated with the old covenant. It even specifies the penalties for altering the covenantal documents (Deut. 4; 30). After Israel is exiled for violating the covenant, the prophets anticipate a renewal of the covenant (Isa. 54–55; Ezek. 37). The final book of the Writings, long after the original exile, awaits the fulfillment of the covenant with David, which will initiate a kingdom of peace and justice (1 Chron. 17; cf. 2 Sam. 7).

Some of the most significant themes that run through the divisions of the old covenant writings are the promises to Abraham, the exodus story, the promises to David, the exile from the land, and the expectation of a messiah who will crush Israel's enemies and establish his dominion to the ends of the earth. These topics are carried into the new covenant writings, making them essential for a canonical reading of the New Testament.

Abrahamic Promises

The promises to Abraham come on the heels of Genesis 1–11 (the creation story and the exile from the garden). Though humanity falls into sin, God

4. See also Gregory Goswell, "The Two Testaments as Covenant Documents," *Journal of the Evangelical Theological Society* 62, no. 4 (2019): 677–92.

5. Andreas J. Köstenberger, L. Scott Kellum, and Charles L. Quarles, *The Cradle, the Cross, and the Crown: An Introduction to the New Testament*, 2nd ed. (Nashville: B&H Academic, 2016), 32.

6. Meredith G. Kline, "Canon and Covenant, Part II: All Scripture Covenantal," *Bulletin of the Evangelical Theological Society* 9 (1966): 179.

7. This is known as the Hebrew order, the *Tanakh* (TNK). The term stands for Torah (Law), Nevi'im (Prophets), and Ketuvim (Writings). Most English Bibles follow a different order: History, Wisdom, and Prophets. On the subject of the order of the Old Testament canon, see Roger T. Beckwith, *The Old Testament Canon of the New Testament Church and Its Background in Early Judaism* (1985; repr., Eugene, OR: Wipf & Stock, 2008), 181–234.

promises that a descendant of Eve will crush the head of the serpent, reversing the curses on creation and returning the world to its prior Edenic state (Gen. 3:15). Christians call this promise the *protoevangelium*, the first announcement of the gospel. Thereafter, humanity looks for one to bring healing to the earth. Lamech, for instance, says this about his son Noah: "Out of the ground the Lord has cursed, he shall bring us relief from our labor and the painful toil of our hands" (5:29). But Noah was not the one to bring relief to creation. Centuries would pass with no sign of a redeemer.

This is where Abraham enters the Genesis narrative. Abraham has no pious background—he is a pagan from the land of Ur. True to his gracious character, God promises Abraham that he "will be a blessing" (Gen. 12:2) and that in him "all peoples on earth will be blessed" (12:3). This means that Abraham will be the vehicle through which diverse peoples from different lands will be incorporated into his family and experience blessing. The visible manifestation of this future blessing is that God will reverse the judgment on creation, restoring paradise for Abraham's descendants.[8] Simply put, Abraham's diverse family will be restored to a cosmic Eden, where they will flourish forever.

This hopeful future is outlined in terms of a covenant, in which God promises Abraham land, innumerable offspring, and blessing (Gen. 15; 17). These promises will be fulfilled when God brings Abraham's *descendants* into a *land* where they will experience all the *blessings* of a new creation. This means much more, but certainly not less, than a new Eden.

From this point on, Scripture's narrative anticipates a descendant of Abraham who will fulfill the Abrahamic covenant promises. Abraham's descendant is one and the same with the offspring of the woman who is expected to reverse the curses and restore Eden.

The Exodus Story

The end of Genesis recounts how Abraham's descendants, Jacob and his sons, make their way to Egypt. It explains that a severe famine drives them to Egypt in search of food (Gen. 42:5). Though Jacob's sons had sold Joseph into slavery, God would exalt Joseph to become the second most powerful official in Egypt. Joseph would use his influence to provide land and food for his family. After the death of Joseph's generation, Jacob's descendants multiply throughout the land of Egypt. The text says that they became "exceedingly

---

8. Craig G. Bartholomew and Michael W. Goheen, *The Drama of Scripture: Finding Our Place in the Biblical Story* (Grand Rapids: Baker Academic, 2014), 53.

fruitful" (Exod. 1:7). The strength of the Israelites threatens Pharaoh, so he decides to make them slaves (1:8–14).

With the Abrahamic promises in peril, God raises up Moses to lead his people out of slavery (Exod. 3–14). Though Moses is the leader, God himself sends ten plagues upon the Egyptians, the final one being the death of the firstborn, and leads them through the waters of the Red Sea (Exod. 15). From there, God leads the Israelites through the wilderness and to the promised land. So important is the story of salvation from Egypt that the psalmist and the prophets use the exodus story as the pattern for a future act of deliverance for God's people. What they anticipate is a "new exodus."

Before God's people exit the wilderness, God calls them to be "a kingdom of priests" (Exod. 19:6). This means that the Israelites are to obey God's law in the land into which he is bringing them, reflecting his character to the nations. The essence of the law is found in the "ten words" or "ten commands" given to Moses at Mount Sinai, which are summed up in loving God and neighbor (Exod. 20). Israel is to be like Adam and Eve in the garden, enjoying the blessing of living in the presence of God. As it did with their parents, covenantal blessing depends on obedience to God's commands, and disobedience brings the curse of exile from the land (Deut. 28). This means that Abraham's people are to live an Edenic existence in the land. Failure to do so will mean expulsion from the (new) garden, much like Adam and Eve were exiled from Eden.

Davidic Promises

After the death of Moses, God raises up a new generation to possess the land, where they are to carry out their priestly vocation (Josh. 1:1–9). Following the period of the judges, Israel establishes itself as a kingdom. The first king, Saul, is tall and handsome but far from one who exemplifies the kind of Torah obedience expected of Israel's monarch (1 Sam. 13:11–13). God then raises up David, a king after God's very heart (13:14).

Though Israel is experiencing rest, God makes a covenant with David, promising, "I will provide a place for my people Israel and will plant them so that they can have a home of their own and no longer be disturbed" (2 Sam. 7:10).[9] There, Israel will experience a better rest. God also promises to establish the eternal reign of David's offspring. Since David is the offspring of Abraham, the one through whom God will establish his people as an eternal

---

9. This section draws on Miguel G. Echevarría Jr., *The Future Inheritance of Land in the Pauline Epistles* (Eugene, OR: Pickwick, 2019), 46–49.

kingdom is a descendant of Abraham. The land in which Israel resides, then, is only a picture of the better land over which a lasting Davidic monarch will reign. This is the figure who will fulfill the promises to Abraham and, ultimately, to humanity.

Exile

The kingdom of Israel flourishes under Solomon, whose reign begins with messianic overtones.[10] He builds the temple and brings the ark of the covenant into the inner sanctuary (1 Kings 6–8). The ark represents God's presence and contains the "ten words" or "ten commands" given to Moses. With the ark in the temple, God is dwelling in the midst of his people. Under Solomon, the people appear to experience rest with God as in the days of Eden, leading readers to imagine that Solomon is the Davidic descendant through whom God will fulfill his promises.

But this hope is short-lived. Echoing the covenantal blessings and curses of Deuteronomy 28, God appears to Solomon and promises to establish his kingdom forever, if he will walk in obedience, or to remove Israel from the land, if he walks in disobedience (1 Kings 9:3–9). Despite the warning, Solomon marries foreign women who turn his heart to other gods (11:1–8). This begins Israel's long and hard road to exile.

Following Solomon's death, the kingdom divides into southern and northern tribes. Most of the kings who succeed Solomon practice idolatry and selfish rule (1 Kings 12–2 Kings 25). The kings do not exemplify covenant faithfulness, falling woefully short of the expectations for David's descendants.

This leads to the inevitable exile promised in Deuteronomy and reiterated to Solomon, the exile about which prophets like Elijah and Elisha warned. The northern tribes are the first to go into exile in 722 BC and are deported to Assyria (2 Kings 17). Later, Babylon takes the southern tribes into exile in 586 BC (2 Kings 24). What God forewarned comes true: the people are driven from their garden, like Adam and Eve were driven from Eden. Their only hope is for God to raise up a deliverer to fulfill the promises.

The Promised Messiah

Although Israel is in exile, the prophets do not lose faith in their covenant-keeping God. Ezekiel, for instance, anticipates that God will deliver his people into an Edenic land over which a Davidic monarch will rule (Ezek. 37:15–28).

10. Echevarría, *Future Inheritance*, 50.

At this time, God will cleanse his people of their sins and place his Spirit in them, enabling them to obey his commands (36:25–27). This time is also associated with the hope that Israel's "dry bones" will come to life. This is Ezekiel's way of anticipating the period when God will resurrect his people to a land where the curses will have been removed and where they will experience peace under the rule of David's promised offspring.

The psalmist describes David's descendant as God's very son (Ps. 2:7). The psalmist also assumes that the land over which this descendant will rule has expanded beyond the original borders of the promised land to include the entire earth (2:8). Isaiah affirms the expanded nature of the land promise when he looks forward to Israel dwelling in a new heavens and earth (Isa. 65–66). Both the psalmist and Isaiah speak of the future deliverance of Israel as a "new exodus" that will culminate in entering a better land.

So strong is Isaiah's hope for a new exodus that he structures chapters 40–66 in view of Israel's original deliverance from Egypt. Only this time the deliverer will not be Moses—it will be God himself. Isaiah 40:3 sets the tone for the section:

> In the wilderness prepare
>   the way for the LORD;
> make straight in the desert
>   a highway for our God.

In other words, Isaiah envisions that God will save his people again, delivering them through the wilderness of this sinful world, ending once and for all their exile from the garden. The cosmic exile will end with an entrance into a new heavens and earth, a new Eden (Isa. 65–66). All this will be made possible through a "suffering servant" who will bear the curses of the covenant to deliver his people from exile (Isa. 52–53). Isaiah's servant, then, takes the curses upon himself, in place of the people, to deliver them from the exile they deserve for sinning against their God (cf. Jer. 33:4–11; Ezek. 36–37).[11]

All in all, the Old Testament expects a royal figure, God's very son, who will suffer to deliver his people from their state of exile outside the promised land. This person is one and the same with the offspring of the woman and descendant of Abraham, who will bring healing to the entire earth. While some may argue that Ezra marks Israel's return to the land, the text is very

11. See N. T. Wright's discussion in *Jesus and the Victory of God* (Minneapolis: Fortress, 1996), 268–74.

DIFFERENT OLD TESTAMENT ENDINGS

Hebrew manuscripts contain a couple of competing endings to the Old Testament. One ending closes with Ezra-Nehemiah, noting that Israel is still enslaved to foreign rulers (Ezra 9; Neh. 9). From this, we deduce that Israel is still in exile, still awaiting the historical return to the land. The other ends with Chronicles, reiterating the promises to David (1 Chron. 17) and Cyrus's edict to return to the land (2 Chron. 36:23). This version assumes that Israel has not yet returned to their rightful territory and is still awaiting the day when the Messiah returns to establish their people in the land promised to them. Neither the Ezra-Nehemiah ending nor the Chronicles ending assumes fulfillment—for both await the future realization of the promises.

clear that the people were "slaves" to foreign rulers, like when they were in Egypt or Babylon (Ezra 9; Neh. 9). The promises have not been fulfilled. The people are still in exile, still expecting liberation from their enemies, still waiting to dwell in a cosmic kingdom that will stretch far beyond the borders of the original promised land. This glorious future will coincide with the time when God makes a new covenant with his people, which will be marked by the work of the Spirit on their hearts, enabling them to obey their God (Jer. 31:33–34; Ezek. 36:26–27; Joel 2:28–29). This expectation, which runs throughout the Old Testament, establishes the covenantal context for the fulfillment of the promises in the New Testament.

New Testament

The New Testament documents were written several centuries after Israel's so-called return to the land. Even before their composition, other historical accounts about the teachings of Jesus existed. Luke, for example, claims to have examined eyewitness accounts closely (Luke 1:1–4), and Paul sometimes appeals to Jesus traditions with which his communities would have been familiar (1 Cor. 7).

Such traditions did not remain isolated from a larger story or context. While we can speculate about their forms or content, the teachings of Jesus were incorporated into canonical books, just like Moses's teachings were incorporated into the Old Testament.[12] Their final form arose out of a need

12. John H. Sailhamer argues for a "text-oriented" approach to the Old Testament (*Introduction to Old Testament Theology: A Canonical Approach* [Grand Rapids: Zondervan,

for new covenant documents—much like the Old Testament arose out of a need for old covenant documents. Moreover, the sequence of books in the New Testament is based on the progression of the story from the Old Testament to its fulfillment in the New Testament. Thus, it is important to discuss the development and canonical function of the order of New Testament books.

Development of the Canon

The arrival of the messianic age brought with it the expectation of new covenant writings. Paul and Peter suggest that, as early as the first century, these writings were considered on par with those of the Old Testament (1 Tim. 5:18; 2 Pet. 3:16). In other words, they were of equal authority, containing many of the same elements as the old covenant writings, such as regulations for obedience (Matt. 5–7) and warnings against disobedience (Gal. 5:18–20). The curses found in Revelation 22:18–19, which bear the influence of Deuteronomy 4 and 30, come at the conclusion of the New Testament writings. This suggests, as Gregory Goswell argues, "that those responsible for shaping the canon in this way viewed the NT *in toto* as a covenantal document."[13] The New Testament authors affirm the covenantal nature of their writings, envisioning themselves as "ministers of a new covenant," writing about the fulfillment of the promises to the renewed covenant community (e.g., 2 Cor. 3:6).[14]

The New Testament's writings were accepted on par with those of the Old Testament. David's son had finally arrived, initiating the time of deliverance from exile and the fulfillment of the Abrahamic promises (2 Sam. 7:10–16). This son is the one who will lead his people on a new exodus to a new creation, just like Isaiah envisioned. He will also place his Spirit in his people, leading them to obey their God, something with which the old covenant community struggled (Jer. 31; Ezek. 36–37; Joel 2). All this necessitated new covenant documents in which authors like Matthew and the author of Hebrews show how Jesus fulfills the promises to their spiritual ancestors.

Since New Testament authors explain how Jesus fulfills the promises, we assume a covenantal connection between the Old and New Testaments. Meredith Kline argues, "For the historical relationship sustained by the new covenant to the old covenant and the place occupied by the New Testament

---

1995], 36–85). I will take a similar approach to the New Testament, focusing on the actual text of Scripture.

13. Goswell, "Two Testaments," 689.

14. Kline, "Canon and Covenant," 198.

as the divine documentation of the new covenant compel us to understand the New Testament as a resumption of that documentary mode of covenant administration represented by the Old Testament."[15]

Criteria for Acceptance in the Canon

The acceptance of these "new" writings was not dependent on the rulings of later councils. In fact, by the second century there was widespread agreement on the canonical status of the Gospels, Acts, the Pauline epistles, 1 Peter, and 1 John.[16] The remaining books were generally accepted by the fourth century. The role of councils like Laodicea (AD 363), Hippo Regius in North Africa (AD 363), and the Third Council of Carthage (AD 397) was to affirm the Scriptures that churches had already recognized as new covenant documents. There was no great debate over the canonical status of the New Testament writings. Nor was there a coordinated political effort that drove the acceptance of certain books over others. The church councils were officially recognizing the writings that were *already* considered authoritative Scripture—in some cases, for centuries.[17]

Early Christians used certain criteria to ascertain the authoritative status of certain writings over others. The first is based on a given writing's conformity to the Rule of Faith, the second on its apostolic origin, and the third on its regular use among the churches.[18] Even with such criteria, it is important to note that there was not unanimity or universal agreement but a general consensus about the twenty-seven books of the New Testament.

RULE OF FAITH

An essential element of canonicity was whether the document conformed to the Rule of Faith.[19] The earliest Christian communities were the initial recipients of and witnesses to the story of how Jesus the Messiah died and

15. Kline, "Canon and Covenant," 196. See also Michael J. Kruger, *Canon Revisited: Establishing the Origins and Authority of the New Testament Books* (Wheaton: Crossway, 2012).

16. Peter T. Balla, "The Canon of Scripture," in *New Dictionary of Biblical Theology*, ed. Desmond T. Alexander and Brian S. Rosner (Downers Grove, IL: InterVarsity, 2000), 30; Köstenberger, Kellum, and Quarles, *Cradle, the Cross, and the Crown*, 17–32.

17. Peter T. Balla, "Evidence for an Early Christian Canon (Second and Third Century)," in *The Canon Debate*, ed. Lee Martin McDonald and James A. Sanders (Peabody, MA: Hendrickson, 2002), 372–85.

18. These criteria are also found in Bruce M. Metzger, *The Canon of the New Testament: Its Origin, Development, and Significance* (Oxford: Clarendon, 1997), 251–54.

19. The Rule of Faith is synonymous with other terms such as "the canon of truth" and "the rule of truth." Metzger, *Canon*, 252.

rose from the dead, initiating a new covenant and the restoration of the entire creation. Understood in this light, the Rule sets the normative beliefs of the Christian tradition, such as the incarnation of Jesus and the bodily resurrection, within the larger cosmic drama of the covenant-keeping God.[20] Jesus, Abraham's descendant and God's very Son, was the key to understanding this unfolding story of redemption. Being a people who had inherited the story of Israel, early Christians grounded their normative beliefs, their Rule, within the expectations of Old Testament Scriptures, which will be fulfilled when Jesus returns to consummate the eschaton.[21]

There are arguments about whether the Rule was circulated in oral or written form, as well as whether its original contents were invariable or flexible enough for teachers to expand on its message to combat heresy. In whatever form it was inherited, Christians were sufficiently aware of its essential contents to discern writings that were in accordance with the normative teachings of the church.

Second-century church fathers Irenaeus and Origen were some of the most ardent supporters of the Rule. In his *Demonstration of the Apostolic Preaching*, Irenaeus explains the nature of the Rule by retelling the biblical narrative, focusing on the promises fulfilled in the work of Jesus the Messiah. In his *Against Heresies*, Irenaeus argues that Gnostics impose a "foreign storyline" on the Scriptures, which is contrary to the one presented in the Rule (1.9.4).[22] The late second-century and early third-century church father Tertullian uses a similar argument when combating heretics (*The Prescription against Heretics*, 39.5–7). Origen operates "within the Rule," as Paul Blowers argues, "honoring the narrative framework of Scripture through his vision of a divine discipline leading fallen humanity progressively toward transcendence and stability from which free beings will ultimately never lapse."[23] While his exegesis betrays a Platonic influence, Origen strives to place the struggle of human beings within the story of creation and redemption.[24] For Irenaeus and Origen, the Rule guides what is normative Christian teaching, separating orthodoxy from heresy.

---

20. See N. T. Wright, *The New Testament and the People of God* (Minneapolis: Fortress, 1992), 456.

21. Christopher Seitz, "Canon, Covenant and Rule of Faith—The Use of Scripture in Communion," *International Journal for the Study of the Christian Church* 8, no. 2 (May 2008): 81–84; Paul M. Blowers, "The *Regula Fidei* and the Narrative Character of Early Christian Faith," *Pro Ecclesia* 6 (1997): 199–215.

22. Blowers, "*Regula Fidei*," 210.

23. Blowers, "*Regula Fidei*," 218.

24. See Origen's discussion on the consummation of all things in *On First Principles*, where he contends that "the goodness of God through Christ will restore his entire creation to one

GNOSTICISM

Full-blown Gnosticism arose in the second century AD. A core belief of Gnosticism was that Jesus came to give people "knowledge" (*gnōsis*) of their true selves—their souls—imprisoned in their bodies. Such insight would result in the salvation of the soul from the fallen, physical realm and into the divine realm of light. Gnosticism likely arose from Platonism, which places a similar emphasis on the spiritual over the material.

This very Rule was used by the wider Christian community to measure books that claimed the status of Scripture. A book was to be in accordance with the story of Scripture, which was inherited from Israel, and in line with assertions about basic Christian orthodoxy. Aside from the incarnation of Jesus and the bodily resurrection, other assertions about Christian orthodoxy were essential teachings like the virgin birth and the physical return of Jesus.

APOSTOLIC ORIGIN

Another important criterion for determining whether a book belonged in the canon was its apostolicity. An example of this criterion is found in the Muratorian Fragment, which was likely written in the late second century,[25] where the author argues against the authoritative status of the Shepherd of Hermas because it was written after the time of the apostles (lines 70–85).[26] On account of this, the letter does not have the same status as the writings of "the prophets," which is shorthand for the Old Testament, or those of the apostles (lines 75–85). From this we see how early Christians regarded apostolic origin as an important element of canonicity. If a book was associated with an apostle, then it stood a greater chance of being considered as authoritative as the writings of the Old Testament, of being considered Scripture. An instance where the New Testament testifies to this standard is when Peter grants Paul's letters the status of "Scripture," alongside those from the Old Testament (2 Pet. 3:16).

---

end, even his enemies being conquered and subdued." *On First Principles*, Christian Classics (Notre Dame, IN: Ave Maria, 2013), 70.

25. See the discussion of the dating of the Shepherd of Hermas in Edmon L. Gallagher and John D. Meade, *The Biblical Canon Lists from Early Christianity: Texts and Analysis* (Oxford: Oxford University Press, 2017), 175–77.

26. Metzger, *Canon*, 253.

CANON LISTS

Canon lists are some of the earliest pieces of evidence for which books early Christian authors and councils deemed worthy of being included in the biblical canon. Perhaps the earliest canon list is the Muratorian Canon, also called the Muratorian Fragment, which was named after its eighteenth-century discoverer, Ludovico Muratori. The document has traditionally been designated to late second-century Rome and includes twenty-two of twenty-seven New Testament writings, particularly the Gospels, Acts, the Pauline epistles, and the majority of John's epistles.[a] Other noteworthy lists are those of Origen, Athanasius, Augustine, and Eusebius. Although canon lists were by no means uniform, they show evidence of general consensus as to the books the church considered worthy of incorporation into the canon. We see this consensus as early as the fourth century.

a. Edmon L. Gallagher and John D. Meade, *The Biblical Canon Lists from Early Christianity: Texts and Analysis* (Oxford: Oxford University Press, 2017), 175–76.

Books like Mark and Luke were accepted into the canon because of their association with Peter and Paul respectively. Luke even claims to have relied on eyewitness testimony to the historical Jesus (Luke 1:1–4). Such testimony likely came from the firsthand accounts of the apostles. Although Hebrews is anonymous, it has historically been associated with the apostle Paul.

In short, the criterion of apostolic origin meant that an apostle was either the author or an influential source of a document. That took some time to sort out in the case of books like 2 Peter and Revelation. Eventually, the apostolic origin of such books was also recognized.

Ecclesiastical Use

A final important criterion for canonicity was a book's regular ecclesiastical use. Lee Martin McDonald argues that this "is what Eusebius had in mind ([*Church History*] 3.25.1–7) when he mentioned that certain writings were 'recognized' among the churches and became 'encovenanted' (*endiathēkē*, lit., 'testamented' or 'canonical')."[27] Documents deemed "covenantal" were received as authoritative for preaching, teaching, and worship.

This one criterion was considered alongside a document's conformity to the Rule of Faith and apostolic origin to determine whether it was canonical or,

27. Lee Martin McDonald, *The Biblical Canon: Its Origin, Transmission, and Authority* (Peabody, MA: Hendrickson, 2007), 414.

as Eusebius would say, "encovenanted." According to Bruce Metzger, "These three criteria (orthodoxy, apostolicity, and consensus among the churches) for ascertaining which books should be regarded as authoritative for the Church came to be generally adopted during the course of the second century and were never modified thereafter."[28]

Canon lists also included extrabiblical works such as the Wisdom of Solomon, Judith, and 1–2 Maccabees. Such books were normally considered profitable and worth reading, even if they were not given canonical status.

Canonical Function of New Testament Books

Each canonical book has a particular historical context and authorial intention. An author like Peter, for instance, intended to encourage believers to maintain their Christian witness in the midst of a hostile culture. While an author's historical intention is important, of greater regard is the function of a book within the biblical canon. The canonical function is what allows the reader to envision how the purposeful sequence of books contributes to the progression of the covenantal storyline from the Old Testament to its continuation and consummation in the New Testament.[29]

An important factor for determining canonical function is, as Goswell notes, "where a biblical book is placed relative to other books."[30] He argues that this "influences the reading of a book on the assumption that the material that is juxtaposed is related in meaning in some way. Consciously or unconsciously, the reader's evaluation of a book is affected by the company it keeps in the library of Scripture."[31] Interpreting a book of Scripture in view of neighboring books will enable us to see textual and thematic links of various kinds, which strengthen a book's association with other scriptural books. All such features contribute to the canonical function of books, which enables readers to see how Scripture speaks beyond its time-conditioned historical audience, bearing witness to a story that will be culminated when Jesus returns to fulfill the promises to people like Abraham and David.

When considering canonical function, we may wonder about the importance of chronology. After all, introductory textbooks often focus on the

---

28. Metzger, *Canon*, 254.
29. On canonical function or canonical intentionality, see Brevard S. Childs, *The New Testament as Canon: An Introduction* (Philadelphia: Fortress, 1984), 37–47.
30. Gregory Goswell, *Text and Paratext: Book Order, Title, and Division as Keys to Biblical Interpretation* (Bellingham, WA: Lexham, 2022), 11.
31. Goswell, *Text and Paratext*, 11.

chronological development of books to explain the progression of themes in the New Testament canon. An example is comparing Paul's earlier eschatological expectation in 1 Thessalonians to his later, more settled anticipation in the Pastorals. Once more, however, we should keep in mind that the placement of the twenty-seven New Testament documents is not based on their date of composition. The Gospels, for instance, were written after the Pauline epistles, but they are positioned prior to them. James was one of the first new covenant writings but does not appear until the section on the Catholic epistles. Although the dates of documents are important, and we will discuss them in the upcoming chapters, the placement of a document within the canonical spectrum has more hermeneutical significance.[32]

Overview of the Order of New Testament Books

Each New Testament document was collected and placed into a particular corpus (or group) and sequential order. The corpora are based on factors such as genre, common authorship, and similar titles. The basic corpora, in the order in which they are located, are the Gospels, Acts, the Pauline epistles, the Catholic epistles, and Revelation. Each book bears important hermeneutical significance within each corpus.

The Gospels are the first and largest body of literature in the New Testament. They are organized as follows: Matthew, Mark, Luke, John. Each Gospel tells its own unique story of the life and teachings of Jesus of Nazareth. Though Mark was written first, Matthew functions at the beginning of the four Gospels to establish the continuation of the biblical storyline, showing that Jesus is the promised son of Abraham and David, the one who has come to deliver his people from exile and into a cosmic kingdom (Matt. 1:1–18). Mark provides an abbreviated, fast-paced account, omitting birth and resurrection narratives already found in Matthew's story. Luke inserts Jesus's genealogy in chapter 3, placing initial priority on reminding readers that Jesus's life and teachings are based on scrupulous eyewitness accounts (Luke 1:1–4). John's Gospel is a fitting conclusion to the Fourfold Gospel witness, confirming the accuracy of eyewitness testimony about Jesus while also conceding that it would be impossible to provide an exhaustive account of his life (John 21:24–25). From this we assume that the Gospel writers have

---

32. We will follow the order in the NA[28] and UBS[5], which is what we find in most Protestant Bibles.

DIFFERENT ORDERS OF NEW TESTAMENT BOOKS

The current order of New Testament books reflects the Western order found in the Latin Vulgate.[a] This sequence is found in most English and Spanish Bibles. We should be aware, however, that the order of New Testament books varies in the manuscript tradition. The only commonality among the witnesses is the placement of the Gospels at the beginning of the New Testament and Revelation at the end.[b] Between these books, a number of variations occur with regard to the order of the corpora and the individual books therein. Some of the more common sequences are Acts, Catholic epistles, Pauline epistles and Pauline epistles, Acts, Catholic epistles. While the present order of the Gospels is the most prevalent in the manuscript tradition, the Western order (Matthew, John, Luke, Mark) represents perhaps the most noted variation within the Fourfold Gospel tradition.[c] The order among the Pauline and Catholic epistles is relatively stable.

While we may speculate about the reason for the varying orders, it is significant that the Gospels and Revelation consistently stand at the beginning and end of the New Testament canon. This suggests that Christians have historically viewed the Gospels as the proper continuation of Israel's story and Revelation as the fitting culmination. Within these canonical bookends, communities had hermeneutical freedom to arrange and rearrange the new covenant writings.

a. Andreas J. Köstenberger, L. Scott Kellum, and Charles L. Quarles, *The Cradle, the Cross, and the Crown: An Introduction to the New Testament*, 2nd ed. (Nashville: B&H Academic, 2016), 28.

b. Kurt Aland and Barbara Aland, *The Text of the New Testament: An Introduction to the Critical Editions and to the Theory and Practice of Modern Criticism*, trans. Erroll F. Rhodes (Grand Rapids: Eerdmans, 1995), 79.

c. Aland and Aland, *Text of the New Testament*, 79.

recorded only what is pertinent for showing that Jesus is the promised Messiah, the one who has come to establish his reign to the ends of the earth.

Acts is an appropriate transition from the Gospels to the Pauline epistles, showing how the Spirit empowers the apostles to spread the kingdom of the resurrected Jesus to the ends of the world. As the kingdom spreads, Jews and increasingly gentiles are added to the people of God. The book concludes with Paul proclaiming the arrival of the kingdom of God while under house arrest in Rome (Acts 28). The ending of Acts solidifies, though by no means concludes, the spread of the good news of the kingdom to gentile lands.

Paul's letters are addressed to churches in certain geographic areas and individual associates throughout the Roman world. The first nine letters are addressed to churches (Romans, 1 Corinthians, 2 Corinthians, Galatians,

Ephesians, Philippians, Colossians, 1 Thessalonians, and 2 Thessalonians) and the next four to individuals (1 Timothy, 2 Timothy, Titus, and Philemon). Beyond this general arrangement, Romans provides an entry point into the Christ-centered theology of Paul, which is then applied to the circumstances of churches and individuals.[33] So, for instance, when the Pastoral epistles speak of "sound doctrine" (1 Tim. 1:10; 6:3; 6:20; 2 Tim. 1:13; 4:3; Titus 1:9, 13), we should assume that this is the very gospel that Paul expounds upon in Romans, the content of which believers are called to guard and entrust to others.

Regardless of its anonymous authorship, Hebrews has historically been situated in the Pauline corpus. In the present order, its placement as the last of the letters associated with Paul serves as a link between the Pauline epistles and the Catholic epistles, encouraging believers to persevere in following Jesus into the kingdom, which saints have long desired to inherit. This message is to be at the front of readers' minds as they read the Catholic epistles, which exhort believers to be mindful of false teachers and to live an obedient life, even amid persecution, as they await the return of Jesus Christ. This corpus was intended for a wide audience—hence the designation "Catholic"—and includes the letters of James, 1 Peter, 2 Peter, 1 John, 2 John, 3 John, and Jude.

Revelation is the capstone of the New Testament canon. This final letter reveals how Jesus the Messiah will return to fulfill the covenantal promises. In so doing, he will raise the dead and re-create the present earth into a new Eden for God's people. He will judge all those who have refused to honor him as king. This letter's placement in the canon is meant to strengthen the faithful's trust in Jesus, assuring readers that the difficulties of the present age will soon give way to an eternal kingdom of peace and justice.

Conclusion

This chapter provides the canonical context for our reading of the New Testament. Of particular importance is the way the old covenant story anticipates new covenant documents, which are synonymous with what we call the New Testament. New covenant documents were accepted based on their conformity to the Rule of Faith, apostolicity, and ecclesiastical use. As these documents were accepted, the church organized them into a particular order and groupings so as to continue the story that was being fulfilled in the person and

33. See the relevant discussion in Brevard S. Childs, *The Church's Guide for Reading Paul: The Canonical Shaping of the Pauline Corpus* (Grand Rapids: Eerdmans, 2008), 2–7, 65–78.

work of Jesus the Messiah. Each canonical book, then, makes a purposeful contribution to the story of Scripture, which is something we will examine in the coming chapters.

SUGGESTED RESOURCES

Childs, Brevard S. *The New Testament as Canon: An Introduction*. Philadelphia: Fortress, 1984.

Emerson, Matthew Y. *Christ and the New Creation: A Canonical Approach to the Theology of the New Testament*. Eugene, OR: Wipf & Stock, 2013.

Goswell, Gregory. *Text and Paratext: Book Order, Title, and Division as Keys to Biblical Interpretation*. Bellingham, WA: Lexham, 2022.

Kruger, Michael J. *Canon Revisited: Establishing the Origins and Authority of the New Testament Books*. Wheaton: Crossway, 2012.

McDonald, Lee Martin, and James Sanders. *The Canon Debate*. Peabody, MA: Hendrickson, 2002.

Metzger, Bruce M. *The Canon of the New Testament: Its Origin, Development, and Significance*. Oxford: Clarendon, 1997.

THREE

THE HERMENEUTICS
OF THE
NEW TESTAMENT AUTHORS

After establishing the canonical context for reading the New Testament, we turn our attention to the hermeneutics of the New Testament authors. We will observe how New Testament authors draw on Old Testament texts to show that Jesus has come to fulfill centuries of covenantal promises. Some of the strategies they employ are quotations, allusions, and typology. The insights of this chapter will establish the hermeneutical principles for our survey of the New Testament writings.

New Testament authors routinely quote or allude to the Greek Old Testament, otherwise called the Septuagint (LXX). Although they may have been familiar with the Hebrew Scriptures, they make frequent use of the Septuagint in their writings—for Greek was the language with which their early Christians audiences were most familiar. Since Septuagint books were produced over the course of two or three centuries, beginning in the third century BC, New Testament authors do not draw from a homogeneous text. By the first century AD, there were various translations of the Hebrew Scriptures and recensions of prior Septuagint versions with which Christian communities would have been acquainted.[1] Some were more formal (word-for-word), others more dynamic (thought-for-thought). This is not unlike the multiple translations we have today, like the ESV (a formal-equivalent translation) and the NIV (a dynamic-equivalent one).[2] So when we say that authors like Paul and Peter quote or allude to the Septuagint, we are not insinuating that they employ a standardized version. We use "Septuagint" as a catchall term for any version of the Greek Old Testament.

When making use of the Old Testament, authors frequently evoke interpretive backdrops that stretch beyond the immediate words of quotations and allusions. This phenomenon is much like a rock that is tossed into a lake and causes several feet of ripples beyond the original place of impact.[3] If we think along these lines, we can imagine how inserting a passage into a New Testament writing evokes a larger context that stretches back into its original Old Testament context. The respective Old Testament context then merges into the conceptual framework of the New Testament passage. One example is in Galatians 3:13, which argues that Jesus has redeemed his followers from the law's curse by "becoming a curse for us," after which Paul cites the Septuagint version of Deuteronomy 21:23: "Cursed by God is every person who hangs upon a pole" (my translation). The citation from Deuteronomy 21:23 brings into view the wider context of Deuteronomy 21, which records the punishment for violating the covenant with Yahweh. Recognizing this interpretive backdrop provides a fuller grasp of Paul's argument: Jesus took on the covenantal curse of death so that believers would not suffer the same fate. What is often missed in Paul's use of Deuteronomy 21:23 is the theme of covenantal curses in the larger context of Deuteronomy 21. This reading is possible when we recognize the more expansive framework the quotation elicits.

Reflecting on how quotations and allusions import Old Testament contexts into New Testament writings enables us to envision the importance of the entire canon for reading Scripture. We realize that a passage's interpretive context extends beyond the immediate page before our eyes. Thus, we should not fear reading too much into a text. If anything, we should

1. For thorough treatments on LXX versions, see Karen H. Jobes and Moisés Silva, *Invitation to the Septuagint* (Grand Rapids: Baker Academic, 2005), 29–102; Natalio Fernández Marcos, *The Septuagint in Context: Introduction to the Greek Version of the Bible*, trans. Wilfred G. E. Watson (Atlanta: SBL, 2000), 35–103.
2. Formal equivalence is a "word-for-word" translation. Dynamic equivalence is a "thought-for-thought" translation.
3. I draw this illustration from Richard B. Hays, *Echoes of Scripture in the Letters of Paul* (New Haven: Yale University Press, 1989), 120.

READING STRATEGIES

Think about some of the ways you have been taught to read Scripture. Have you been told that context is limited to the words on a single page? Have you been encouraged to read like Jesus and the apostles? What are some of your apprehensions when reading beyond an author's immediate historical context?

fear reading too little. We should be cautious about constraining our readings to the immediate context without considering the entire witness of Scripture. Since the biblical authors felt no such apprehensions as they imported texts from prior settings to recall different canonical stories and images, we have a similar freedom. We have the liberty to read as much as textual citations and allusions elicit in our imaginations, so long as our readings are faithful to a passage's argument and the larger canonical storyline.

The remainder of this chapter will examine the hermeneutics of the New Testament authors. We will first explore the use of Old Testament quotations and allusions in the New Testament. We will then show how the biblical authors use these hermeneutical strategies to make typological associations between the Old and New Testaments. Such typological connections display the interconnectedness of the Testaments, which tell one coherent story about Jesus Christ. We will also argue that Jesus and Paul expect that believers will employ their hermeneutical strategies for reading Scripture. Thus, we are free to read Scripture like Jesus and the apostles, who stretched readings beyond their immediate historical contexts.

■ Quotations

Quotations are the most transparent uses of the Old Testament in the New Testament. Authors quote from Old Testament passages verbatim or alter them slightly.[4] The former occurs when an author quotes word-for-word from a prior text. Altered quotations occur when an author reproduces most of

---

4. G. K. Beale argues that a "quotation is a direct citation of an OT passage that is easily recognizable by its clear and unique verbal parallelism" (*Handbook on the New Testament Use of the Old Testament: Exegesis and Interpretation* [Grand Rapids: Baker Academic, 2012], 29). Moisés Silva provides a helpful chart of Old Testament citations in Paul's epistles. "Old Testament in Paul," in *Dictionary of Paul and His Letters*, ed. Gerald F. Hawthorne and Ralph P. Martin (Downers Grove, IL: InterVarsity, 1993), 631.

the exact words and structure of an Old Testament verse but makes minor changes for the sake of conforming the quotation to its new context, such as altering the case of a noun, changing the tense of a verb, and inserting or omitting select words.

Galatians 3:13 is again an appropriate example. Here Paul quotes from Deuteronomy 21:23, using the noun form of "cursed" (*epikataratos*), rather than the participial form (*kekatēramenos*), and dropping the prepositional phrase "by God" (*hypo theou*). In its original context, Deuteronomy 21:23 reads, "Cursed by God is every person who hangs upon a pole." Paul likely expects readers to be familiar with this passage, so as to understand that God is the one who pronounces the curse. The change to the noun form of "cursed" from the participle makes no significant interpretive difference. Like this example from Galatians 3:13, altered quotations are usually recognizable. Their significance for exegesis, though, must be assessed on a case-by-case basis.

Authors often introduce quotations using introductory formulas, such as "so was fulfilled" (Matt. 2:15), "as it is written" (Rom. 3:4), or "it says" (Eph. 4:8). When an author uses no introductory formula, their quotations are often so parallel to an Old Testament passage that it is feasible to discern the source of the quotation (e.g., Gal. 3:6; Eph. 6:2, 3). The following are examples of explicit quotations of the Old Testament in the New Testament; some include introductory formulas, while others exclude them.

Matthew 1:23

When recording the events surrounding the promised birth of Jesus, Matthew inserts the Septuagint version of Isaiah 7:14 into his narrative, applying the verse to Jesus: "All this took place to fulfill what the Lord had said through the prophet: 'The virgin will conceive and give birth to a son, and they will call him Immanuel' (which means 'God with us')" (Matt. 1:22–23). Since Matthew takes this quotation from the broader context of Isaiah 7–9, he reveals that the promise that the virgin will bear a son, though in a sense partially fulfilled in the birth of Maher-Shalal-Hash-Baz (Isa. 8:1), finds its ultimate fulfillment in Mary's conception of Jesus, who is the very God who has returned to dwell with his people and establish the promised throne of David.[5] We see this connection when considering the context from which Matthew draws his citation.

5. Craig L. Blomberg, *Matthew*, New American Commentary 22 (Nashville: Broadman, 1992), 60.

John 1:23

While being interrogated about his identity, John the Baptist responds by quoting Isaiah 40:3:

> [I am the] voice of one calling:
> "In the wilderness prepare
>   the way for the LORD;
> make straight in the desert
>   a highway for our God."[6]

One of the significant alterations to this citation is the inclusion of the pronoun *egō* ("I"). The first clause in the Septuagint version simply reads, "The voice of one crying in the wilderness."[7] The insertion of the pronoun therefore strongly suggests that John believes himself to be the one of whom Isaiah speaks. And since Isaiah 40–66 is the broader backdrop of the quotation, John's quotation further elicits the hope of a new exodus. John's role in this story is to prepare the people of God for the arrival of Jesus, the new Moses, who will lead his people on a sojourn that will culminate in the inheritance of a new heavens and earth.

Hebrews 1:5

In arguing for the superiority of Jesus over angels, the author of Hebrews quotes verbatim from the Septuagint versions of Psalm 2:7 and 2 Samuel 7:14. Hebrews 1:5 reads,

For to which of the angels did God ever say,

> "You are my Son;
>   today I have become your Father"?

Or again,

> "I will be his Father,
>   and he will be my Son"?

The quotation from Psalm 2:7 brings to mind the entire psalm, displaying that Jesus is God's very Son, the one who will inherit a worldwide kingdom.

---

6. My translation departs from the NIV in explicitly translating *egō eimi* as "I am."

7. I translate *phōnē boōntos en tē erēmō* as "the voice of one crying in the wilderness" (Isa. 40:3 LXX).

The subsequent quotation from the context of 2 Samuel 7:14, on which the Chronicler also draws (1 Chron. 17:13), links Jesus to the royal descendant of David, who is also identified as God's son. Taken together, these quotations in Hebrews 1:5 leave no doubt that Jesus is the promised ruler of the cosmos, who is unquestionably superior to angelic beings.

These examples reveal that it is not enough to merely recognize when New Testament authors are quoting from Old Testament texts. Since a quotation is tethered to its original context, the reader must discern the Old Testament context from which an author draws their quotation. This enables the reader to envision the backdrop for interpreting a New Testament passage.

Allusions

An allusion is when an author shares enough of a portion of Scripture to evoke a prior context.[8] This may include embedding several words or concepts from the Old Testament into their writings. Unlike quotations, allusions do not reproduce the wording of a passage verbatim. We must listen more closely to the creative ways in which the biblical authors employ portions of texts to allude to prior Old Testament contexts. This raises the level of the reader's involvement by asking them to discern the passages from which an author may be drawing.[9]

---

8. My discussion on allusions leans on my coauthored volume with Benjamin Laird, *40 Questions on the Apostle Paul* (Grand Rapids: Kregel, 2023). I also draw on Beale, *Handbook on the New Testament Use of the Old Testament*, 31–34.

9. Since we cannot avoid subjectivity in reading texts, Hays proposes seven criteria for discerning proposed allusions and echoes in the writings of Paul: (1) availability (the echo's availability to the original author and audience), (2) volume (mainly repetition of words and syntactical patterns), (3) recurrence (the frequency of Paul's use of the same scriptural passage elsewhere), (4) thematic coherence (the echo's fit into Paul's argument), (5) historical plausibility (whether Paul's readers would have understood the echo), (6) history of interpretation (whether other interpreters have heard such echoes), and (7) satisfaction (appeases competent readers) (*Echoes of Scripture in the Letters of Paul*, 31–32). I have summarized these categories

Ephesians 6:10–20

In this passage, Paul lists the various pieces of the armor of God that allow believers to withstand the schemes of the devil. Scholars commonly argue that the armor of God follows the example of a Roman suit of armor. While it is helpful to note parallels with Roman armor, the various allusions to Isaiah suggest that Paul's use of prior scriptural contexts should take interpretive priority.

In Ephesians 6:14, the call to "gird your loins in the truth" bears a striking resemblance to Isaiah's description of God: "He shall be girded with righteousness around the loins and enclosed with truth on the sides" (Isa. 11:5).[10] The similarities between Ephesians 6:14 and Isaiah 11:5 revolve around the notions of "girding the loins" and "truth," which Paul takes up into one phrase. Also, in Ephesians 6:17 the exhortations to "put on the breastplate of righteousness" and to "receive the helmet of salvation" recall the activity of God in Isaiah 59:17: "He clothed himself with righteousness as a breastplate and he put the helmet of salvation upon his head." Although he does not employ verbatim quotations, Paul alludes to enough of the terminology of Isaiah 11 and 59 to bring to mind these prior contexts. When we detect these allusions, we envision how the apostle uses metaphorical language about God in Isaiah to exhort believers to take up the warrior-like character of God in spiritual battles.

John 10:11

In this verse, Jesus calls himself the "good shepherd." Of the contexts where shepherding imagery is used, perhaps Ezekiel 34 is the most prominent, where Israel's leaders are described as bad shepherds. Within this context, God promises to one day be like a "shepherd" who will gather and care for his poorly treated flock (Ezek. 34:11–14). When Jesus calls himself the "good shepherd" in John 10:11, he alludes to Ezekiel 34 to reveal himself as Israel's good shepherd, the one who has come to care for his sheep. One would be hard-pressed to read John this way without discerning the allusion to the prior context of Ezekiel 34.

Matthew 1–4

Matthew 1–4 is an example of how an author may allude to several passages to bring a common Old Testament theme into view. The exodus story is one

---

similarly in my book *The Future Inheritance of Land in the Pauline Epistles* (Eugene, OR: Pickwick, 2019), 25–26n22.

10. I provide my own translations of the passages in this paragraph.

RECOGNIZING ALLUSIONS

Recognize the allusions of Old Testament texts in Galatians 4:21–31 and 1 Peter 2:18–25. Determine what significance the Old Testament contexts of the allusions have for the interpretation of each New Testament passage. Follow the same process with two other New Testament texts.

such theme, which spans from the book of Exodus to the book of Joshua, recalling how God led his people out of slavery in Egypt, through the Red Sea, and into the wilderness and ultimately the promised land. Among the many places where the exodus theme appears in the New Testament, Matthew 1–4 portrays Jesus as a Moses-like figure whose young life was threatened by Herod—much like Moses's life was endangered by Pharaoh (Matt. 2:16–23; cf. Exod. 2:1–22). Jesus rises up out of the waters of baptism, as the Israelites rose out of the waters of the Red Sea (Matt. 3:13–17; cf. Exod. 14:1–31). Jesus then enters the wilderness, where he encounters temptation, akin to the way Israel was tempted in their wilderness journey (Matt. 4:1–11; cf. Exod. 15–Deut. 34). Unlike the Israelites, Moses included, Jesus does not succumb to temptation, showing that he is a better Moses who will lead his people into the cosmic inheritance. It is possible to continue the exodus-story theme throughout the Gospel of Matthew. For now, the above example is sufficient to show how New Testament authors may use a string of texts to allude to larger themes or stories, showing how Jesus has come to fulfill the promises to his people.

▪ Typology

Typology is another important category for understanding the hermeneutics of the New Testament authors. In its most rudimentary sense, a "type" is an Old Testament shadow that is fulfilled in a New Testament "antitype."[11] New Testament writers envision people, places, and institutions as shadows realized in new covenant writings. As a result, typological exegesis expands the boundaries of scriptural readings beyond the immediate context of a passage to include the whole canon.

11. E. Earle Ellis, *Paul's Use of the Old Testament* (1981; repr., Eugene, OR: Wipf & Stock, 2003), 126. See also Mitchell L. Chase, *40 Questions about Typology and Allegory* (Grand Rapids: Kregel, 2020), 36–39.

I succinctly define typology as follows: typology occurs when historical people, places, institutions, and things in the Old Testament act as "types" that anticipate an escalated fulfillment in the New Testament. Two essential components of this definition are the words "historical" and "escalated." The former assures that a typological connection is grounded in the history of redemption. The latter requires there to be escalation (or intensification) between a type and its fulfillment. Examples of escalation are when the author of Hebrews contends that Jesus is greater than Moses (Heb. 3:1–6) and when Matthew records that Jesus is greater than Jonah and Solomon (Matt. 12:38–42).

The nature of typology necessitates that readers interpret Scripture "backwards" to grasp connections between Old Testament types and New Testament antitypes. The most helpful way to do this is by envisioning how Jesus fulfills old covenant patterns. It is not necessary for old covenant writers to have been conscious about how types, such as the priesthood and the temple, were to be realized in the person of Jesus (1 Pet. 1:10–12).

Authors and their communities were bound to particular times and places in history. Once their writings are inserted into the timeless context of the canon, these writings are no longer restricted to their original historical setting. The sixty-six biblical books of the canon now become the fresh context for reading the writings of Scripture. This allows new covenant writings to shed light on old covenant ones, opening possibilities for envisioning types that old covenant authors may have been unaware of.

While the original historical intention of an author is important, what matters most for typological exegesis is what the divine author has intended to reveal in all the pages of Scripture. That means, for instance, that God may use Matthew to reveal that the original exodus on which Hosea reflects foreshadows Jesus's later departure from the same land (Matt. 2:15; cf. Hosea 11:1). It is not necessary, and rather unlikely, for Hosea, centuries earlier, to have envisioned how his reflection on the exodus would be realized in Jesus. What matters is that God intended for Matthew to reveal the greater typological intent for the exodus event.

In later chapters, we will observe how the New Testament writings illuminate typological connections across the canon. So, it will be important to examine examples of typology to gain further clarity about this hermeneutical category. While observing such examples, we will notice how authors often use quotations and allusions to make typological connections between the testaments.

Romans 5:12–21

This passage alludes to the creation account in Genesis 1–3 to relate Adam to Christ, explicitly stating that Adam "was a type of the one who was to come" (Rom. 5:14).[12] According to Paul, as death came to the world through Adam's sin, so salvation comes to the world through Christ. E. Earl Ellis argues that Christ's redemption extends to the entire created order, something elucidated in Romans 8.[13] Considering that the entire creation was cursed because of Adam's sin, it is right to see that the new Adam's salvation extends to the entire earth. Paul makes a similar typological connection in 1 Corinthians 15, where Adam's sin brings death, but Christ brings life to all. What we witness in Romans 5:12–21, and by extension in 1 Corinthians 15, is an association between two historical figures, Adam and Christ, with the latter intensifying the comparison, making this a legitimate instance of typology.

1 Corinthians 10:1–13

This passage draws a connection between Israel's wilderness generation and the Corinthians. The recollection of the wilderness generation testing the Lord and being judged serves as a "type" or "example" from which the Corinthians should learn (1 Cor. 10:6, 11). Essential to Paul's argument is the historical connection between Israel and the Corinthians, and he even draws a familial connection between the two groups. Escalation in Paul's comparison occurs when he claims that the events in the wilderness function as a "type" for the Corinthians, "on whom the culmination of the ages has come" (10:11). As Israel's wilderness generation was judged, never entering the promised land, the Corinthians are in danger of perishing without ever inheriting the coming age. Paul employs typology to exhort the Corinthians to avoid the sins that beset the Israelites, like sexual immorality and idolatry, so that they might complete their own journey through the present wilderness of sin and receive the world that God's people have longed to inherit.

Hebrews 9:11–28

The author of Hebrews contends that the priests offered yearly sacrifices, while Jesus offered himself once for all "at the culmination of the ages" (Heb.

---

12. The NIV translates *typos* as "example." I have rendered *typos* as "type" because it suits the "typological" context.
13. Ellis, *Paul's Use of the Old Testament*, 129.

9:26). The finality of Jesus's eschatological sacrifice makes his self-offering better than the ones presented by the priests. Thus, there is historical correspondence between the priestly sacrifices and Jesus, with escalation occurring in Jesus's final offering for sins. After Jesus made his superior offering, the priestly sacrifices became obsolete. The author of Hebrews recognizes the typological fulfillment of priestly sacrifices by interpreting these events in view of Jesus's death for sins. This is a prime example of how reading backward allows an author to envision typological fulfillment.

In sum, typology opens our eyes to how Old Testament shadows find eschatological fulfillment in the New Testament. We see these in terms of associations between Old Testament types and New Testament antitypes. Most types are realized in the person and work of Jesus. The necessity of both testaments for typological exegesis is another reason for reading both the Old Testament and the New Testament as Christian Scripture.

Beyond Explicit Types

So far, we have done the easy job of identifying explicit instances of typology. But should we push beyond explicit types? In other words, should we identify types in the Old Testament that are not identified as such in the New Testament?

Some argue against seeing implicit types in Scripture. So even if a reader may be able to discern historical correspondence and escalation between an Old Testament type and a New Testament antitype, such an exegetical maneuver would be unwarranted or even dangerous. Consequently, we should only discern explicit typological associations. Richard Longenecker, for instance, argues that our goal should not be to reproduce the exegetical practices of New Testament authors. Longenecker contends that authors like Paul evidence culturally conditioned Jewish practices of exegesis, such as pesher and midrash, which we should not replicate. We should replicate the essential truths of the Christian faith that authors proclaim, not the interpretive patterns they use to proclaim them.[14]

Longenecker presents fair concerns about going beyond what is written. Exegetical excess should concern all responsible readers of Scripture. A responsible interpreter, however, would also take seriously the interpretive expectations of Jesus and Paul, who anticipate that believers will emulate their interpretive practices. Their ways of reading texts press beyond the historical contexts of Old Testament writings.[15] Since believers are expected to emulate Jesus and Paul, our interpretive habits are not bound to any particular cultural context. Our practices for reading Scripture should conform to Jesus's and Paul's, which move beyond minimalist approaches to the use of the Old Testament in the New Testament.

Emulating Jesus

Luke 24:13–35 and John 5:1–47 are windows into Jesus's hermeneutic for reading Scripture. Each passage reveals how Jesus expects us to envision him as the one who fulfills the old covenant Scriptures. This is the case even in passages with no explicit promises of messianic fulfillment.

LUKE 24:13–25

After his resurrection, Jesus encounters two of his followers, Cleopas and an unnamed companion, on their way to a village named Emmaus. They converse about the death of Jesus and the messianic expectations associated with him (Luke 24:13–15). Their hopes were all but extinguished after Jesus's crucifixion at the hands of the authorities (24:17–21). It is clear that these disciples do not understand that the Old Testament witnesses to the suffering and resurrection of the Messiah. And this not just from a few explicit passages, like Isaiah 53, for the entirety of the old covenant Scriptures point to his death and resurrection. So Jesus teaches them about how the books of Moses and the Prophets—another way to describe the Old Testament—testify about him (24:25–27).

After his impromptu teaching session, Jesus agrees to a meal with his followers. When he breaks the bread, their eyes are "opened" to his true identity (Luke 24:31). In other words, they now understand that Jesus is the

14. See Richard N. Longenecker, *Biblical Exegesis in the Apostolic Period*, 2nd ed. (Grand Rapids: Eerdmans, 1999), xxxiv–xxxix.

15. See Chase, *Typology and Allegory*, 47–52; Hays, *Echoes of Scripture in the Letters of Paul*, 178–92.

Messiah—the very one who has died and risen from the grave, just as the Old Testament Scriptures promised. They are so deeply impacted by this experience that they ask, "Were not our hearts burning within us while he talked with us on the road and opened the Scriptures to us?" (24:32). They then testify to the eleven disciples about their encounter with the risen Christ (24:33–35).

Luke's record of this encounter reveals that Jesus expects his followers to read the entire Old Testament in light of himself, the risen Christ. So much so that Jesus initially calls Cleopas and his unnamed companion "foolish" for being slow to recognize the Christocentric testimony of Moses and the Prophets (Luke 24:25). The Old Testament writings still speak to specific historical circumstances. But we ought to read these accounts in a way that preserves their historical witness while imagining how they anticipate the arrival of Jesus the Messiah. We are to envision how the *historical* persons, figures, and institutions find their *escalated* fulfillment in Jesus. This should motivate us to reread Luke's words so that we can find, as Richard B. Hays argues, "submerged correspondences between 'Moses and the prophets' and the mysterious stranger who chastises us as 'slow of heart' for failing to discover such correspondences on our first reading."[16]

JOHN 5:1–47

Jesus's hermeneutical lesson comes at the conclusion of a conflict with religious leaders for healing a lame man on the Sabbath (John 5:2–9). Their audacity at Jesus's legal violation boils over when he claims that his authority to work on the Sabbath is sourced in his status as God's Son (5:17). The religious leaders then "tried all the more to kill him; not only was he breaking the Sabbath, but he was even calling God his own Father, making himself equal with God" (5:18). Since they do not understand why he has the authority to make this claim, they must be taken to the very Scriptures on which they trust, but sorely misunderstand, since they are claiming that they bear witness to Jesus (5:39). Jesus argues that Moses, "on whom [their] hopes are set," will accuse them before the Father (5:45). He tells them, "If you believed Moses, you would believe me, for he wrote about me. But since you do not believe what he wrote, how are you going to believe what I say?" (5:46–47).

For all their study of Moses's writings, Jesus's opponents have failed to understand the ultimate referent of these writings. They have focused so much

16. Richard B. Hays, *Echoes of Scripture in the Gospels* (Waco: Baylor University Press, 2016), 223.

IMPLICIT TYPOLOGY

Replicating the hermeneutical patterns of biblical authors is more art than science. Most artists will testify that it takes years, in some cases a lifetime, to master their craft. Biblical interpretation is no different: it takes lots of practice. So consider this your first exercise in typological interpretation of Scripture: discern two typological associations between the Old and New Testaments. Remember that the two criteria for discerning types and antitypes are *historical correspondence* and *escalation*. As you become more comfortable with the practice, try to discern typological associations in your own reading of Scripture.

on the literal, historical sense that they have neglected to understand that Jesus is the one in whom Moses's writings find their escalated fulfillment. Consequently, they reject Jesus, the one who fulfills the Scriptures.

Jesus's hermeneutical instructions also serve as a lesson for us: we must read the Old Testament Scriptures in light of Jesus. We should, in other words, read them typologically, envisioning how the historical utterances in the old covenant writings find their escalated fulfillment in the person and work of Jesus the Messiah. Even if the correspondences are not explicit, the New Testament functions as our hermeneutical key, empowering us to envision typological associations previously unbeknownst to Old Testament authors. Failure to do so puts us at risk of being just as disobedient as the religious leaders.

Emulating Paul

Unlike the Gospels, Paul's letters do not provide examples of how believers are expected to interpret Scripture. What we see are exhortations to imitate Paul (1 Cor. 4:16; 11:1; Phil. 3:17). Hays argues that to do so "faithfully we must learn from him the art of reading and proclaiming Scripture."[17] He then asks an insightful question: "If we did imitate Paul's interpretive practices, how would our reading of Scripture be shaped by his example?"[18] Would we read Scripture as participants in the eschatological drama of redemption? If we read Scripture as Hays suggests, would we not be free to make typological associations like those in Paul's letters, such as identifying the relationship between a husband and a wife as a picture of the relationship between Christ and his church (Eph. 5:31–32; cf. Gen. 2:24)? Would we not be free to

17. Hays, *Echoes of Scripture in the Letters of Paul*, 183.
18. Hays, *Echoes of Scripture in the Letters of Paul*, 183.

THE NEW TESTAMENT IN THE NEW TESTAMENT

Beyond the use of the Old Testament in the New Testament, we will also explore how the shape and order of the New Testament canon allow us to envision how later New Testament writings may recall earlier ones. Could it be, for instance, that James's instructions allude to Jesus's Sermon on the Mount in Matthew's Gospel? Could it be that 1 John brings into view similar teachings about themes like the Word and the Spirit in John's Gospel? Could it be that Romans calls readers to trust in the Jesus who is more fully revealed in the Gospels? Some connections we find may be intentional, while others may not be. Historical intentionality, however, does not limit the allusions of earlier New Testament writings in later ones. The ordering of the books of the New Testament canon enables readers to envision how later words, themes, and accounts bring to mind prior New Testament writings. All sixty-six books, after all, are the interpretive context for reading Scripture, regardless of historical intention.

claim that things like old covenant festivals and Sabbaths are but shadows of "the things that were to come" (Col. 2:16–17)? Are these not examples of typological exegesis that exhibit *historical correspondence* between old covenant persons, places, and institutions and *escalated* fulfillment in Christ's realization of the new covenant?

Paul's call for believers to imitate his example also includes his typological reading of Scripture. If we are concerned only about reading the literal words on a page, we should reread Jesus's rebuke to the religious leaders in John 5. That should jolt us into being more like Paul than like those whom Jesus reproved. And if we are going to be like Paul, we should feel free to make typological associations in Scripture, now evident through the arrival of the eschatological age in which we are living, the one initiated by Jesus the Messiah. We should, then, replicate the hermeneutical strategies of the New Testament authors. This, after all, seems to be the way that both Jesus and Paul expect us to read Scripture.

Conclusion

Our discussion in this chapter lays a hermeneutical foundation for how we will interpret the twenty-seven New Testament books. We will observe quotations and allusions of Old Testament passages in the New Testament, which will broaden our contexts beyond the immediate historical setting of a given passage. We will also tune into the way New Testament authors use quotations and allusions from the Old Testament to make typological connections in their writings, often showing how persons and institutions find their fulfillment in Jesus the Messiah. All this assumes a canonical framework for reading Scripture: that we read individual books within the canonical story of Scripture.

Since we are expected to emulate Jesus's and Paul's hermeneutic, we will also draw out typological associations not identified as such by New Testament authors. The two prerequisites for typological exegesis will be *historical correspondence* with an Old Testament type and its *escalated fulfillment* in a New Testament antitype, which we will witness by reading Scripture retrospectively. Such typological connections across the canon will repeatedly show how all of Scripture is a unified whole—with the Old Testament finding its ultimate fulfillment in Jesus Christ.

SUGGESTED RESOURCES

Beale, G. K. *Handbook on the New Testament Use of the Old Testament: Exegesis and Interpretation.* Grand Rapids: Baker Academic, 2012.

Chase, Mitchell L. *40 Questions about Typology and Allegory.* Grand Rapids: Kregel, 2020.

Goppelt, Leonhard. *Typos: The Typological Interpretations of the Old Testament in the New.* Translated by Donald H. Madvig. Grand Rapids: Eerdmans, 1982.

Hays, Richard B. *Echoes of Scripture in the Letters of Paul.* New Haven: Yale University Press, 1989.

———. *Reading Backwards: Figural Christology and the Fourfold Gospel Witness.* Waco: Baylor University Press, 2014.

Leithart, Peter J. *Deep Exegesis: The Mystery of Reading Scripture.* Waco: Baylor University Press, 2009.

FOUR

THE GOSPELS AND ACTS

The Fourfold Gospel corpus consists of the accounts about the historical Jesus attributed to Matthew, Mark, Luke, and John. Each Gospel has a common title that contains the preposition *kata* ("according to") followed by the name of the author. These titular features attest to the inclusion of a book into the Fourfold Gospel corpus. The First Gospel is titled "according to Matthew," the Second Gospel "according to Mark," and so on. Gospel titles like those in modern Bibles (e.g., Gospel of Luke) are found in codices like Alexandrinus (A) and Washingtonianus (W).

We will evaluate the contribution of each Gospel in view of its canonical arrangement. Whereas the majority of manuscripts arrange the Gospels according to their traditional sequence (Matthew, Mark, Luke, John), the Western order attested in manuscripts such as Codex Bezae (D) and Papyrus 45 ($\mathfrak{P}^{45}$) puts the Gospels of apostles Matthew and John before those of the apostles' disciples, Mark and Luke (Matthew, John, Luke, Mark). Since this sequence is not prevalent in the majority of manuscripts, I will assume the established order associated with the Fourfold Gospel corpus.[1]

When we consider the diverse, yet unified, message of the Fourfold Gospel corpus, we see that Jesus is the promised descendant of Abraham and David, who will deliver his people from bondage in the present age and lead them into a kingdom of permanent peace and flourishing. He does so in the humblest of ways—by giving his life on a cross, fulfilling the vocation of Isaiah's suffering servant. After his humiliating death, he lies in a tomb for

---

1. Appendix 1 covers the relationship between the Gospels.

BOOK TITLES

Titles of books are not original to the New Testament autographs—they were added by later editors or redactors. Their postauthorial nature, however, does not negate their importance for interpreting the New Testament. Quite the opposite: the early inclusion of titles and their persistence in the manuscript tradition strongly suggest that they function as invaluable hermeneutical aids for identifying the authors and corpora with which books are associated. David Trobisch even argues that "the present form of the titles" is the "result of a single, specific redaction."[a] Trobisch calls this the original *Canonical Edition,* which set the standard for the format of titles associated with specific corpora like the Gospels and the Pauline epistles.[b] While some doubt the existence of an original *Canonical Edition,* we can (at least) agree that manuscript titles are invaluable postauthorial aids for canonical interpretation.

a. See discussion in David Trobisch, *The First Edition of the New Testament* (Oxford: Oxford University Press, 2000), 38–43.
b. See appendix 2 for a discussion of New Testament manuscripts and codices.

WHY FOUR GOSPELS? WHY NOT JUST ONE?

Some view having four Gospels—rather than a single definitive one—as problematic. We should recognize that Christians have historically valued the witness of the Fourfold Gospel. The second-century theologian Tatian is a notable exception, choosing to harmonize Matthew, Mark, Luke, and John into one account called the Diatessaron ("through the four"). While Tatian's harmony was popular in areas such as Syria, it was eventually rejected in favor of the fourfold testimony of Matthew, Mark, Luke, and John. This historical development underscores how the church preferred to maintain the mystery between diversity and unity among the four canonical Gospels.

three days and then rises from the dead. His miraculous resurrection begins the restoration of the entire creation. Though humanity longs for restoration, the Gospels provide believers hope that their present sufferings will give way to life in a kingdom where they will exhibit the love for God and others that has been so difficult since the exile from Eden. Jesus's disciples are charged with taking this "good news" to the ends of the earth. Before his ascension, Jesus commands his followers to wait for the Holy Spirit, who will empower them to take this message to the nations.

THE GOSPELS AS ANCIENT BIOGRAPHIES

Until the early twentieth century, scholars generally followed the conclusions of form critics like Rudolf Bultmann, who argued that the Gospels were *sui generis* ("their own genre"). It was assumed that the Gospels were unique literary productions of early Christians based on the preaching and teaching of the church. The "uniqueness" of the Gospels, and thereby the lack of comparable literature, is the very thing that makes this view untenable. Recently, scholars have shifted their view on the genre of the Gospels, comparing them to ancient Greek biographies, which focus on a historical person's ancestry, birth, childhood, important speeches and sayings, great deeds, virtues, and death within a chronological framework.[a]

a. See Richard A. Burridge, *What Are the Gospels? A Comparison with Greco-Roman Biography*, 25th anniv. ed. (Waco: Baylor University Press, 2018).

The book of Acts continues the story of the Gospels, showing how the promised Spirit arrives, empowering the apostles to take the message of the kingdom from Jerusalem, Judea, and Samaria to the ends of the earth (Acts 1:8). That Acts ends with Paul in Rome tells the reader that the good news has made its way into gentile lands. The kingdom is extending into the world that Jesus is in the process of making new. While some manuscripts include the Pauline or Catholic epistles after the Gospels, the Gospels-Acts order—attested in manuscripts such as Papyrus 45 ($\mathfrak{P}^{45}$) and Papyrus 53 ($\mathfrak{P}^{53}$), the Muratorian Fragment, Eusebius's *homologoumena* ("recognized writings"), and the Latin Vulgate—provides a smooth continuation of the storyline of Scripture, showing how the message of the Messiah's kingdom in the Gospels spreads to the ends of the earth in Acts.[2]

Matthew

The Gospel of Matthew is strategically placed at the head of the New Testament canon. Interpreters have proposed several arguments for Matthew's literary position. Augustine, for one, argues that the Gospels are organized according to their order of composition, allowing for later Evangelists to use

2. On the placement of Acts in the New Testament canon, see Gregory Goswell, "The Place of the Book of Acts in Reading the NT," *Journal of the Evangelical Theological Society* 59, no. 1 (2016): 67–82.

the material of earlier ones (*Harmony of the Gospels* 1.4). Most modern scholars, however, argue that Mark was the earliest written Gospel. That would mean that Matthew likely draws from Mark, not the other way around. Another view is linked to Papias, Origen, and Chrysostom, who contend that Matthew was placed first because it was originally written to Jews in Hebrew or Aramaic and later translated into Greek. We have no evidence of an original Hebrew or Aramaic Gospel of Matthew. We have more warrant to argue that the position of Matthew is due to its theological relationship to the Old and New Testaments, showing that Jesus is the descendant of David and Abraham, Israel's promised Messiah who offers salvation to Jew and gentile. No other Evangelist links the Old and New Testaments as well as Matthew.

Matthew uses direct quotation formulas, such as "this was to fulfill what was spoken through the prophet" (Matt. 8:17; cf. 1:22–23; 2:15), and quotations from the Old Testament to explain how Jesus fulfills Israel's scriptural hopes (13:14; 24:15).[3] While writing in such a way that the Israelites would understand the significance of the life, death, and resurrection of Jesus, Matthew also shows how a Jewish Jesus extends salvation to the gentiles.[4] This should come as no surprise, for God promised to Abraham that through him "all nations on earth will be blessed" (Gen. 18:18; 22:18). In short, Matthew reads the promises to Israel through the lens of Jesus, who brings salvation to Jews and gentiles.

Outline and Overview

The Gospel of Matthew tells the story of Jesus in five major sections.[5] Chapters 1 and 2 narrate the genealogy, birth, and early childhood of Jesus. The Gospel then fast-forwards to Jesus's adulthood appearance as the Messiah and his temptation in the wilderness in 3:1–4:11. Matthew mentions nothing about the years between Jesus's early childhood and his adulthood. (The only account about anything in these intervening years is found in Luke 2:41–52.) Matthew then tells of Jesus's ministry as Messiah in 4:12–20:34. Subsequently, his Gospel narrates Jesus heading toward Jerusalem as he prepares to offer his life for his people in 21:1–26:1. Although Jesus continues to minister and prophesy, the main focus of this section is his road to the cross.

---

3. Richard B. Hays, *Reading Backwards: Figural Christology and the Fourfold Gospel Witness* (Waco: Baylor University Press, 2014), 36–37.

4. See Francis Watson, *The Fourfold Gospel: Theological Reading of the New Testament Portraits of Jesus* (Grand Rapids: Baker Academic, 2016), 26–27.

5. There is much disagreement about the outline of Matthew's Gospel. See Donald A. Hagner, *Matthew 1–13*, Word Biblical Commentary 33a (Waco: Word, 1993), l–liii.

Last, Matthew tells of Jesus's passion, resurrection, and great commission to his followers in 26:2–28:20. The overall contours of Matthew's "chronological or biographical outline," as Constantine Campbell and Jonathan Pennington argue, is "common to all four of the Gospels, and it likely stems from Mark's original story."[6]

Five major discourses are woven into Matthew's outline: the Sermon on the Mount (chaps. 5–7); Jesus's commissioning of twelve disciples (chap. 10); parables of the kingdom (chap. 13); ecclesial expectations (chap. 18); and woes and judgment (chaps. 23–25). It is possible that Matthew's five discourses reflect the fivefold organization of the Pentateuch, cohering well with his presentation of Jesus as a new Moses. The clear sense from these discourses is that Jesus is the promised Messiah, who invites Jews and gentiles to partake in the saving promises to forefathers like Abraham and David.

Prologue: Genealogy, Birth, and Early Childhood of Jesus (1:1–2:23)

The very first verse in Matthew's Gospel claims that Jesus is the offspring of David and Abraham (Matt. 1:1). The genealogical connection to David alludes to 2 Samuel 7, showing that Jesus is the promised king who will establish a perpetual kingdom over Israel. We should not assume that his kingdom will be relegated to a spiritual realm. The context of 2 Samuel 7 reveals that the Israelites anticipated that the promised king—the Messiah—would establish an earthly kingdom for his people, where they would experience perpetual rest from enemies (7:10). The permanency of this kingdom suggests that it will be far better than the original kingdom in Canaan, making the monarchy in Canaan a type of the greater one established through the promised Davidic king.

The genealogical connection to Abraham alludes to chapters such as Genesis 12 and 18, which promise that the nations will experience blessing through Abraham. This second allusion allows readers to envision Jesus as the descendant of Abraham who extends the blessing of salvation to the nations. Taken together, the allusions to Genesis and 2 Samuel enable readers to see that Jesus will establish a cosmic reign over the nations of the earth. Matthew's explanation of the premonarchial and monarchial periods (Matt. 1:2–11), Israel's deportation to Babylon (1:12–16), and the deportation to the arrival of Christ conclude the genealogical section, insinuating that Jesus is the one

6. Constantine R. Campbell and Jonathan T. Pennington, *Reading the New Testament as Christian Scripture: A Literary, Canonical, and Theological Survey* (Grand Rapids: Baker Academic, 2020), 91.

who will deliver his people from exile (1:17). Since the allusion to Abraham cosmically expands the promises, we see that Jesus delivers the nations out of the present sinful world and into his kingdom on a renewed earth.

The remainder of the section deepens the connection between Jesus and Old Testament expectations. Matthew shows that Jesus's virgin birth fulfills Isaiah's expectation of God returning to dwell with his people (Matt. 1:18–25; cf. Isa. 7:14). As Pharaoh unsuccessfully attempted to kill the Israelite newborns in Egypt (Exod. 1:15–2:20), Herod futilely attempts to kill the promised king of Israel, the one who will topple all kingdoms, including Herod's own (Matt. 2:1–12; cf. Mic. 5:2). Jesus and his family escape to Egypt until the death of Herod, when they return to Israel (Matt. 2:13–23). Matthew connects Jesus's calling out of Egypt to the verbatim words of Hosea 11:1 ("Out of Egypt I called my son"), underscoring that Jesus is the promised Israelite who will deliver his people out of slavery to sin and into a kingdom that will extend beyond the original borders of Canaan.

The profound connections between Jesus and old covenant expectations set the stage for the remainder of Matthew's Gospel, which will show that Jesus is the promised Messiah, who will deliver Jews and gentiles into the promised kingdom.

Jesus's Adulthood Appearance as the Messiah and His Temptation in the Wilderness (3:1–4:11)

The narrative of Matthew's Gospel leaps from Jesus's early childhood to his public life as an adult. Before Jesus's public appearance, Matthew introduces John the Baptist in the wilderness, calling Israel to repent before the arrival of the promised kingdom (Matt. 3:1–2, 8, 11). Using an almost verbatim quotation from Isaiah 40:3, Matthew 3:3 evokes the image of Jesus leading his people on a new exodus through the present wilderness of sin. God's people should heed John's warning and prepare themselves for Jesus's arrival, so that they might partake of this new act of deliverance. Otherwise, they will face God's wrath (3:7–12).

When Jesus appears in the wilderness, he expects to be baptized by John (Matt. 3:13). Jesus says that this is necessary "to fulfill all righteousness" (3:15). Jesus's baptism symbolizes that God is fulfilling the Old Testament expectation of a new exodus to a new creation. This connection is even more pronounced when we consider that the quotation of Isaiah 40:3 is in the context of Isaiah 40–66, which begins with the announcement of a new exodus (chap. 40) and concludes with God reigning over his people in a new heavens and earth (chaps. 65–66). The baptism of Jesus concludes with a heavenly voice asserting that Jesus is God's Son, strengthening the notion that he will reign over the people of the earth (Matt. 3:17; cf. Ps. 2).

The location of the temptation of Jesus after his baptism solidifies him as God's true Son (Matt. 4:1–11). Unlike Adam and Eve in Eden or Israel in the wilderness, Jesus resists the temptation to obey Satan. Although Satan offers Jesus "all the kingdoms of the world" (4:8), Jesus's baptism has already revealed him to be the true ruler of the cosmos. Satan cannot give to Jesus what the Father has already promised as an inheritance (Ps. 2). That Jesus obeys his Father, and thereby resists Satan, proves that he is the faithful Son who will receive the covenant promises. This sets the stage for the ministry of Jesus, where he calls people to follow him and share in the promises of the Father.

The Messiah's Ministry (4:12–20:34)

Jesus's ministry begins with a public announcement about the arrival of the kingdom (Matt. 4:17). So central is the kingdom that Jesus's preaching focuses on the "good news of the kingdom" (e.g., 4:23; 9:35; cf. 24:14). While modern evangelicals may be inclined to think that the gospel is only about forgiveness of sins, Matthew's Jesus preaches a gospel that is centered on the arrival of God's sovereign rule, which brings wholeness to people and to the entire earth. That is why Jesus goes around healing the sick, the leprous, the paralyzed, the blind, and the mute, renewing people afflicted by sin's dominion over the present age (4:23–25; 8:1–4; 9:1–7, 18–26, 27–34; 20:29–34). The wholeness Jesus brings to people fulfills the eschatological expectations of the prophet Isaiah, who anticipated the day when God would heal the sick, the blind, the mute, the paralyzed, and the lame (Isa. 35; 52–53). Jesus even casts out demons (Matt. 8:28–34) and raises the dead (9:23–26), showing that his kingdom is nullifying the rule of Satan and the forces of darkness. Jesus's followers preach this very "gospel of the kingdom" (10:35–38).

Matthew inserts a lengthy section focused on Jesus's Sermon on the Mount (Matt. 5–7). The sermon explains the nature of the kingdom, which alludes to Moses instructing the Israelites on Mount Sinai (Exod. 19–23). Jesus explains that his rule does not abolish the Mosaic law—it fulfills it, showing its true intent (Matt. 5:17–20). In so doing, Jesus teaches that God expects both inward and external devotion—he expects an entire person's life will be devoted to God. The Mosaic law always expected that God's people would dedicate their entire selves to loving him and the people under his rule. Jesus expects a righteousness that "surpasses" that of the Pharisees and the teachers

SHARING THE GOSPEL OF THE KINGDOM

Matthew's section on Jesus's ministry reveals that the gospel is about more than forgiveness of sins or salvation of souls—it is about delivering people into a place where they will experience the healing and wholeness for which humanity has longed. How should Matthew's presentation of the gospel influence the way we preach or teach the message of salvation? What kind of hope should we offer people—one that delivers them into heavenly bliss? Or one that delivers them into a place of restoration?

of the law (5:20). While perfection was not required, Jesus did expect that his followers would reflect the whole devotion expected of those awaiting the fulfillment of the kingdom, one that was distinct from the devotion of Israel's religious leaders.

Following the Sermon on the Mount, Matthew includes accounts of Jesus teaching in parables to explain the nature of the kingdom (e.g., Matt. 13:1–58; 18:21–35; 19:1–11). This is akin to the way Old Testament prophets used parables to speak to the hardened people of Israel after they had refused the plain speech of people like Moses and Elijah (cf. Isa. 6:9–10; Ezek. 24).[7] Jesus's parables sometimes fall on deaf ears; other times, willing recipients understand the "secrets of the kingdom" (Matt. 13:11). When understood correctly, Jesus's parables reveal that the kingdom has arrived. Soon Jesus will restore his people to life under his promised reign. We can think of him as the final prophet, who brings final parables to his people. If they are wise, they will prepare themselves for the consummation of the kingdom, lest they be judged as enemies (cf. 24:1–25:46).

The present section on Jesus's ministry makes additional connections between Jesus and Moses. We see this in the accounts of Jesus feeding five thousand (Matt. 14:13–21) and four thousand (15:32–39), which allude to God using Moses to provide abundant provision for Israel's wilderness generation (Exod. 16). Whereas God used Moses to provide manna for Israel, Jesus is the God who multiplies the sparse loaves and fish to provide for the people in the wilderness, showing that he is greater than Moses.

Matthew strengthens the presentation of Jesus's deity when he recalls Jesus walking on water (Matt. 14:25–26), which alludes to Yahweh trampling on the

---

7. G. K. Beale and Benjamin L. Gladd, *The Story Retold: A Biblical-Theological Introduction to the New Testament* (Downers Grove, IL: IVP Academic, 2020), 58.

waves of the sea in Job 9:8, and when he records Jesus's transfiguration before Moses and Elijah (Matt. 17:1–9), revealing that Jesus is the God who has come to fulfill the Law and the Prophets.[8] Jesus is also one and the same with Isaiah's suffering servant (Isa. 52–53) and Daniel's son of man (Dan. 7:13–14), who will go to Jerusalem to cement his reign over the cosmos through his suffering and death (Matt. 16:21–28; 17:22–23; 20:17–19).

Jesus's Road to the Cross (21:1–26:1)

Matthew 21 marks Jesus's triumphal entrance into Jerusalem. The people rightly hail him as the "Son of David" (21:9, 15). Soon he will go to the cross and take his rightful place as king. Along the way, Jesus clashes with the religious leaders, claiming they have corrupted the temple (21:12–17) and relating a series of parables that expose their wickedness and hypocrisy (21:28–32; 22:15–40). Though the leaders refuse to praise him, Jesus shows how even children understand that he is the promised Davidic king (21:16). Jesus stupefies them, showing from Scripture that he is the Messiah and son of David (22:41–46).

As Jesus continues his journey to the cross, he prophesies judgment on the teachers of the law and Pharisees (Matt. 23:1–36) and on Jerusalem (23:37–39). Both are full of murder and hypocrisy. Jesus's Olivet Discourse even speaks of the future tribulation and judgment coming on the earth, leading to his eschatological return (Matt. 24–25). Before all this, Jesus must first go to the cross, beginning the eschatological period associated with the events foretold in the Olivet Discourse.

Jesus's Passion, Resurrection, and Great Commission (26:2–28:20)

Matthew's final block of material is the darkest and most sinister of his entire Gospel. The religious leaders plot to kill Jesus (Matt. 26:1–5). But they need a betrayer, so they contract Judas for thirty pieces of silver, and he hands Jesus over in the Garden of Gethsemane (26:14–16, 47–56). Jesus then undergoes court trials before Caiaphas, the Sanhedrin, and Pilate, where he is sentenced to die on the cross (26:57–68; 27:1–2, 11–31). To make matters worse, Peter denies him, just as Jesus predicted (26:30–35, 69–75), as do the remainder of his male followers (26:56). Contrary to the cowardice of the

---

8. Richard B. Hays, *Echoes of Scripture in the Gospels* (Waco: Baylor University Press, 2016), 166–67.

men, "many women" remain as Jesus suffers on the cross, including Mary Magdalene, Mary the mother of James and Joseph, and the mother of the sons of Zebedee (27:55–56). Shortly after, Jesus dies and is buried (27:32–61).

What seems so dark and hopeless was foretold in the Scriptures, fulfilling the promises of what Israel's anticipated king would endure before entering his glory (Matt. 26:56). As Israel's God, Jesus understood that his suffering and death were necessary to fulfill the promises of a king who would establish his eternal reign over the cosmos. We see this, for instance, in the way Jesus institutes the Lord's Supper to anticipate how the new covenant would be established in his blood and to anticipate the consummation of the kingdom (26:26–29).

Jesus's death gives way to his resurrection (Matt. 28:1–9). As at his death, only women are present to witness the resurrected Jesus (28:1–6). As a result, Jesus gives women the privilege of proclaiming his resurrection to the men who had abandoned him (28:7–10). After the disciples receive the report, the resurrected Jesus gives them the commission to go into all the nations and make disciples of the resurrected Messiah (28:18–20). Those who receive the message will dwell in the promised kingdom, where the dominion of sin will have been abolished and the entire creation restored. God promises to be with his followers as they carry this message to the ends of the earth (28:20).

Canonical Function

That the Gospel of Matthew is positioned at the head of the New Testament should cause us to reflect on its significant—arguably the most significant—position in the canon. No other book continues the story of the Old Testament like Matthew does. We see this as soon as Matthew opens his Gospel with a genealogy, showing how Jesus is the descendant of Abraham and David, fulfilling the promise of a messianic ruler who brings the blessings of salvation to the nations by leading them out of exile and into a cosmic kingdom (Matt. 1:1–17).[9] In the remainder of his Gospel, Matthew incorporates Jesus's teachings about the kingdom, miracles of healing, exorcisms, parables, and suffering, death, and resurrection to underscore what he reveals in his genealogy. The opening of Matthew's Gospel is therefore

---

9. David R. Nienhuis argues, "Among the four canonical Gospels, none is better suited than Matthew to help readers transition out of the Old Testament (OT) and into the New Testament (NT). It is sometimes referred to as a transition or 'bridge' text, or even the 'hinge' on which the two Testaments pivot and swing." *A Concise Guide to Reading the New Testament: A Canonical Introduction* (Grand Rapids: Baker Academic, 2018), 18–19.

CANONICAL ORDER

Our modern Bibles conclude the Old Testament with the prophet Malachi and begin the New Testament with Matthew followed by Mark. Hebrew manuscripts, however, often conclude with Chronicles, and New Testament manuscripts usually begin with Matthew and Mark. Consequently, an alternate order would be Chronicles, Matthew, Mark. Consider this exercise: interpret the canonical function of Matthew in view of a Malachi, Matthew, Mark order. What are the similarities with the Chronicles, Matthew, Mark order? What are the differences? Which order most effectively continues the Old Testament storyline?

the most consequential section in the entire biblical canon, immediately connecting Jesus to the fulfillment of old covenant hopes and expectations. Without it, we are left to infer Jesus's messianic vocation from other sections of Matthew's Gospel—which is certainly possible, but it is not as clear without the genealogy that establishes his identity. We should think of Matthew's genealogy as a thesis statement for the entire Gospel and, by extension, the entire New Testament. After all, Jesus is the Messiah, Israel's God in the flesh, who initiates a cosmic restoration and about whom the entire New Testament canon testifies.

Authorship, Dating, and Audience

The early church held that the apostle Matthew authored the First Gospel (Eusebius, *Church History* 1.7.10; 3.24.5). While modern scholars may argue against this testimony, the evidence in the Gospel leans toward Matthew, the former tax collector turned follower of Jesus, as the author (Matt. 9:9).[10] Another important piece of evidence is that the manuscript tradition consistently identifies the author of the First Gospel with the title *Kata Matthaion* ("according to Matthew"). While titles are sometimes overlooked in discussions about authorship, it is important to recognize, as Martin Hengel argues, that the Gospels never circulated without the titles of their authors.[11] David Trobisch argues that the titles of the Gospels were added by the editors of the earliest edition of the New Testament as early as the

10. See references to taxation in Matt. 9:9; 10:3; 17:24.

11. Martin Hengel, *The Four Gospels and the One Gospel of Jesus Christ: An Investigation of the Collection and Origin of the Gospels*, trans. John Bowden (Harrisburg, PA: Trinity Press International, 2000), 96–105.

second century.[12] If true, we see that early Christians attributed authorship of the First Gospel to Matthew.

Matthew likely penned his Gospel in Syria, shortly after the composition of the Gospel of Mark. Since Matthew's Jesus predicts the future destruction of the temple, Matthew must have written his Gospel several years before this event in AD 70 (Matt. 24:2). We are therefore on relatively safe ground to date Matthew's composition to the mid- to late 60s. Matthew's later composition enabled him to draw from the earlier Gospel of Mark, which was likely penned in the mid-50s.

While there is no explicit mention of the audience, Matthew's explicit use of the Old Testament to show that Jesus is the Messiah points to an original Jewish audience. Since Matthew was included in the canon, the church intended for Matthew to have a broad, universal audience, making it applicable for all Christians throughout history.

Mark

Early theologians justified Mark's canonical position on the assumption that he abbreviated Matthew's Gospel.[13] They held that Mark did not have much to contribute to the tradition of the life, death, and resurrection of Jesus. Although this was a popular opinion throughout much of church history, most modern scholars rightly argue that Mark was the first Gospel, not Matthew. Although Mark was not an apostle and eyewitness to the historical Jesus, Papias confirms that his Gospel is based on the testimony of the apostle Peter (Eusebius, *Church History* 3.39.15). Consequently, it was Matthew who borrowed from the earlier Gospel of Mark, not the other way around.

We should not view the placement of Mark's Gospel as the result of its lesser importance or later composition. We should appreciate the Gospel's unique contribution to the Fourfold Gospel corpus—it is a fast-paced narrative that jumps quickly from scene to scene, almost like an action-packed movie. Whereas Matthew explicitly shows how Jesus is the promised Messiah, Mark takes readers on a high-octane journey that emphasizes the importance of Jesus's suffering as well as that of his followers. Mark is therefore an important reality check in the Gospel corpus. The triumphant call to "make disciples of all nations" at the conclusion of Matthew's Gospel is quickly

12. David Trobisch, *The First Edition of the New Testament* (Oxford: Oxford University Press, 2000), 38–43.

13. Augustine, *Harmony of the Gospels* 1.2.4.

tempered by Mark's Gospel, which disabuses readers of any dreams of glory without suffering.

Outline and Overview

Mark's Gospel follows a discernible geographic progression from Galilee to Jerusalem. Scholars often break the Gospel's progress into three stages: Jesus's Galilean ministry (Mark 1:1–8:26), Jesus's journey from Galilee to Jerusalem (8:27–10:52), and Jesus's final week in Jerusalem (11:1–16:8).[14] While this outline is helpful, it would be more accurate to argue that Mark uses the geographical progression of his Gospel to make a theological point: Jesus is the Son of God and Messiah who suffers for sinners. Mark therefore uses geography in service of theology.[15] As a result, we will follow an outline that makes two progressive theological points. First, Mark 1:1–8:26 presents Jesus as the Son of God and Messiah. Second, Mark 8:27–16:8 describes Jesus as the Son of God and Messiah who suffers for sinners.[16] In all this, Mark is more discreet than Matthew in showing the identity of Jesus, using more scriptural allusions than direct citations or fulfillment formulas. On some occasions, Mark uses the phrase "let the reader understand" to draw readers' minds to an intertextual allusion.[17] On the whole, readers must pay close attention to understand how Mark's Jesus fulfills old covenant expectations.

JESUS AS THE SON OF GOD AND MESSIAH (1:1–8:26)

Mark's first verse establishes that his Gospel is all about Jesus the Messiah, the Son of God (Mark 1:1). This line recalls 2 Samuel 7, where God promises David that one of his offspring will reign over his people, and Psalm 2, where God promises that his messianic Son will inherit a kingdom of multitudinous nations stretching to the ends of the earth. The remainder of the Gospel supports the thesis that Jesus is God's Son and Messiah while providing realistic expectations for those who desire to follow Jesus.

14. R. T. France, *The Gospel of Mark*, New International Greek Testament Commentary (Grand Rapids: Eerdmans, 2002), 11–15; Campbell and Pennington, *Reading the New Testament*, 106; Beale and Gladd, *Story Retold*, 71.

15. Stated otherwise: the progression of Mark's geography is linked to the progressive revelation of Jesus's identity.

16. Andreas J. Köstenberger, L. Scott Kellum, and Charles L. Quarles, *The Cradle, the Cross, and the Crown: An Introduction to the New Testament*, 2nd ed. (Nashville: B&H Academic, 2016), 286–90.

17. Hays, *Reading Backwards*, 17.

Mark supports his proposal by claiming to quote "Isaiah the prophet" (Mark 1:2). On closer examination, there is actually a short catena of citations—one from Malachi 3:1: "I will send my messenger ahead of you, who will prepare your way" (Mark 1:2); and one from Isaiah 40:3: "a voice of one calling in the wilderness, 'Prepare the way for the Lord, make straight paths for him'" (Mark 1:3). Since Mark mentions Isaiah to introduce and close the catena, we should assume that he wants readers to understand Malachi 3:1 through the lens of Isaiah. More to the point, since the Isaiah quotation recalls Isaiah's hope of second exodus in chapters 40–66, which culminates in the reception of a new heavens and earth in chapters 65–66, we envision that Mark is eliciting a vision of one preparing the way (Mal. 3:1) for a new exodus (also Isa. 43:2; 49:9–10; 52:12). As Moses led Israel out of slavery to Egypt, so Jesus now leads his people on a new exodus from the power of Satan, sin, and death. This "good news" is the source for Mark's own story about Jesus, who fulfills Israel's prophetic hopes. Like Matthew, for Mark the gospel is about more than just forgiveness of sins—it is about a Messiah and Son of God who will lead his people on a new exodus to a new heavens and earth.

Following the string of quotations in Mark 1:2–3, Mark inserts the account of John the Baptist proclaiming a baptism for the forgiveness of sins (1:4–8). To avoid overly spiritualizing "forgiveness of sins," we should recall that Israel's end of exile was tied to the forgiveness of their transgressions against their God (Isa. 40; Dan. 9). When this happened, God would once more extend mercy to his people, delivering them through a new exodus. So when John announces "a baptism of repentance for the forgiveness of sins" (Mark 1:4), Israel was to envision that the time of their deliverance had arrived, compelling them to turn from their unfaithfulness and to prepare themselves for the arrival of their saving God. John's public baptism of Jesus identifies him as God's royal Son and leader of the exodus (1:11; cf. Ps. 2). Jesus is the one on whom God has bestowed his Spirit (Mark 1:10), fulfilling Isaiah's expectation of one who will bring justice to the people of the earth after leading them out of slavery (Isa. 42:1–9). Jesus will baptize his people with the Spirit, enabling them to overcome their time in the present wilderness (Mark 1:8).

After his baptism, Jesus enters the wilderness and is tempted by Satan for forty days (Mark 1:12–13). Unlike Israel, who succumbed to Satan's temptations in the wilderness, Jesus overcomes, showing he is God's true Son (1:13). He then enters Galilee, announcing the good news of the transformative reign of God, which will be fulfilled after the completion of the new exodus (1:14–15).

Jesus begins his Galilean ministry by calling his first disciples (Mark 1:16–20). These first followers were not among society's elite—they were common fishermen who spent their lives casting nets into the sea to support their families. The scene sets a pattern for the kinds of followers whom Jesus draws—everyday people who drop everything to follow Jesus. In turn, Jesus will entrust them with the task of gathering more people into his kingdom.

Mark then inserts several healing stories into his narrative. Jesus heals a man with an unclean spirit (Mark 1:21–28). He also heals Simon's mother-in-law (1:29–31) and many diseased persons (1:32–34). He heals a leper (1:40–45), a paralytic (2:1–12), and a man with a withered hand (3:1–6). These accounts recall texts such as Isaiah 35, which anticipates the day when God will return to heal the blind, deaf, lame, and mute. We should assume the presence of Isaiah 35 whenever we read accounts of Jesus restoring the blind, deaf, lame, and mute, as well as performing other various healings, revealing how Jesus brings wholeness to people oppressed by the debilitating reign of sin.

In addition to healing accounts, Mark includes stories of Jesus delivering people from unclean spirits and demons (Mark 1:23–27, 34, 39). In such contexts, Jesus presents himself as one who forgives sins (2:5; cf. Isa. 44:22) and as the Son of Man (Mark 2:10; cf. Dan. 7). These accounts serve to reveal that Jesus, the Son of God and Messiah, is one and the same with the God of Israel, who has come to free the world from the power of sin (Isa. 44) and establish his eternal dominion over the earth (Dan. 7).

An account about Jesus preaching in Galilee rests in the midst of Mark's stories of healing and restoration (Mark 1:35–39). From this, we see that Mark wants readers to grasp the content of Jesus's preaching through the framework of Jesus healing and restoring people afflicted by the power of sin and demonic forces. So Jesus's preaching "throughout Galilee" is focused on the arrival of God's restorative reign to the earth (1:39). Soon the entire cosmos will be liberated from the reign of sin and death and renewed into a new creation. But not all people accept this "good news." The scribes, for instance, question Jesus's divine prerogative to forgive sins, accusing him of blasphemy (2:6–8). Others accept the testimony of Jesus, confessing him as God's divine Son, who has come to establish his reign over the earth (3:7–12).

At this point in the narrative, Mark organizes accounts that reveal increasing opposition to Jesus's transformative ministry (Mark 3:13–6:6). While we would certainly expect incredulity from religious leaders, Mark makes a point to include how Jesus's family reacts to Jesus's increased notoriety: "He is out of his mind" (3:21). Mark includes this account right after he provides

PARABLES

Jesus uses parables (metaphorical forms of instruction) to convey truths about the kingdom. Some would argue that parables have only one meaning. While this is possible for some parables, we should be open to envisioning that Jesus uses parables to draw his audiences into the story, pushing them to identify with a particular group or character. Assuming parables have different meanings for different readers, we should view them as having the potential for polymorphic meaning rather than one static sense.

a list of Jesus's twelve apostles (3:13–19). These two accounts insinuate the reaction Jesus's followers should expect, even from their own families: that they too are "out of their minds." Many believers have had to endure these very words from loved ones who are incredulous about the work of Jesus. Yet, those who have suffered such rejection can be sure that they have not been abandoned. Jesus explains that our primary familial ties are not with those who share biological connections but with "whoever does God's will" (3:35).

Mark 4:1–34 contains a series of Jesus's parables. He includes a parable about a sower (4:1–20), a lamp under a basket (4:21–25), scattered seed (4:26–29), and a mustard seed (4:30–32). Such parables encourage readers to discern their standing in relation to the kingdom that is progressively expanding to encompass the entire earth.

Mark follows the series of parables with several stories that reveal Jesus's identity. In the first story, Jesus calms a storm, showing his power over nature (Mark 4:35–41). In the second, Jesus heals a man possessed by a demon, displaying his mastery of the spiritual realm (5:1–20). In the third, Jesus performs two miracles, healing a woman who had suffered from an incurable discharge of blood (5:21–34) and raising a dead girl to life (5:35–43). These stories continue to prove that Jesus is the Son of God and Messiah, who has come to restore the world and bring wholeness to people who have longed for deliverance. Despite these identity-revealing miracles, many prefer that Jesus depart from their presence (5:17). Others display their unwavering faith in the transformative power of Jesus (5:34).

The remainder of the first half of Mark's Gospel continues the pattern of increased opposition to Jesus's ministry (Mark 6:1–8:26). Some of his stiffest opposition comes from the religious leaders (7:1–13; 8:11–13) and his hometown of Nazareth (6:1–6). With the mention of Nazareth, it is clear that resistance to and incredulity regarding Jesus are everywhere. In the midst of these stories of rejection, however, Mark continues to include stories that reveal the identity of Jesus. One of several such stories is Jesus feeding the five thousand in a desolate place (6:30–44), which recalls Moses providing manna for the Israelites in the wilderness (Exod. 16). There is also a similar story about Jesus feeding four thousand people (Mark 8:1–10), which alludes to the exodus tradition. Such accounts bring to mind that Jesus is a greater savior than Moses.

Jesus walking on water (Mark 6:45–52) alludes to Yahweh, the one who "treads on the waves of the sea" in Job 9:8. Jesus healing a deaf person again recalls Isaiah 35, which anticipates the return of Yahweh to restore the diseased. All in all, these accounts strengthen the identity of Jesus in Mark's Gospel: he is the divine Son of God and Messiah, who has come to lead his people to a place of restoration, just as the prophets foretold. Mark's Gospel is shaped in such a way that readers are compelled to trust in the one whom he unveils to readers but who remains hidden from his contemporaries.

Jesus as the Son of God and Messiah Who Suffers for Sinners (8:27–16:8)

Peter's confession that Jesus is the Messiah shifts our attention to the second half of the Gospel (Mark 8:27–30). In this section, Mark teaches readers about the suffering believers should expect when they commit to following Jesus on a new exodus. He begins by inserting three accounts in which Jesus explains the necessity of the Son of Man suffering, dying, and rising from the grave (8:31–33; 9:30–32; 10:32–34). But the disciples fail to understand that suffering is the path to glory (9:32). Despite the dullness of the disciples, Mark presents Jesus in such a way that readers should grasp that the Messiah and Son of God are one and the same with Isaiah's suffering servant (Isa. 52–53). If we hear Jesus's teaching about his suffering, death, and glory in light of the context of Isaiah 52–53, we envision that Jesus suffers to deliver his people on a new exodus into a new heavens and earth (Isa. 40–66). All who will follow Jesus out of the present wilderness of sin and death should expect to follow his path of suffering.

The accounts of Jesus's teaching about his death and resurrection are interspersed with insightful stories about the nature of the messianic kingdom.[18] We read, for instance, stories of Jesus healing a boy with an unclean spirit

---

18. Campbell and Pennington, *Reading the New Testament*, 113.

(Mark 9:14–29), Jesus teaching on true greatness in the kingdom (9:33–37; 10:35–45), and receiving the kingdom as a child (10:13–16). Such stories reveal that Jesus's restorative reign is unlike anything ever experienced on the earth. It is one in which the loftiest of rulers—almighty God himself (9:2–13)—will offer his life in service of others (10:45).

Chapter 11 begins with Jesus riding into Jerusalem on a donkey, what is often called the triumphal entry (Mark 11:1–10). This event alludes to Genesis 49:10–11, which sets the expectation for a messianic ruler in 2 Samuel 7.[19] Genesis 49:10–11 claims that Judah's future ruler will have dominion over the nations. What links this figure to Jesus is the reference to the ruler binding "his donkey to a vine, his colt to the choicest branch" (49:11). When Jesus rides into Jerusalem on a donkey, Mark portrays him as the one who fulfills the expectation of a ruler from Judah. In turn, this figure is linked to messianic hopes in 2 Samuel 7. Mark tempers the triumphal entry with accounts of Jesus cleansing the temple (Mark 11:15–19) and challenging the teachings and practices of religious leaders such as the Pharisees and scribes (12:1–40). He also inserts the Olivet Discourse, which anticipates the future destruction of Jerusalem (13:1–37). All of this paints the picture of the arrival of the king who will soon consummate his reign. In the meantime, his followers should ready themselves for his return, lest they be judged along with those who refuse his rule.

Mark 14–16 begins with the plot to kill Jesus (14:1–2) and culminates with his reported resurrection (16:1–8). Along the way, Mark includes accounts about a woman who exhausts a costly bottle of perfume to anoint Jesus for his upcoming burial (14:3–9) and Jesus's final Passover with his disciples (14:12–31). The former account shows how a woman forsakes wealth to prepare Jesus for death. She stands in contrast to Judas, who hands Jesus over to the authorities for financial gain (14:10–11, 43–50).[20] The final Passover scene recalls the original one, just before Israel was delivered from Egypt (Exod. 12), while also anticipating Jesus's death as the final Passover lamb. Through Jesus's death, God will accomplish a greater deliverance than anything witnessed in Egypt. This comparison allows readers to envision that the original exodus through Moses functioned as a type of the greater exodus through Jesus the Messiah.

When the crowd of chief priests, scribes, and elders comes for Jesus, his remaining followers abandon him (Mark 14:50). Even worse, Peter denies

---

19. See Chrysostom, *Homilies on Genesis* 67.9.

20. James R. Edwards, *The Gospel according to Mark*, Pillar New Testament Commentary (Grand Rapids: Eerdmans, 2002), 413.

THE ENDING OF MARK'S GOSPEL

Many of our Bibles include a note saying that Mark 16:9–20 is not in the earliest manuscripts. The abrupt ending to the Gospel of Mark did not sit well with scribes. At the risk of sounding overly simplistic, I note that some scribes added a fuller ending to the Gospel of Mark (including accounts such as resurrection appearances and the Great Commission) that harmonized with the endings of Matthew and Luke. This ending was then copied for centuries in several manuscript traditions and is found in translations such as the King James Version. The correct ending of Mark is found in two of the most reliable codices from the fourth century, Sinaiticus (ℵ) and Vaticanus (B), which do not include 16:9–20. The more abrupt ending of Mark coheres with some of the earliest manuscripts and the theological emphasis of the Gospel, which encourages fear and trembling before committing to follow Jesus.

Jesus during his condemnation before the Jewish council (14:53–72), which was just as Jesus had predicted (14:27–31). Jesus is then handed to Pilate, who delivers Jesus to be crucified (15:1–15). Like Matthew's Gospel, Mark mentions that only women were present for Jesus's death (15:40–41). He also notes that only women—Mary Magdalene, Mary the mother of James, and Salome—intended to anoint Jesus's dead body (16:1–2). This is in stark contrast to the male disciples, who had already fled from the presence of Jesus. Since the women remain loyal to Jesus even after his death, they are rewarded with the opportunity to share the good news of Jesus's resurrection with the disciples (16:5–7).

The Gospel of Mark closes on an ominous note: "Trembling and bewildered, the women went out and fled from the tomb. They said nothing to anyone, because they were afraid" (Mark 16:8). No confirmation that the women announced the resurrection to the disciples. No accounts of Jesus appearing to his followers. No Great Commission to spread the good news among the nations. We are left with only fear and trembling—which is actually an appropriate ending to Mark's Gospel. Although the Gospel has shown that Jesus is the divine Son of God and Messiah, whose Passover death accomplishes a new exodus to a new creation, Mark consistently calls readers to count the cost of following Jesus. Readers should question whether they are prepared to remain faithful to the very end—just like the women. Readers should consider such a question with much fear and trembling.

Canonical Function

Matthew's announcement of the promised Messiah (Matt. 1:1) and the consequent call to make disciples of all nations (28:19–20) may leave us with the impression that following Jesus is all about triumph and glory. After all, the king has come! So we should tell everyone about it! But then we turn to Mark's Gospel, which provides a realistic account of what it means to follow the Messiah. Jesus has undoubtedly initiated a new exodus from the power of sin and death that will culminate in the entrance into a new creation. But readers must remember that we are currently in the wilderness, where sin still inflicts suffering on God's people. Our experience is analogous to what Israel endured during the original exodus, as they underwent a painful journey to Canaan. It is also comparable to what Jesus endured, as he suffered and died before entering glory.

We should not take lightly the commitment to follow Messiah Jesus. We should consider Mark's emphasis on the suffering that Jesus's followers should expect to endure before entering their glorious existence on a new earth. Consequently, we must approach the journey with much fear and trembling, knowing that it may cost us our very lives. But we should not be deterred from the journey. Nor should we be deterred from making followers of the Messiah. Peter, the very source for Mark's Gospel, gives the reason why: "And the God of all grace, who called you to his eternal glory in Christ, after you have suffered a little while, will himself restore you and make you strong, firm and steadfast" (1 Pet. 5:10).

Authorship, Dating, and Audience

The title *Kata Markon* ("according to Mark") is the only indicator of the authorship of the Second Gospel. This Mark is likely one and the same with John Mark in Acts (Acts 12:12, 25; 13:5, 13; 15:37), who was an associate of Paul (Col. 4:10; 2 Tim. 4:11; Philem. 24) and Peter (1 Pet. 5:13). Since he was not an eyewitness or apostle, authors such as Papias (Eusebius, *Church History* 3.39.15), Irenaeus (*Against Heresies* 3.1.2), Tertullian (*Against Marcion* 4.5), and Origen (*Commentary on Matthew* in Eusebius, *Church History* 6.25.5) claim that Mark drew his information from the apostle Peter. This makes sense when we consider that Mark's Gospel follows Peter's sermon outline in Acts 10:36–43[21] and when we notice the correlation between the emphasis on

21. Peter Stuhlmacher, *Biblical Theology of the New Testament*, trans. Daniel P. Bailey (Grand Rapids: Eerdmans, 2018), 561.

suffering in 1 Peter and in Mark's Gospel. In short, the authorship of Mark's Gospel is tied to John Mark, the associate of apostles such as Paul and Peter.

Mark wrote his Gospel before Matthew and Luke composed theirs. If Matthew and Luke wrote their accounts somewhere between the mid- to late 60s AD, we can date Mark's Gospel to the mid- to late 50s AD. This would have given Matthew and Luke enough time to familiarize themselves with Mark's work before using it to compose their own accounts. Luke likely refers to Mark's Gospel when he claims that "many have undertaken to draw up an account of the things that have been fulfilled among us" (Luke 1:1).

Mark's use of Latinisms—such as *lepta* (two Roman coins, Mark 12:42), *praetorium* (governor's home, 15:16), *legion* (cohort of Roman soldiers, 5:9), and *centurion* (Roman soldier, 15:39)—points to a Roman audience familiar with such terminology.[22] While this may have been Mark's original audience, the Gospel's inclusion in the canon of Scripture suggests that it is intended for all Christians.

Luke

The Gospel of Luke is the first of two volumes known as Luke-Acts. Both volumes are addressed to Theophilus, whose name means "friend of God" (Luke 1:3; Acts 1:1). Acts even refers back to the "former book" Luke addressed to Theophilus, where he wrote about "all that Jesus began to do and teach until the day he was taken up to heaven" (Acts 1:1–2). While Theophilus was likely a real person, possibly the patron of Luke's writings, the fact that the Gospel of Luke is in the canon means that it is intended for more than a single historical figure in the first century. Luke himself insinuates that his Gospel is for the broadest audience possible—especially vulnerable members of society, such as women and the poor, and social outcasts, such as shepherds, Samaritans, and lepers.

That Luke and Acts were volumes in a single literary work does not mean that we should read them consecutively. The manuscript tradition reveals that Luke has always been read in the context of the Fourfold Gospel. Acts has always followed the Gospels, joined to either the Pauline or the Catholic epistles. As a result, Luke is meant to be heard among the other Evangelists.

We last heard Mark calling readers to consider the cost before following Jesus. Now Luke encourages us to see the salvation that Jesus brings to Jew

---

22. Köstenberger, Kellum, and Quarles, *Cradle, the Cross, and the Crown*, 281–82.

and gentile, regardless of age, gender, social class, or infirmities. Luke is the most inclusive of all the Evangelists, showing how Jesus's kingdom is for all people, erasing boundaries that kept women in their place and social outcasts outside the people of God. There is little doubt that Luke abolishes restrictions on who is permitted to benefit from Jesus's salvific reign.

Outline and Overview

The Gospel of Luke has three major sections. The first section reveals the identity of Jesus, beginning with the events surrounding his promised birth, followed by his childhood, continuing into his ministry of teaching and healing (Luke 1:1–9:50). The second section narrates Jesus's journey to Jerusalem, what is commonly called the travel narrative (9:51–19:27). While Jesus continues to teach and heal, unique to this section are parables such as the good Samaritan (10:25–37) and the prodigal son (15:11–32). The third and final section focuses on Jesus's arrival in Jerusalem and the passion narrative (19:28–24:53). The book concludes with Jesus's resurrection appearances to his followers, explaining how all the Law and Prophets are fulfilled in him.

Campbell and Pennington observe that these sections are all "centered on Jerusalem, which is known as the city of David and the center of Jewish worship and culture."[23] Luke's choice to organize his Gospel around Jerusalem may be linked to his focus on the fulfillment of messianic promises to Israel—which he often accomplishes by employing Old Testament allusions. We see this at the very inception of the Gospel, when Luke claims to write an orderly account of the events "fulfilled among us" (Luke 1:1) and when Elizabeth exclaims to Mary, "Blessed is she who has believed that the Lord would fulfill his promises to her!" (1:45; also 1:32–33, 54–55, 68–75).[24] For Luke, it is fitting to situate his Gospel around the place where the kingdom was originally centered and where it would be fulfilled through the promised Davidic king, who would expand the kingdom to include Jews and gentiles of every gender, class, and tribe.

THE IDENTITY OF JESUS: BIRTH, CHILDHOOD, AND MINISTRY (1:1–9:50)

Luke concedes that his Gospel is based on accounts about the historical Jesus (Luke 1:1–4). He likely used the Gospel of Mark, with which he

23. Campbell and Pennington, *Reading the New Testament*, 121.
24. These examples of fulfillment are from Nienhuis, *Concise Guide*, 56.

and Matthew share material in common. Since he has material in common with Matthew not found in Mark, Luke may have drawn on the earlier Gospel of Matthew. It is also possible that Luke and Matthew drew their common material from another early Christian source or tradition, what scholars refer to as Q.[25]

After the dedication to Theophilus, the remainder of Luke 1–2 establishes that the time has come for God to fulfill the promises to his people. We see this as early as the account about the promised birth of John the Baptist, who will prepare the people for the Lord's return (1:5–25). His father, Zechariah, doubts the promised birth, for he and his wife are advanced in age (1:18), so the angel swears that Zechariah will remain mute until the birth of his son (1:19–20).

After John's birth, Zechariah's tongue is loosed, and he blesses the God who fulfills his promises through the barrenness of humanity, as he did through Sarah, Rebekah, and Leah (Luke 1:57–66). We also see that God—once more through an angel—promises Mary that she, though a virgin, will give birth to the son of David, the one who will reign over his people forever (1:26–45). Unlike Zechariah, Mary shows great faith, even singing a song of praise to the God who "has helped his servant Israel, remembering to be merciful to Abraham and his descendants forever, just as he promised to our ancestors" (1:54–55). The arrival of God's salvation recalls the exodus, when God acted through Moses to deliver his people out of oppression in Egypt. In the present time, he acts through Jesus the Messiah to save his people from oppressive powers such as Rome, through which sin exercises its dominion.

Luke records that Jesus, the king of the universe, is born in a stable and visited by lowly shepherds (Luke 2:1–20). Unlike Matthew, Luke excludes the magi from his Gospel so that he might draw attention to Jesus's salvation of the downtrodden. The angel of the Lord, after all, says to the shepherds that Jesus is "for all the people" (2:10). Luke's Jesus removes any hints of the exclusivity of salvation readers may have drawn from Matthew and Mark.

Following Jesus's appearance in the temple as a twelve-year-old (Luke 2:41–52), Luke 3–4 shows that Jesus begins the process of transforming the present order into a new creation (cf. Isa. 65–66; Ezek. 36–37).[26] We see this as

---

25. The letter Q is short for the German word *Quelle*, meaning "source." Appendix 1 includes a brief discussion on the Q source.

26. See the helpful discussion in Beale and Gladd, *Story Retold*, 104–8.

John baptizes Jesus in the wilderness, proclaiming "a baptism of repentance for the forgiveness of sins" (Luke 3:3). Earlier, we noted that "forgiveness of sins" is tied to the end of exile and the restoration of God's people.[27] Luke's more universalized use of the exodus tradition warrants further discussion regarding the connection between "forgiveness" and "restoration." In Daniel 9:16, Daniel's prayer admits that Israel's state of exile among the nations is because of "our sins" and "the iniquities of our ancestors." He appeals to God's "great mercy" to "forgive" his people so that they might experience restoration (9:18–19).[28] The link between "forgiveness" and "end of exile" is even more pronounced considering that Luke 3:4–6, after mentioning that John's baptism is "for the forgiveness of sins," contains a quotation of the new exodus context of Isaiah 40:3–5. Although Matthew and Mark quote Isaiah 40:3, Luke extends his quotation to include Isaiah 40:4–5 to universalize the nature of salvation through Jesus. This is affirmed at the close of Luke 3:6, which draws the reader to Isaiah 40:5: "and all people will see God's salvation." Luke's extended quotation reveals the cosmic nature of the new exodus. For Luke, Jesus has come to deliver all people from exile under the dominion of sin and into a kingdom in a new creation, just like Isaiah foresaw in his vision of a new heavens and earth (Isa. 65–66) and Daniel saw in his vision of a son of man "coming with the clouds of heaven" (Dan. 7:13).

Furthermore, Luke's portrayal of John's baptism specifies that the new exodus is not restricted to those who think their ethnic privilege makes them the rightful children of Abraham (Luke 3:7–9). God's mercy extends to those who were formerly considered outside the boundaries of the covenant, such as tax collectors and Roman soldiers (3:10–14). John's baptism concludes with Jesus passing through the baptismal waters (3:21–22), alluding to Israel passing through the Red Sea (Exod. 14). After Jesus rises from the waters, the Holy Spirit descends on Jesus "like a dove," and God announces from heaven that Jesus is his "Son, whom [he] loves" (Luke 3:22). This event alludes to Ezekiel 36:25–27 and Joel 2, where the presence of the Spirit is linked to the arrival of the new age and the restoration of God's people. The pronouncement from heaven recalls Psalm 2, which confirms that God's Son will rule over the nations. These passages broaden the interpretive framework for Jesus's baptism, envisioning that, through the empowerment of the divine Spirit, Jesus will forgive his people's sins, delivering them from exile in the fallen world and into his kingdom in a new creation.

27. N. T. Wright, *Jesus and the Victory of God* (Minneapolis: Fortress, 1996), 270–71.
28. Wright, *Jesus and the Victory*, 271.

Luke includes a genealogy of Jesus (Luke 3:23–38) between the baptism narrative (3:21–22) and the temptation of Jesus (4:1–13). Luke 4:1 encourages readers to link Jesus's baptism and temptation accounts: "Jesus, full of the Holy Spirit, left the Jordan and was led by the Spirit into the wilderness." This statement draws on the exodus overtones in Jesus's baptism and carries them into his temptation, underscoring that Jesus is the Son of God, who overcomes the devil's temptation through the empowerment of the Spirit. Although God sent his Spirit to lead Israel through the wilderness (Neh. 9:20–21; Isa. 63:11–14), the exodus story reveals how Israel falls into idolatry (Exod. 32) and puts God to the test (Exod. 17). In overcoming the very temptations to which Israel succumbs, Jesus displays his victory over the devil and the arrival of eschatological salvation. Soon he will lead his people on a triumphant exodus journey that will culminate in the final defeat of Satan and the Spirit's restoration of the cosmos.

We see vivid pictures of this new reality in the way Jesus teaches in the synagogue, claiming he fulfills Isaiah's foretold renovation and undoing of sin's curse on the "prisoners," "blind," and "oppressed" (Luke 4:16–21; cf. Isa. 61:1–2). He will do so, as Isaiah 61:1 mentions, because "the Spirit of the Lord is on" him (Luke 4:18). He also heals people of diseases (4:38–40) and exorcises demons (4:33–37, 41), showing that Satan is losing his authority over people. All this activity is associated with the "good news of the kingdom of God," which Jesus has come to proclaim (4:43).

Luke 5:1–9:50 focuses on Jesus's ministry in Galilee, just before he begins his journey to Jerusalem (9:51). The section opens with Jesus calling three fishermen—Peter, James, and John—to become his first disciples (5:1–11). Jesus promises that they will "fish for people," which signifies a change of vocation—from drawing fish into nets to gathering people into the kingdom (5:10).[29] Jesus gains a large group of followers, from which he chooses twelve apostles (6:12–16). The Twelve, which recall the twelve tribes of Israel, represent a new people whom Jesus will lead into a new creation, fulfilling the covenant promises to Abraham.

Between these accounts, Luke inserts stories of Jesus cleansing a leper (Luke 5:12–16), healing a paralytic (5:17–26), and healing a man with a withered hand (6:6–11). As in Matthew and Mark, such accounts allude to the healings associated with Isaiah's expectation of a new creation (Isa. 35:1–6). What is more, Isaiah links the restorative acts of the new age with the new exodus

---

29. Darrell L. Bock, *Luke 1:1–9:50*, Baker Exegetical Commentary on the New Testament (Grand Rapids: Baker Academic, 2004), 460–62.

(35:8–10). Contrary to the Pharisees' expectations, the disciples do not fast, because Jesus is the bridegroom who has come to bring his people into an age of celebration and rejoicing (Luke 5:33–39).

Jesus continues to reveal his identity as the powerful Davidic king when he heals many people's diseases (Luke 6:17–19). So great is his restorative power that many "tried to touch him, because power was coming from him and healing them all" (6:19). Luke also includes stories of Jesus healing a centurion's servant (7:1–10), raising a widow's son (7:11–17), healing a man with a demon (8:26–39), healing a woman with an incurable rush of blood (8:40–48), and restoring a ruler's daughter (8:49–56). These powerful events are reported to John the Baptist, who in turn commands two of his disciples to question Jesus about whether he is "the one who is to come" (7:18–20; cf. Ps. 118:26; Mal. 3:1).[30] After the question, Luke records, "At that very time Jesus cured many who had diseases, sicknesses and evil spirits, and gave sight to many who were blind" (Luke 7:21). This suggests that the answer to John's question is linked to Jesus's restorative miracles and his power over demons. In Luke 7:22, Jesus's response draws on passages from Isaiah: "the blind receive sight, the lame walk, those who have leprosy are cleansed, the deaf hear" (Isa. 35:3–4), "the dead are raised" (26:19), and "the good news is proclaimed to the poor" (61:1–2).[31] His reply confirms that he is the one whom God has sent to deliver his people from the powers of sin and darkness.

Luke also includes accounts that reveal the nature of Jesus's messianic kingdom. The Beatitudes reveal that the reign of Jesus will bring a great reversal of fortunes: the marginalized (the poor, the hungry, and those who weep) will be raised to enjoy the blessings of the kingdom, whereas the powerful (the rich, the satisfied, and those who laugh) will taste no such benefits (Luke 6:20–26). Also significant are the kingdom-reversing expectations to love your enemies (6:27–36) and withhold hypocritical judgment (6:37–42), as well as Jesus forgiving a woman whom the Pharisees deemed unworthy of salvation (7:36–50). Such stories show that the nature of the kingdom is radically different from the expectations of the present age.

Jesus then commissions the Twelve to proclaim the kingdom that undoes the power of sin over humanity (Luke 9:1–2). Upon their return, Jesus reveals another picture of the kingdom by providing bread in the wilderness

---

30. David W. Pao and Eckhard J. Schnabel note that "the one to come" alludes to Mal. 3:1 and Ps. 118:26. "Luke," *Commentary on the New Testament Use of the Old Testament*, ed. G. K. Beale and D. A. Carson (Grand Rapids: Baker Academic, 2007), 299.

31. Pao and Schnabel, "Luke," 299.

(9:10–17). Although Moses provided manna in the original exodus, his generation eventually died in the wilderness (Exod. 16). In the new exodus, Jesus sustains his people until they enter the promised kingdom on a new earth. Peter recognizes that Jesus is the Messiah, the promised king of Israel (Luke 9:18–20). Jesus's kingdom will not be fulfilled by overpowering enemies. Just the opposite: Jesus predicts that his reign will be established through the weakness of death (9:21–22). Since Jerusalem is where his reign will be established, Jesus begins the journey to the place where he will suffer to deliver his people from the grip of sin and the devil so that he will fulfill the promise of a new exodus into a cosmic kingdom (9:51).

Jesus's Journey to Jerusalem (9:51–19:27)

As he heads to Jerusalem, Jesus appoints "seventy-two" to go into "every town and place where he was about to go" (Luke 10:1). This group is a "new humanity . . . reconstituted around King Jesus,"[32] who commands his followers to heal the sick and announce the arrival of the kingdom of God (10:9–12). Once more, Luke pairs the themes of "healing" and "kingdom." As I have argued, the kingdom brings deliverance from diseases associated with the present dominion of sin. Those who respond to the preaching of the kingdom are united to the reconstituted humanity, who will experience all the benefits of living under the reign of Jesus. Since the kingdom has not yet been consummated, the Lord's Prayer teaches Jesus's followers to pray for the fulfillment of the kingdom (11:1–4). Only then will the benefits of God's reign be fully realized on the earth.

Luke includes a parable about a rich man (Luke 12:13–21) and Jesus's teaching about avoiding anxiety over provisions (12:22–34) to stress that God's people should not worry about money and provisions (12:31). Those anxious about such things show themselves to be like gentiles, who do not worship the king who provides all good things for his people (12:31). Since Jesus will soon bring a sword of division, separating believers and unbelievers, it is important to know in whom we have really placed our trust (12:49–53).

While continuing to include miraculous healings associated with the reign of Jesus (Luke 13:10–17; 14:1–6; 17:11–19), Luke increases the number of parables about the kingdom (13:1–19:27). The parables about the steadily growing mustard seed and the slowly expanding yeast show that the kingdom

---

32. Beale and Gladd, *Story Retold*, 116.

REFLECTION QUESTIONS

Jesus's journey to Jerusalem raises several questions. Are we willing to prioritize his kingdom over biological family (Luke 9:57–62)? Are we willing to suffer, just like Jesus (11:37–12:59)? The way we answer these questions determines whether we are "fit for service in the kingdom of God" (9:62).

WHOM DOES THE CHURCH VALUE?

Luke's esteem of the outsider raises some important questions. Do we value the same people Luke does—sinners, widows, tax collectors, women, and the diseased? Or do we esteem the rich, powerful, and influential—those from whom we can profit? Otherwise stated, do our values align with those of Luke? Or do they align with those of the passing age?

arrives gradually (13:18–21).[33] This is an adjustment from the old covenant expectations of prophets like Isaiah and Daniel, who foresaw an instantaneous transition between the old age and the one to come (Isa. 63:4–6; 65:17–25; 66:15–24; Dan. 2:44). Moreover, the growth of the mustard seed into a tree where the "birds perched in its branches" (Luke 13:19) alludes to Psalm 104:12 and Daniel 4:9–21, which anticipate the gentiles under God's care. Such allusions underscore the progressive expansion of the kingdom, which will gather Jews and gentiles under the care of the true God.

Jesus's parables about the wedding feast (Luke 14:7–24) and the rich man and Lazarus (16:19–31), as well as stories about the Pharisees and the tax collector (18:9–14) and children coming to Jesus (18:15–17), reveal that the kingdom is for outsiders, the poor, and the lowly. This is radically different from the kingdoms of the present age, which value people of notoriety, wealth, and high status. The kingdom of Jesus brings a radical transformation of values regarding who is "in" and who is "out" of the reign of God.

What is more, Jesus's parables of the lost sheep (Luke 15:1–7), the lost coin (15:8–10), and the prodigal son (15:11–32) reveal that the kingdom welcomes those who have wandered from God. Jesus even welcomes a chief tax collector like Zacchaeus, who many consider too sinful to be a beneficiary of God's salvation (19:1–10). Perhaps Luke includes the story of Zacchaeus

---

33. James R. Edwards, *The Gospel according to Luke*, Pillar New Testament Commentary (Grand Rapids: Eerdmans, 2015), 398.

toward the end of the travel narrative, just before Jesus makes his way to his execution in Jerusalem, to emphasize that Jesus's salvific sacrifice is even, perhaps especially, for those considered outsiders to the promises of God.

Jesus's Arrival in Jerusalem and the Passion Narrative (19:28–24:53)

Luke 19:28–24:53 begins by narrating Jesus's entrance into Jerusalem, the place from which Israel's kings ruled. Of all the kings, David directly foreshadows the reign of Jesus—for to him God promised a descendant who would reign perpetually over God's people (2 Sam. 7). So when Jesus arrives in Jerusalem, he comes to rule over his people. Although Luke does not quote Zechariah 9:9, it is impossible to ignore the image of Jesus as Israel's king, who approaches Jerusalem on a humble donkey, symbolizing the reign of peace that will begin in Jerusalem and spread to the ends of the earth (Luke 19:28–40).

As Jesus enters Jerusalem, a large crowd proclaims him "the king who comes in the name of the Lord" (Luke 19:38). Such display of belief is also mixed with incredulity, as the Pharisees call for Jesus to rebuke his disciples for acknowledging his royal status (19:39). Jesus retorts that the silence of his disciples will not preclude even the stones from crying out about the arrival of the king of Israel (19:40). Jesus's response recalls that his rule brings about the restoration of the entire creation, even the very stones of the earth that languish under sin's tyranny (cf. Isa. 24–25).

Jesus weeps over the future destruction of obstinate Jerusalem (Luke 19:41–44). Luke stresses Israel's unbelief in the accounts about the religious leaders challenging Jesus's authority (20:1–8), the scribes and the chief priests questioning Jesus about paying taxes to Caesar (20:20–26), and the Sadducees interrogating Jesus about the resurrection (20:27–40). The rejection of the king will result in the destruction of the sacred temple (21:5–9) and the city of Jerusalem (21:20–28). These events will crescendo in the return of the Son of Man to establish his reign over the world (21:25–28; cf. Dan. 7). Although the cross marks the inception of his reign, Jesus will consummate his kingdom only when he returns "in a cloud with power and great glory" (Luke 21:27) to put the world to rights (21:28).

As his crucifixion draws near, Jesus celebrates the Passover with his disciples, which looks back on the original exodus and anticipates Jesus's new exodus as the final Passover lamb (Luke 22:7–23). This meal also foreshadows the day when Jesus and his followers will dine together when his kingdom is established over the earth (22:28–30; cf. Rev. 19). After being betrayed and arrested, Jesus stands trial before an assembly of Israel's elders, then Pilate, and later Herod (Luke 22:3–6, 47–53; 22:66–23:10). When he is returned to Pilate, the Roman governor acquiesces to the crowd and delivers Jesus to be crucified (23:11–24).

Jesus's death, burial, and resurrection show that he is the rightful king who takes his throne through the weakness of death and the power of the resurrection (Luke 23:26–24:12). After his resurrection, Jesus encounters two disciples on the road to Emmaus (24:13–35). The disciples express disappointment about the death of Jesus, for they "had hoped that he was the one who was going to redeem Israel" (24:21). It is ironic that the disciples are blind to the resurrected Jesus who stands before them, whereas the women proclaim the resurrection of the one whom they have not yet seen (24:1–12). Jesus has to explain to the male disciples on the Emmaus road that he fulfills prophetic expectations: that "the Messiah" had "to suffer these things and then enter his glory" (24:26). Jesus then explains how Moses's writings and the Prophets should be interpreted through the lens of the life, death, and resurrection of the Messiah (24:27). After their eyes are finally opened to Jesus's identity, the two disciples proclaim to the eleven apostles, "The Lord has risen!" (24:34).

At the conclusion of the Gospel, Luke includes another unique account about the resurrected Jesus appearing to his followers in Jerusalem (Luke 24:36–49). After displaying his resurrected body, Jesus again explains that his death and resurrection fulfill the Scriptures, calling his followers to take this message to all nations (24:44–49; cf. Matt. 28:19–20). Jesus then leads them to Bethany and ascends into the heavens, which anticipates the day he will return to complete the new exodus journey and consummate his reign over the earth (Luke 24:50–53).

Canonical Function

Mark's ominous tone may have left readers wondering whether they should embark on a journey marked by suffering. Luke's tone is more hopeful than Mark's, showing that the Messiah has enacted a cosmic kingdom for all people, regardless of gender, ethnicity, ability, or social status. For Luke, the kingdom inaugurated through Jesus's death and resurrection welcomes the marginalized and reverses the fortunes of the downtrodden. Although the crucifixion marks the inauguration of the kingdom, believers anticipate the day Jesus returns to complete the restoration of the earth. Luke 24:47 even includes a summary of the Great Commission, likely abbreviated from Matthew's Gospel, which calls Jesus's followers to proclaim the message of King Jesus "to all nations, beginning at Jerusalem." This summary statement draws the strings together on the first three Gospels: after Matthew concludes his Gospel with the commission to make people of all nations beneficiaries of the promised kingdom (Matt. 28:19–20), Mark highlights the suffering expected for those who respond to this call, only for Luke to return to the cosmic mission for which believers should be willing to suffer, which will bring diverse groups of people under the reign of Jesus in a restored creation (Luke 24:45–47). Reading the Synoptics this way should ease any fears of purposeless suffering. Though at present we face difficulties and opposition, we respond to the call of Matthew and Luke, knowing we will inherit a glorious kingdom, where the lowly people of God will be raised to dwell with their exalted Messiah.

Authorship, Dating, and Audience

The title *Kata Lukon* ("according to Luke") identifies the author of the Third Gospel. Since the Gospel of Luke and the book of Acts are two volumes of the same work, the authorship of Acts is also attributed to Luke. In Acts, Luke includes "we" passages, revealing that he was one of Paul's travel companions (e.g., Acts 16:10; 20:5–15). Paul himself refers to Luke as an associate (Col. 4:14; 2 Tim. 4:11; Philem. 24). Although he was not an apostle, Luke argues that his Gospel is based on prior testimony, to which he may have had access through his relationship with those in the Pauline circle (Luke 1:1–4).

Since Luke 21 predicts the fall of Jerusalem and the destruction of the temple, which happened in AD 70, we may date the Gospel prior to that event. Luke's dependency on Mark's Gospel means his work should be dated somewhere between the composition of the Third Gospel and the destruction of Jerusalem and the temple, somewhere between the late 50s and the late 60s. At face value, the intended audience for Luke's Gospel is the "most excellent Theophilus" (Luke 1:4). Luke intended for his Gospel to provide "certainty" about the faith (1:4). Although Theophilus's exact identity alludes us, we are certain that Luke's Gospel was included in the canon of Scripture, confirming its authority for all Christians.

John

The Gospel of John is positioned between Luke and Acts. While some choose to read Luke-Acts as a literary unit, manuscripts testify to the church's preference for reading John as the conclusion to the Fourfold Gospel corpus before encountering Acts. Even the less attested Western order of the Gospels separates Luke from Acts, placing Luke between John and Mark (John, Luke, Mark, Acts). We will follow the more attested canonical placement of John's Gospel after Luke's and before the narrative of Acts (Luke, John, Acts). In this position, John functions as the conclusion to the Gospel corpus and the canonical bridge to the Acts narrative.

As far as content, John excludes much of the material found in Matthew, Mark, and Luke, such as Jesus's baptism and temptation, the transfiguration, exorcisms, and parables.[34] While following the basic outline of the Synoptics, John's Gospel includes unique stories, teachings, and signs not found in the other Gospels. John organizes his account in a way that reveals Jesus as the creator of the cosmos who has come to restore all things. John's Jesus does not come to deliver people from the earth and into a spiritualized existence in heaven. Through strategically placed quotations and allusions, John's Jesus cares so profoundly about his creation that he gives his life for the redemption of the cosmos.[35] Viewed in this light, John's Gospel enlarges the boundaries of salvation beyond Luke's, showing that the scope of salvation extends beyond human beings to encompass the redemption of all things.

Outline and Overview

The Gospel of John includes a prologue (John 1:1–18) and an epilogue (21:1–25).[36] Some scholars argue that the epilogue was added by the redactors of John's Gospel. Others contend that it was included by the editors of the first canonical edition of the New Testament.[37] Among other evidence, the first-person statements "we know" (21:24) and "I suppose" (21:25) suggest that later redactors affirmed the content of the Gospel. Whatever our view on the editorial work of the Gospel of John, the manuscript tradition testifies to the inclusion of John 21, making it likely that the published copy

---

34. Nienhuis, *Concise Guide*, 68–69.

35. Richard B. Hays makes an important observation about the relatively few quotations in John's Gospel: "Precisely because there are relatively few quotations, each citation that does appear in John's uncluttered narrative assumes proportionately greater gravity as a pointer to Jesus' identity. If Luke is the master of the deft, fleeting allusion, John is the master of the carefully framed, luminous image that shines brilliantly against a dark canvas and lingers in the imagination." *Reading Backwards*, 78.

36. My outline follows Andreas J. Köstenberger, *A Theology of John's Gospel and Letters: The Word, the Christ, the Son of God*, Biblical Theology of the New Testament (Grand Rapids: Zondervan, 2009), 167.

37. Trobisch, *First Edition*, 53–55.

of the Gospel of John always circulated with the twenty-one chapters found in our modern Bibles.

Between the prologue and the epilogue are the two main sections of John's Gospel: the book of signs (John 1:19–12:50) and the book of exaltation (13:1–20:31). The book of signs progressively reveals the identity of Jesus through seven messianic signs. The book of exaltation focuses on the crucifixion, resurrection, and ascension of the Messiah. The seventh sign, the raising of Lazarus, bridges these two sections, anticipating Jesus's own resurrection for the entire cosmos (11:1–44; 12:1–11, 17–19).[38]

Prologue (1:1–18)

John begins his prologue by quoting three noteworthy words from Genesis 1:1: "In the beginning." These words stretch the interpretive context of John's Gospel to the pages of Genesis, revealing that Jesus is the Word who has come to renew all he made at the inception of creation (John 1:1–3). In so doing, he shines his renewing "light" into a world darkened by sin and death, bringing about a new creation (1:1–3; cf. Gen. 1).

John the Baptist testifies about the renewing work of Jesus (John 1:6–9, 15). Those who trust in Jesus have the privilege of being called "children" who have been "born of God," meaning they are new creations who will experience a restored existence in the renewed cosmos (1:11–13; cf. Ezek. 36:25–27). The entire world benefits from such "grace" (John 1:16).

Book of Signs (1:19–12:50)

The book of signs revolves around seven identity-revealing signs that progressively confirm the message of the prologue: Jesus is the Messiah, who has come to restore all things. Woven into this section are important accounts that strengthen the identity and mission of Jesus.

Before the first sign, John the Baptist announces that Jesus is the "Lamb of God, who takes away the sins of the world," identifying Jesus as the new Passover lamb, whose death will remove the power of sin over the cosmos (John 1:29; cf. Exod. 12). After his baptism, Jesus calls his first disciples (John 1:35–51). The narrator then affirms that Jesus is the Son of God, who will extend his rule to the ends of the earth (1:34; cf. Ps. 2).[39]

---

38. Köstenberger, *John's Gospel and Letters*, 168.
39. The NIV follows the variant reading *ho eklektos* ("the chosen") found in manuscripts such as the uncorrected version of Sinaiticus (א). I am following the majority of witnesses that read *ho huios*. Along with the modifying phrase *tou theou*, the correct translation is "the Son of God."

The first sign at a wedding in Cana in Galilee hints at Jesus's restorative reign (John 2:1–11). Jesus's mother and disciples are present at the wedding, where wine is customary. But there is a problem: the wine has run out. So Mary informs Jesus of the unfortunate circumstances (2:3). She then instructs the servants, "Do whatever he tells you" (2:5). Her words recall Pharaoh's in Genesis 41:55, when he commands the starving Egyptians to find Joseph and "do what he tells you." The intertextual link between Genesis 41:55 and John 2:5 suggests a typological connection between Joseph and Jesus. Although Joseph's food sustained the Egyptians for a time, what Jesus provides will sustain his people forever.

Jesus turns the water in six stone jars into wine (John 2:6–10). Turning water into wine recalls Isaiah 25:6–7, where wine symbolizes the arrival of the messianic age, when God will restore his broken people. If we trace the allusion to Isaiah 25:8, we envision that Jesus's messianic reign will soon spread over all people and remove death from the earth forever.

The accounts following the first sign strengthen the notion that Jesus has come to enact a new creation. The cleansing of the temple reveals that this institution is becoming obsolete (John 2:13–22). Jesus has begun the process of renewing the present earth, creating a cosmic temple, which prophets like Ezekiel anticipated, where God will dwell with his people forever (Ezek. 40–48). Additionally, Jesus's conversation with Nicodemus emphasizes that a person must be born of "water and the Spirit" to enter the kingdom of God (John 3:5–7). The words "water and the Spirit" allude to Ezekiel 36–37, where water is associated with the cleansing of God's people and the Spirit with the giver of life. Trusting Jesus will result in a new birth into the renewed kingdom Jesus is bringing to the earth (John 3:7). John encapsulates this reality with the language of "eternal life" (3:16–18). Jesus's conversation with a Samaritan woman, which results in many Samaritans trusting in Jesus (4:1–42), emphasizes that the Messiah's redemption extends beyond the boundaries of Israel to include all who worship "in the Spirit and in truth" (4:23). The Samaritans rightly confess that Jesus is the "Savior of the world" (4:42).

This brings us to the second and third signs: the healing of an official's son (John 4:46–54) and the healing of a lame man at a pool (5:1–15). These signs reveal that Jesus delivers people from sickness and disease associated with the present age of darkness (cf. Isa. 35). While certainly miraculous, these works are windows into the greater work Jesus will accomplish when he raises the dead, completing the work of restoration (John 5:19–29). Despite these signs, many refuse to believe that Moses's writings point to Jesus's arrival (5:30–47).

Such people will be raised not to life in a new creation but to judgment (5:29; cf. Dan. 11:2–3).

John's fourth sign is the feeding of the five thousand (John 6:1–15), and the fifth is Jesus walking on the sea (6:16–21). The former account alludes to Moses providing manna in the wilderness (Exod. 16), and the latter recalls his leading of Israel through the Red Sea (Exod. 14).[40] The crowd who witnesses the fourth sign recognizes the connection to Moses: "After the people saw the sign Jesus performed, they began to say, 'Surely this is the Prophet who is to come into the world'" (John 6:14). Jesus is certainly one "like Moses," only his "signs and wonders" are mightier and greater than anything Moses did in Egypt "in the sight of all Israel" (Deut. 34:10–11). John presents Jesus as the new Moses, who will accomplish a cosmic deliverance far greater than the one from Egypt.

The bread of life discourse and the Feast of Booths accounts are situated between the fifth and sixth signs. In the bread of life discourse, Jesus tells the crowds that he is a better Moses: "Your ancestors ate the manna in the wilderness, yet they died. . . . I am the living bread that came down from heaven. Whoever eats this bread will live forever" (John 6:49, 51). During the Feast of Booths, the people are deeply divided over whether Jesus is the Prophet, whether he is the Messiah, or whether they should wait for someone else (7:40–44). Regardless of the signs he performs or the claims he makes, such as his claim to being "the light of the world" (8:12) or being greater than Abraham (8:48–59), the religious authorities are intent on killing him (7:1). Unbeknownst to them, this is how he will redeem the world from the powers of darkness.

The sixth sign is the healing of a man born blind (John 9:1–41). Blindness is an ailment associated with the fallen creation. Isaiah 35:5–6 anticipates that the age of restoration will restore sight to the blind as well as speech to the mute, hearing to the deaf, and walking to the lame. So Jesus's healing of a blind man shows that he is the God who fulfills the prophetic hopes of Israel. Soon healing "waters" will overcome the present wilderness and restorative "streams" will overwhelm the desert, re-creating the present earth into a new creation (Isa. 35:6). The sixth sign is thick with irony: Although the Jewish leaders witness the miracle with their eyes, they remain blind to the true identity of Jesus (John 9:31–32). Yet, the one who was once blind can now "see" that Jesus is the Lord who restores the earth (9:35–41).

---

40. See John H. Sailhamer, *NIV Compact Bible Commentary*, NIV Compact Series (Grand Rapids: Zondervan, 1994), 488.

"I AM" SAYINGS

The Gospel of John includes several "I am" (*egō eimi*) statements, which allude to Exodus 3:14 to link Jesus to Israel's God.

- I am the bread of life. (John 6:35)
- I am the light of the world. (8:12)
- I am the gate for the sheep. (10:7)
- I am the good shepherd. (10:11, 14)
- I am the resurrection and the life. (11:25)
- I am the way and the truth and the life. (14:6)
- I am the true vine. (15:1)

Before the seventh and final sign, Jesus claims to be the "good shepherd" (John 10:1–42). This account alludes to Ezekiel 34:1–10, where Israel's leaders are chastised for being bad shepherds, caring more about themselves than their sheep. As a result, God promises to seek and care for his people through a Davidic ruler who will "shepherd" his people (Ezek. 34:11–24). Jesus's claim to be the good shepherd fulfills the words of Ezekiel. Soon he will make his sheep "lie down in good grazing land, and . . . in a rich pasture" (34:14).

All this leads to a climactic seventh sign (John 11:1–44). The account begins with the death of Lazarus (11:1–16). After Lazarus's death, Jesus boldly declares to Lazarus's sister Martha, "I am the resurrection and the life. The one who believes in me will live, even though they die; and whoever lives by believing in me will never die" (11:25–26). Jesus's statement affirms that all resurrection life comes through him. He proves his claim by raising Lazarus from the grave, performing the final messianic sign in the Gospel of John (11:43–44). The seventh sign points forward to the resurrection of Jesus, which in turn points to the final restoration of the cosmos.

After Jesus raises Lazarus, the religious leaders set their sights on crucifying Jesus (John 11:45–57). In view of his looming crucifixion, Mary anoints Jesus, which symbolically prepares him for his death and burial (12:3–7). Later, Jesus enters triumphantly into Jerusalem on a donkey (12:12–15). Like in the Synoptics, this account recalls Zechariah 9:9, signifying that Jesus is the Israelite king who will establish a reign of peace. In John's Gospel, Jesus's peaceful reign extends to the ends of the earth. Before taking his throne, Jesus must be "lifted up" to deliver the entire creation out of exile in the fallen world and into his kingdom in a restored cosmos (John 12:27–36).

BOOK OF EXALTATION (13:1–20:31)

The second major section of John's Gospel begins with Jesus arriving in Jerusalem for the Passover celebration (John 13:1). The Gospel gives this event a twofold significance: it looks back on Israel's exodus from Egypt and forward to a new exodus out of the present dark age. John 13–17 narrates the upper room discourse, in which Jesus prepares his followers for his departure from the present world (13:1).

The discourse begins with Jesus washing his disciples' feet, which communicates two significant truths (John 13:1–17). First, "washing" signifies the need to be "cleansed" from sins, alluding to the new covenant promise in Ezekiel 36:25: "I will sprinkle clean water on you, and you will be clean; I will cleanse you from all your impurities." So strong is the need for cleansing that Jesus tells Peter, "Unless I wash you, you have no part with me" (John 13:8). Only those who have been washed of their transgressions can experience life in the renewed world. Second, foot washing is reserved for servants, linking Jesus to Isaiah's suffering servant (Isa. 52:13–53:12).[41] In washing his disciples' feet, Jesus prepares his followers for the cleansing they will receive through the suffering he will endure on the cross, which will enable them to partake of the new exodus to the new creation.

In the discourse, Jesus also gives his followers "a new command" to "love one another" (John 13:34; cf. 15:12–17). This command is in keeping with the new covenant expectation that the law will be written on people's hearts, enabling them to love others, which was so difficult under the old covenant. While the command is grounded in the old covenant, what is new is that Jesus will send his Spirit, empowering his people to "follow my decrees and be careful to keep my laws" (Ezek. 11:20). Jesus will send the promised Spirit, just like Ezekiel foretold, to empower them to obey all he taught them (John 14:15–18, 25–26; 16:5–15). Their love for others, in obedience to Jesus's command, is how the world will recognize that they are followers of the Messiah (13:35).

Also in the discourse, Jesus foretells his betrayal (John 13:21–30) and the world's hatred of his followers (15:18–25). While persecutions are inevitable, Jesus reassures his followers that he has "overcome the world" (16:33). Suffering will therefore lead to life in a new creation, where believers will experience eternal peace in the presence of God.

The upper room discourse concludes with Jesus's high priestly prayer for his followers (John 17:1–26). Jesus prays not for the Father to "take them out

41. Beale and Gladd, *Story Retold*, 145.

of the world" but for him to "protect them from the evil one" (17:15). Jesus will send his followers "into the world" to which the Father sent him so they can share the "good news" that Jesus has begun the process of delivering the earth from the powers of darkness (17:18). Jesus prays that his followers' mission will mirror the unity exemplified in the relationship between the Father and the Son (17:18–26).

After his high priestly prayer, Jesus goes with his disciples to a garden across the brook of Kidron, where he is arrested by a band of soldiers (John 18:1–11). Jesus is then led to trial before high priests Annas (18:12–14, 19–23) and Caiaphas (18:24). Since Jews did not have the right to exercise capital punishment, Jesus is sent to Pilate, the Roman governor of Judea (18:28–19:16), who succumbs to the pressure to crucify Jesus (19:15–16). Consequently, both Pilate and the Jewish leadership are responsible for Jesus's death.

Pilate places an inscription on the cross: "Jesus of Nazareth, the King of the Jews" (John 19:19). Although this is mentioned in other Gospels, only John records that Jesus's charge was written in Aramaic, Latin, and Greek. Marianne Meye Thompson makes an insightful observation: "On the one hand, these three languages attest the exchange of Jewish, Hellenistic, and Roman language, culture, and architecture in the eastern end of the Mediterranean, including first-century Jerusalem. On the other hand, the three languages on the placard show that the death of Jesus is intended for all the world."[42]

Just before his death, Jesus says, "*Tetelestai*" (John 19:30). While many translations render the word "it is finished," a more suitable translation is "it is fulfilled." Jesus knows that he has fulfilled the role of the servant whose suffering leads to the end of exile and the beginning of the new exodus from the present earth (Isa. 40–66). The fact that the soldiers "did not break his legs" (John 19:33) points to Jesus as the Passover lamb, whose legs were not to be broken (Exod. 12:46; Num. 9:12). As the lamb's blood on the doorframes of Israel led to their deliverance from death and their exodus from Egypt, so Jesus's death leads to humanity's deliverance from the darkness of the present age and a new exodus into the renewed world. Unlike the original exodus, this new exodus will be for all the people of the earth.

After the resurrection, Jesus appears to Mary Magdalene (John 20:11–18), who then announces to the disciples that she has "seen the Lord" (20:18). As in the Synoptics, John's Gospel reveals that a woman is the first witness to the resurrection of Jesus. Jesus then appears to his disciples, who fear they will

---

42. Marianne Meye Thompson, *John: A Commentary*, New Testament Library (Louisville: Westminster John Knox, 2015), 398.

also be killed (20:19–23). He breathes the Holy Spirit on them, empowering them to be witnesses to his restorative work (20:22–23). This account is akin to Matthew's Great Commission passage, where Jesus authorizes his followers to go into all the earth to make followers of the one who announces the end of exile and the arrival of the promised kingdom (Matt. 28:19–20).

John 20:30 states that what has been written in the Gospel of John is not an exhaustive record of the signs Jesus performed. What has been recorded, however, is intended to elicit faith in Jesus the Messiah and Son of God, resulting in "life in his name" (20:31). This life should be understood as dwelling in the new creation.

EPILOGUE (21:1–25)

The epilogue contains three additional stories and some final comments. The first story is about the resurrected Jesus eating fresh-caught fish with his disciples (John 21:1–14). During the course of the meal, the disciples comprehend Jesus's identity. This account alludes to the similar one in Luke 24:28–35.

The second story is about Jesus questioning Peter about whether he loves him, and each time Peter responds with the sentence "You know that I love you" (John 21:15–19). The three questions allude to earlier in the Gospel when Peter denies Jesus three times (18:15–27). At the conclusion of the story, Jesus exhorts Peter, "Follow me!" (21:19).

The third story corrects a rumor that the beloved disciple would not die before Jesus returned (John 21:20–23; cf. 13:23). The Gospel rebuffs the rumor: "Jesus did not say that he would not die" (21:23). Why this account is included in the last chapter is quite puzzling. Some argue that it was inserted by later editors of the Gospel to correct a misunderstanding about the beloved disciple among some of the earliest Christian communities.

The Gospel of John's concluding comments have a twofold purpose (John 21:24–25). First, they affirm the testimony of the beloved disciple throughout the Gospel: "We know that his testimony is true" (21:24). Second, they affirm that the entire Fourfold Gospel corpus is sufficient testimony about the historical Jesus: "Jesus did many other things as well. If every one of them were written down, I suppose that even the whole world would not have room for the books that would be written" (21:25).

Canonical Function

John is a fitting conclusion to the Fourfold Gospel corpus. His salvific vision expands beyond that of Matthew, Mark, and Luke, providing readers with a cosmic perspective of the new exodus, which will culminate when Jesus restores the earth that has fallen into the darkness of sin. In Revelation, we will see that the restoration anticipated in John's Gospel is fulfilled when God raises the dead and renews the earth into an Edenic paradise (Rev. 21–22). Until then, the final strategic words in John's Gospel testify that all the Four-fold Gospel says about Jesus is true (John 21:24–25). So readers have reason to believe all that Matthew, Mark, Luke, and John say about Jesus the Messiah, God's very Son, whose kingdom will stretch beyond the boundaries of ancient Israel to encompass all the nations of the earth.

We may presuppose the Gospel accounts about the historical Jesus as we continue into Acts, the Pauline and Catholic epistles, and Revelation. We need no more accounts about the life of Jesus. The Gospels have provided sufficient testimony about the Messiah, whose kingdom spreads in Acts, whose teachings are applied to various ecclesial contexts in the Epistles, and about whose eschatological return Revelation prophesies.

Authorship, Dating, and Audience

The author of the Gospel of John does not reveal his identity. We know the authorship of the Gospel because of the title *Kata Iōannēn* ("according to John"). This John is one and the same with "the disciple whom Jesus loved" (John 13:23; cf. 19:26; 20:2; 21:20), who was one of the twelve apostles (13:23) and a son of Zebedee (21:2). Early church fathers such as Irenaeus (*Against Heresies* 3.1.2) and Clement (quoted by Eusebius, *Church History* 6.14.7) affirm the beloved disciple's authorship of the Fourth Gospel.

Scholars have dated the Gospel of John to anywhere between AD 55 and AD 200. The discovery of Papyrus 52 (a short fragment containing portions of John 18), which may be ascribed to the early second century, rules out any date after the mid-second century. A plausible date range for the Gospel of John is therefore anywhere from the late first century to the early second century (ca. AD 80–120).[43]

John's historical audience in Asia Minor may have struggled with matters related to the incarnation and resurrection of Jesus and the goodness of God's creation. That is why John dedicates considerable space to these matters (e.g., John 1:1–18; 1:19–28; 1:35–42; 3:22–36; 10:40–42; 21:1–25). Yet, we should not assume that John was combating full-blown Gnosticism. His audience's

---

43. Colin Kruse, *John: An Introduction and Commentary*, Tyndale New Testament Commentaries 4 (Downers Grove, IL: InterVarsity, 2003), 30; Raymond E. Brown, *The Gospel according to John (I–XII)*, Anchor Bible 29 (New York: Doubleday, 1966), lxxx–lxxxvi.

views were likely influenced by Platonism, which itself contributed to the rise of the Gnostic movement. As with other Gospels, that John is included in the Fourfold Gospel corpus signifies that it is intended for all audiences throughout history.

Acts

Acts is the second volume of Luke-Acts. Although Acts was written to complement the Gospel of Luke, the manuscript tradition separates Luke from Acts. In the canonical order of our modern English Bibles, attested in earlier witnesses like Codex Alexandrinus (A) and later ones associated with the Byzantine tradition, the Gospel of John comes between Luke and Acts. We should prefer to read Acts in this order (Luke, John, Acts) over its original historical composition as Luke-Acts.

As it stands, Acts provides a canonical bridge between the Gospels and the Epistles. First, Acts shows that the Spirit who empowers Jesus to proclaim the arrival of the kingdom in the Gospels also empowers the apostles to preach the kingdom in Acts. Second, the Epistles assume that the messianic kingdom has spread to the ends of the earth. This is why Paul's letters are addressed to congregations in Rome, Corinth, and Colossae, cities in gentile lands. It is also why James writes to "the twelve tribes scattered among the nations" (James 1:1) and why Peter writes to exiles dispersed throughout Asia Minor (1 Pet. 1:1). Third, Acts links the presentation of the historical Jesus in the Gospels to the Epistles. So as we read about Jesus Christ in the Pauline and Catholic epistles, we can assume the historical details about him mentioned in the Gospels. Last, Acts supplies historical details about apostles Paul, James, Peter, and John that will help readers understand the authors before they dive into their letters. In all this, we see the pivotal canonical role of Acts.

Outline and Overview

The outline of Acts flows from this programmatic statement: "But you will receive power when the Holy Spirit comes on you; and you will be my witnesses in Jerusalem, and in all Judea and Samaria, and to the ends of the earth" (Acts 1:8).[44] In Acts 1:1–7:60, the Spirit empowers the apostles' ministry in Jerusalem. In Acts 8:1–12:25, the Spirit empowers their witness in Judea, Samaria, and beyond. In Acts 13:1–28:10, the Spirit empowers their witness

---

44. Campbell and Pennington, *Reading the New Testament*, 158.

beyond the borders of Israel. In Acts 28:11–31, the Spirit empowers their witness to the "ends of the earth."

Spirit-Empowered Witness in Jerusalem (1:1–7:60)

Before his ascension, Jesus exhorts his followers to be "witnesses . . . to the ends of the earth" so that they will fulfill the call to extend God's dominion over the cosmos (Acts 1:8; cf. Gen. 1:26, 28). Initially, Adam and Eve failed at this pursuit. Later, Israel was to be a new Adamic race who would be a "light for the Gentiles," extending God's "salvation . . . to the ends of the earth" (Isa. 49:6). Yet, they rebelled against the God who led them out of Egypt. Jesus promises that the Spirit will empower people to witness to the reign of God throughout the entire world (Acts 1:8).

When God pours out his Spirit at Pentecost, he immediately brings conviction about Jesus the Messiah, who died and rose from the grave (Acts 2:1–41). The Spirit then enables the apostles to perform signs and wonders (2:43; 5:12). As in the Gospels, signs and wonders testify to the arrival of Jesus's restorative reign (cf. Isa. 35; 53; 61). We see this as onlookers are filled with "wonder and amazement" at the lame beggar who is healed in the name of Jesus Christ (Acts 3:1–10). This is an appropriate response to the restorative acts of Jesus, which signal the arrival of his cosmic reign.

Following the arrival of the Spirit, believers provide for the needs of others (Acts 2:45). Believers even sell property and homes and lay the proceeds at the feet of the apostles, who distribute them to the needy (4:34–35). A spirit of generosity and equity was so evident among the earliest believers that "no one claimed that any of their possessions was their own, but they shared everything they had" (4:32). This kind of Christian economy comes only through the work of the Spirit. So important is generosity that Ananias and Sapphira are struck dead for holding back proceeds that could have gone to helping the poor (5:1–11).

The growth in the number of believers in Jerusalem coincides with an increase in problems. First, Greek widows are overlooked in the daily distribution of provisions (Acts 6:1). As a result, seven Spirit-filled men are appointed to oversee the equitable distribution of food (6:2–6). Then Stephen is brought before the Jewish council on fabricated charges (6:8–15). When he is questioned, Stephen takes the opportunity to recite the history of Israel, leading to the arrival of the Messiah, whom the religious leaders crucified (7:1–53). This only enrages the council, which proceeds to stone Stephen (7:54–60). Just before his death, Stephen asks the Lord not to "hold this sin

SHARING POSSESSIONS

Acts reveals how the early Christians shared their possessions with one another. What would it look like for modern Christians to follow the same practice? What cultural contexts facilitate the practice? Those with a strong sense of private property? Or those that are more communal? What are some of your concerns about sharing goods with others? Would Luke have those same concerns?

against them" (7:60). Luke seems to frame Stephen's death in the pattern of Jesus, who faced similar false accusations and suffered and died unjustly. In his Gospel, Luke even records Jesus, as he hangs on the cross, uttering a prayer similar to that of Stephen: "Father, forgive them, for they do not know what they are doing" (Luke 23:34).

Spirit-Empowered Witness in Judea, Samaria, and Beyond (8:1–12:25)

Saul approves of Stephen's execution and, subsequently, incites a great persecution against the church in Jerusalem (Acts 8:1–3). This causes believers to scatter throughout Judea and Samaria (8:1). In God's providence, he uses persecution to advance the preaching of the gospel beyond Jerusalem and into Samaria (8:4–8). As is typical in the Gospels and Acts, the proclamation of the kingdom is linked to works of healing and exorcisms, alluding to texts such as Isaiah 35 and 53, which anticipate the restoration of people in the new age (Acts 8:6–7).

As the message of the kingdom is received beyond the boundaries of Jerusalem, the Samaritans rejoice to see God working in their midst (Acts 8:8). The apostles John and Peter lay hands on the Samaritans, and they receive the Holy Spirit, just like the Jews at Pentecost, marking their inclusion into the new covenant (8:14–17). The eschatological Spirit whom Joel and Ezekiel foresaw is now being bestowed on those outside the traditional boundaries of Judaism. As the gospel of the kingdom spreads to the Samaritans, the mandate given to Adam and Israel is being fulfilled through the new covenant people of God.

Subsequently, Saul journeys on the road to Damascus so he can continue his persecution of Jesus's followers (Acts 9:1–2). Along the way, Saul encounters the risen Jesus—an event that radically alters the course of his life, what many associate with his "conversion" (9:3–6). We should not assume that

FROM SAUL TO PAUL

Many argue that God changed Saul's name to Paul after his conversion on the road to Damascus. Yet, there is no scriptural evidence for this view. The reality is that he continues to be called Saul in the book of Acts. In Acts 13:9, he is even called by both names: "Saul, who was also called Paul." The significant transition from Saul to Paul happens in Acts 13:13, when he sets out into gentile lands. Thus, the shift from the Jewish name Saul to the Greek name Paul is a result of his ministry among the gentiles. The name Paul would have been more conducive for serving among people at "the ends of the earth."

PERSECUTION SPREADS THE GOSPEL

Acts reveals how persecution spreads the message of the gospel. We have seen modern examples of governments in Iran, China, and Cuba that have attempted to repress the good news. The result is similar to what we see in Acts—the gospel spreads and the number of believers increases! What can we learn about the way God works in persecuted contexts? What are some hindrances to the spread of the gospel in areas where believers experience little to no suffering?

Saul's conversion results in a departure from Judaism. Rather, his Damascus road encounter marks the point at which he believes that Jesus is the Jewish Messiah his ancestors, like Abraham, David, and Isaiah, anticipated. From this point on, Saul mainly goes by the name Paul.

Shortly after his encounter with Jesus, Paul proclaims in the synagogues in Damascus that Jesus is the Son of God (Acts 9:19–20; cf. Ps. 2). Though this confounds the Jews in Damascus, Paul is successful in proving that Jesus is the Messiah (Acts 9:22).

Later, the gentiles come to faith through Peter's preaching (Acts 10:34–48). As a result, God pours out his Spirit on the gentiles, leading them to speak in tongues and praise God (10:46). This event is analogous to the one in Acts 2 when the Spirit is poured out on Jews. This time, the Spirit coming upon gentiles testifies that the followers of Jesus include those beyond Jerusalem, Judea, and Samaria. Peter then commands that the gentiles be baptized, marking their inclusion in the people of God (10:47–48).

When the news gets out, Peter convinces the believers in Jerusalem that the gentiles are followers of Christ who are beneficiaries of the same Spirit

(Acts 11:1–18). As a result, no one should stand against their inclusion in the covenant community (11:17). Peter's hearers agree and glorify God for giving the gentiles "repentance that leads to life" (11:18).

Herod then incites a persecution of the church (Acts 12:1). He executes James, the brother of John, and arrests Peter (12:2–5). An angel miraculously delivers Peter from prison (12:6–19). An angel also kills Herod for receiving praise fitting for God (12:20–23). Despite all that happens, the word of God continues to spread throughout the earth (12:24).

Spirit-Empowered Witness beyond Samaria (13:1–28:10)

In Acts 13:1–28:10, the Spirit empowers the apostles to witness beyond Samaria to the arrival of the kingdom. Paul journeys to gentile cities like Iconium, Lystra, Philippi, Thessalonica, Athens, Corinth, Antioch, and Ephesus. Some of his traveling partners are Barnabas, John Mark, Timothy, Silas, and Apollos. As the kingdom spreads, certain Jews enforce circumcision on gentile converts (15:1). Paul and Barnabas appear before the Jerusalem Council—which includes apostles James, Peter, and John—on behalf of the gentiles, testifying to their reception of the Spirit and arguing that no unbearable "yoke" should be placed on their necks (15:2–11). The council agrees, asking only that the gentiles abstain from practices associated with idolatry and food sacrificed to idols, which Jews naturally abhor (15:12–21). The ruling is so important that the council commissions several of their own men, along with Paul and Barnabas, to deliver a letter explaining their decision to the gentile believers in Antioch, Syria, and Cilicia (15:22–35).

Despite their success before the council, not all remains harmonious between Paul and Barnabas. Luke records that, "some time later," Paul and Barnabas disagree sharply over whether John Mark should accompany them on their journey to "believers" where they had "preached the word of the Lord" (Acts 15:36). Consequently, Barnabas takes Mark to Cyprus, and Paul takes Silas to Syria and Cilicia (15:39–41).

As he travels to different cities, Paul continues to preach about the resurrected Jesus and the arrival of the kingdom. The Spirit empowers Paul to perform miraculous deeds, such as raising a young man named Eutychus from the dead after he had fallen asleep while Paul was preaching and had fallen out a window (Acts 20:7–12). Acts records that Paul's miracles were so extraordinary that "even handkerchiefs and aprons that had touched him were taken to the sick, and their illnesses were cured and the evil spirits left them" (19:12). The reports about Paul's miraculous deeds become so well known that seven sons of the

PAUL'S MISSIONARY JOURNEYS

Acts records Paul's three missionary journeys.[a] The first journey begins in Antioch. From there, Paul travels to areas like Cyprus, Pamphylia, Pisidia, South Galatia, and back to Antioch (Acts 13:1–14:28). The second journey takes Paul from Antioch to places like Troas, Philippi, Thessalonica, Berea, Athens, Corinth, Ephesus, and back to Antioch (15:36–18:22). The third journey also begins in Antioch. From there, Paul journeys again to Ephesus and to places like Miletus and eventually Jerusalem (18:23–21:16). The motivation for these journeys is to spread the gospel of the kingdom.

a. For a discussion on the missionary journeys, see Robert J. Cara, "Acts," in *A Biblical-Theological Introduction to the New Testament: The Gospel Realized*, ed. Michael J. Kruger (Wheaton: Crossway, 2016), 152–58.

Jewish high priest Sceva try to cast out demons "in the name of Jesus whom Paul preaches" (19:13). They do not expect that the man possessed by evil spirits will beat them so badly that they will flee "naked and bleeding" (19:16). Even this causes the word of the Lord to spread among the people (19:20).

Paul encounters persecution and resistance to the gospel at almost every turn. For instance, he is almost mauled by a crowd in Ephesus (Acts 19:23–41), and he is arrested and dragged out of the temple in Jerusalem (21:27–36). Chapters 22–26 focus on Paul's captivity and hearings before governors Felix, Festus, and Agrippa, before whom he unashamedly preaches the resurrected Jesus. Agrippa is astonished by Paul's boldness: "Do you think that in such a short time you can persuade me to be a Christian?" (26:28). Agrippa realizes that Paul is guilty of no crime and could have been released from his imprisonment if he had not appealed to Caesar (26:32; cf. 25:12).

Later, Paul is placed on a ship with other prisoners and sails for Rome (Acts 27:1–12). Along the way, the ship encounters a fierce storm and runs aground on the island of Malta (27:13–28:10). While there, Paul is bitten by a viper and suffers no effects (28:1–6). He even heals the sick on the island (28:7–10). This is what we have come to expect of those whom the Spirit empowers to testify to the work of Jesus.

Spirit-Empowered Witness to the Ends of the Earth (28:11–31)

After three months in Malta, the crew sets sail for Rome (Acts 28:11). After arriving in the city, Paul is placed under house arrest (28:16). Paul has enough freedom to spend his days proclaiming the kingdom of God and teaching about Jesus from Israel's Scriptures (28:23, 30–31). Some are persuaded by Paul's preaching, while others are not (28:24). In response to the Jewish people who reject his preaching, Paul draws on Isaiah 6:9–10 to underscore his ministry to the gentiles (Acts 28:25–28).

Although Acts ends without word about Paul's trial in Rome, we know from Paul's letters that he spends his ministry career taking the gospel to the gentiles—those who "will listen" (Acts 28:28). The ending of Acts anticipates Paul's ministry to predominantly gentile churches in his epistles.

Canonical Function

The placement of Acts between John and the Epistles is the key to unlocking the book's canonical function. In this position, Acts shows how the historical Jesus of the Gospels is the very one about whom the apostles preach in Acts. It also reveals that the Spirit who empowers Jesus's ministry in the Gospels also empowers his followers in Acts. Additionally, the messianic kingdom that breaks into the world in the Gospels spreads from Jerusalem, Judea, and Samaria and to the "ends of the earth" in Acts. Moreover, the programmatic verse in Acts 1:7, which anticipates the mission to the gentiles in Acts 28:27–28 (cf. Isa. 6:9–10), is being fulfilled in epistles addressed to believers living in gentile lands like Rome, Corinth, and Ephesus. The kingdom is undoubtedly spreading to the "ends of the earth." That Acts introduces readers to apostles Paul, James, Peter, and John before readers encounter their letters strengthens the literary connection between Acts and the Epistles. All in all, Acts transitions the reader from the narrative of the Gospels to the Pauline and Catholic epistles.

Authorship, Dating, and Audience

Acts is associated with the author of the two-volume work Luke-Acts. As with the Gospel of Luke, the evidence points to Lukan authorship. Luke inserts himself into the narrative of Acts by using the first-person plural form "we" (Acts 16–28). In so doing, he shows himself to be a travel companion of Paul and eyewitness to the historical events he describes in the book. Paul's epistles witness to his friendship (Col. 4:14) and familiarity with Luke (1 Tim. 5:18). Early confirmation of Luke's authorship of Acts is found in the second-century Muratorian Canon, the Anti-Marcionite Prologue to the Third Gospel, and Irenaeus's *Against Heresies* (3.1.1; 3.14.1).[45]

---

45. David G. Peterson, *The Acts of the Apostles*, Pillar New Testament Commentary (Grand Rapids: Eerdmans, 2009), 1.

The dating of Acts is tied to its relationship with the Gospel of Luke. Since the Gospel draws on Mark, Acts must have been written after Mark, which was composed in the mid-50s, and Luke, which was composed between the late 50s and late 60s. To be more precise, we should also consider Acts 28, which records Paul's first Roman imprisonment (around AD 60–62), establishing a date range for Acts anywhere between the early to late 60s.

The explicit audience of Acts is Theophilus (Acts 1:1). Luke addresses his Gospel to the same person (Luke 1:3). Although we do not know the exact identity of Theophilus or his relationship to Luke, we do know that Acts is included in the canon of Scripture. As a result, Acts is for all Christians.

SUGGESTED RESOURCES

Brown, Jeannine K. *The Gospels as Stories: A Narrative Approach to Matthew, Mark, Luke, and John*. Grand Rapids: Baker Academic, 2020.

Hays, Richard B. *Echoes of Scripture in the Gospels*. Waco: Baylor University Press, 2016.

Osvaldo, Padilla. *The Acts of the Apostles: Interpretation, History and Theology*. Downers Grove, IL: IVP Academic, 2016.

Pennington, Jonathan T. *Reading the Gospels Wisely: A Narrative and Theological Introduction*. Grand Rapids: Baker Academic, 2012.

Straus, Mark L. *Four Portraits, One Jesus: A Survey of Jesus and the Gospels*. Grand Rapids: Zondervan, 2007.

Watson, Francis. *The Fourfold Gospel: A Theological Reading of the New Testament Portraits of Jesus*. Grand Rapids: Baker Academic, 2016.

FIVE

THE PAULINE EPISTLES

Most modern Bibles include the Pauline epistles after the book of Acts. Yet, this is not the order found in all New Testament manuscripts. Another arrangement is found in fourth-century codices such as Sinaiticus (א) and Vaticanus (B) and fifth-century Codex Alexandrinus (A), which position Acts before the Catholic epistles. Such evidence leads David Trobisch to argue that the Acts–Catholic epistles organization should be preferred over the Acts–Pauline epistles arrangement.[1] Brevard Childs offers a more balanced perspective: "The manuscript evidence shows that the position of Acts developed along two different traditional lines. On the one hand, Acts was positioned after the Gospels and before the Pauline corpus in a tradition reflected in the Muratorian fragment, Irenaeus, Tertullian, and Origen. On the other hand, in a second, equally old tradition, it was represented in codices 01, A, and B that Acts was connected to the Catholic Epistles and then followed by the Pauline corpus."[2]

Acts also precedes the Pauline epistles in Eusebius's *homologoumena* ("acknowledged or recognized writings") and the Vulgate.[3] Although some prefer to

1. David Trobisch, *The First Edition of the New Testament* (Oxford: Oxford University Press, 2000), 21–44.
2. Brevard S. Childs, *The Church's Guide for Reading Paul: The Canonical Shaping of the Pauline Corpus* (Grand Rapids: Eerdmans, 2008), 225. Also quoted in Matthew Y. Emerson, *Christ and the New Creation: A Canonical Approach to the Theology of the New Testament* (Eugene, OR: Wipf & Stock, 2013), 65.
3. Gregory Goswell, "The Place of the Book of Acts in Reading the NT," *Journal of the Evangelical Theological Society* 59, no. 1 (2016): 75.

ARRANGEMENT OF LETTERS

Scholars commonly argue that the arrangement of the Pauline corpus is based on the length of the books. This is certainly a valid perspective, especially when we consider that the longest Pauline epistles (Romans and 1 and 2 Corinthians) are at the head of the corpus and the shortest (Titus and Philemon) are at the conclusion. But we must remember that Hebrews is also included in the Pauline corpus. If our argument depends on the length of the documents, then Hebrews should be placed toward the front of the corpus, along with Romans and 1 and 2 Corinthians. The reality is that the position of Hebrews varies: (1) it may be positioned between 2 Thessalonians and 1 Timothy, as in Codex Vaticanus (A); (2) it may be placed after Romans, as in Papyrus 46 ($\mathfrak{P}^{46}$); or (3) it may be included at the conclusion of the Pauline corpus, as in the Byzantine tradition of manuscripts. In the first position, it is longer than 2 Thessalonians and 1 Timothy. In the second position, it is shorter than the prior letter, Romans, and the following letter, 1 Corinthians. In the third position, it is longer than the prior letter, Philemon. Consequently, length may not be the deciding factor in the arrangement of the Pauline letters.[a] It is possible that the arrangement depends on the theological contribution of each letter and that the various placements of Hebrews represent a struggle to envision the letter's contribution to the Pauline corpus. Even if the contested authorship of Hebrews is the reason for its placement at the conclusion of the corpus, the position of the letter still exerts a certain hermeneutical pressure on the Pauline letter collection. When we consider the widely attested order for the Pauline epistles, we envision that Romans at the head of the Pauline epistles and Hebrews at the conclusion are the theological bookends for the corpus, providing the interpretive framework for reading the letters positioned between them.

a. David Trobisch argues that $\mathfrak{P}^{46}$ organizes the Pauline letters according to length. Although Hebrews is shorter than 1 Corinthians, he argues that the former is placed after Romans and before 1 Corinthians so as not to break up 1 and 2 Corinthians, which were addressed to the same recipients (Trobisch, *Paul's Letter Collection* [Bolivar, MO: Quiet Waters, 2001], 17). Although this may very well be the case, elsewhere the canonical order does separate Luke and Acts, which were both addressed to Theophilus.

read Acts along with the Catholic epistles, reading Acts along with the Pauline epistles is also attested in early witnesses. This arrangement provides important theological connections between the book of Acts and the Pauline letters.

The order of the Pauline letters is attested in fourth-century codices Vaticanus (B) and Sinaiticus (𝕏) and fifth-century codices Alexandrinus (A) and Ephraemi Rescriptus (C).[4] These codices testify to the arrangement in our

4. See David Trobisch, *Paul's Letter Collection* (Bolivar, MO: Quiet Waters, 2001), 17–24.

modern Bibles: Romans, 1 and 2 Corinthians, Galatians, Ephesians, Philippians, Colossians, 1 and 2 Thessalonians, 1 and 2 Timothy, Titus, and Philemon. These manuscripts, along with others like Papyrus 46 ($\mathfrak{P}^{46}$, ca. 200) and Claromantanus (Dp, ca. 700), also include Hebrews in the Pauline corpus. Although the authorship of Hebrews is contested, the manuscript tradition consistently includes Hebrews in the Pauline letter collection.[5]

The only inconsistency is the placement of Hebrews within the Pauline corpus. The position of Hebrews in our modern Bibles (after Philemon) is attested in the majority of late Byzantine manuscripts and Erasmus's *Textus Receptus*.[6] Since Hebrews is placed within the Pauline letter collection and the majority of witnesses puts this letter at the conclusion of the corpus, this is a suitable order for our study of the letters attributed to the apostle Paul.

▪ Romans

Romans is widely regarded as the most significant Pauline epistle. The letter presents Jesus Christ as the offspring of Abraham and the recipient of all God promised his people. Those in Christ are fellow beneficiaries of the promises, chief among them being the inheritance of a renewed cosmos, where the Spirit will empower believers to love God and neighbor. Paul's argument relies on carefully placed quotations (e.g., Rom. 3:10–18; 4:7–8) and abundant allusions to the Old Testament (e.g., 4:9–25; 5:5).

One of the characteristic features of Paul's letter collection is the distinct pattern of titles, in which the preposition *pros* ("to") precedes the addressee(s). Romans is titled *Pros Romaious* ("to the Romans"). Other epistles follow this titular pattern: *Pros Kolossaeis* ("to the Colossians"), *Pros Philippēsious* ("to the Philippians"), and *Pros Philēmona* ("to Philemon"). The titles of the Pauline corpus are different from those of the Gospels, which all begin with the preposition *kata* ("according to") followed by the name of the author (i.e., "according to Matthew"). The pattern of titles first established in Romans is an important distinguishing marker of the Pauline letter collection.

The placement of Romans at the head of the Pauline corpus testifies to its primacy in the letter collection. In this position, it sets the literary and theological expectations for the remainder of Paul's epistles. Childs argues for the theological primacy of Romans at the head of the Pauline canon: "One can conjecture that . . . when the corpus was read together liturgically, the

---

5. Trobisch, *Paul's Letter Collection*, 20–22.
6. Trobisch, *First Edition*, 25.

prominent role of Romans, with its unique features, took on a special canonical function."[7] He adds, "Not only was it the longest letter, but also it exposited Paul's theology with greatest detail, showed less historical particularity (except chapter 16), and seemed to provide the final and most profound formulation of Paul's theology."[8] Read in this light, Romans provides the theological foundation for the remainder of the Pauline epistles, making it the appropriate entryway into this letter collection.

Outline and Overview

Romans can be divided into four main sections. Chapters 1–4 argue that the genuine heirs of Abraham are those who share his faith. Chapters 5–8 show that the Spirit makes people new creations who will dwell in a renewed cosmos. Chapters 9–11 contend that there is still a place for Israel in God's plan of redemption. Chapters 12–15 call Abraham's children to live holy lives as they await the reception of their cosmic inheritance. Chapter 16 closes the letter with final greetings and instructions.

GENUINE HEIRS OF ABRAHAM (1:1–4:25)

Paul identifies himself as a slave of Jesus Christ, whose gospel was promised through Israel's prophets (Rom. 1:1–2).[9] Paul explains that the content of the gospel is about God's very Son, "who as to his earthly life was a descendant of David, and who through the Spirit of holiness was appointed the Son of God in power by his resurrection from the dead: Jesus Christ our Lord" (1:3–4). This explanation condenses the hope of 2 Samuel 7, which anticipates the future Davidic king establishing God's people in the promised land, and that of Psalm 2, which foresees God's royal Son ruling over the cosmos. It also condenses the message of the Gospels, which testify to the Spirit raising Jesus from the dead, declaring his victorious reign over the cosmos. All this is packed into the gospel that Paul is commissioned to take to the nations (Rom. 1:5).

Paul's mission to the nations recalls his earlier comment in Acts 28:28: "Therefore I want you to know that God's salvation has been sent to the Gentiles." His words create a canonical link between Acts and Romans, underscoring his mission to the nations.[10] In the remainder of Romans 1–4,

---

7. Childs, *Church's Guide for Reading Paul*, 7.
8. Childs, *Church's Guide for Reading Paul*, 7.
9. N. T. Wright, "The Letter to the Romans," in *The New Interpreter's Bible Commentary* 9 (Nashville: Abingdon, 2015), 333.
10. Emerson, *Christ and the New Creation*, 67.

THE NEW PERSPECTIVE

The New Perspective on Paul rejects the traditional Protestant reading of letters such as Romans and Galatians, which is influenced by figures such as Martin Luther and John Calvin: that Paul counters his Jewish opponents' emphasis on attaining righteousness by keeping all the works of the law, what is commonly called "legalism." In place of this reading, New Perspective authors such as N. T. Wright and James Dunn draw on E. P. Sanders's monumental *Paul and Palestinian Judaism* to argue that first-century Judaism was not legalistic—it was a religion of grace.[a] Keeping the law was Israel's proper response to a gracious God who had called them into a covenant relationship, what Sanders calls "covenantal nomism." Consequently, Paul does not oppose legalists—he opposes Jewish believers compelling gentile converts to adopt the traditional "boundary markers" that distinguished those "in" the covenant from those who were "out," such as circumcision and food laws. Paul urges gentiles to resist all such pressures, for all that is required for covenant membership is faith in the Messiah, who makes people of all nations members of the people of God and recipients of the promises to Abraham.

a. See E. P. Sanders, *Paul and Palestinian Judaism: A Comparison of Patterns of Religion*, 40th anniv. ed. (Minneapolis: Fortress, 2017); N. T. Wright, *What Saint Paul Really Said: Was Paul of Tarsus the Real Founder of Christianity?* (Grand Rapids: Eerdmans, 1997); James D. G. Dunn, *The New Perspective on Paul* (Grand Rapids: Eerdmans, 2005).

Paul develops the themes associated with the gentile reception and the Jewish rejection of the Messiah. As the letter develops, at the point where readers have all but dismissed the salvation of Israel, Romans 9–11 unveils the mystery surrounding the place of Israel in the plan of God.

In view of this overarching framework, in Romans 1:18–3:20 Paul declares that all humanity is worthy of God's just condemnation for worshiping other gods and living unfaithfully. No one is exempt from God's judgment: "There will be trouble and distress for every human being who does evil: first for the Jew, then for the Gentile" (2:9). For Paul, "God does not show favoritism" (2:11). All humanity is unrighteous and accountable before God (3:1–18).

The bleak picture in Romans 1:18–3:20 prompts the question "Is there hope for humanity?" In Romans 3:21–4:25, Paul responds with an emphatic yes.[11] He argues that God reveals his "righteousness" through Jesus the Messiah. What exactly Paul means by righteousness may be discerned from books like

11. Wright, "Letter to the Romans," 333.

RIGHTEOUSNESS

Protestants have traditionally interpreted righteousness as being "right" before a holy God. New Perspective proponents interpret righteousness as membership in the covenant people who will receive eschatological vindication and the new creation promised to Abraham. These views are not mutually exclusive. It is reasonable to argue that faith in Jesus makes a person righteous, meaning that a person is brought into the covenant people who are in right relationship with God. A person is then called to live out their righteous status by loving God and others with whom they are in covenant. On this reading, righteousness is understood within a gracious covenantal framework that brings together vertical (right with God) and horizontal (right with others) elements of salvation.

THE *PISTIS CHRISTOU* DEBATE

An ongoing debate among scholars is whether to translate *pistis Christou* as "faith in Christ" or "faithfulness of Christ" (Rom. 3:22, 26; Gal. 2:16a; 2:16b; 2:20; 3:22; Phil. 3:9). The "faith in Christ" translation depends on an objective genitive reading of the phrase and stresses the importance of human faith. The "faithfulness of Christ" translation depends on a subjective genitive reading of the phrase and emphasizes Christ's fidelity to redeem God's people through his life, death, and resurrection. Faithful scholars hold to both translations of *pistis Christou*. Gordon Fee and James Dunn, for instance, hold to the "faith in Christ" translation, and Dan Wallace and Richard Hays argue for the "faithfulness of Christ."[a] Since the matter is not one of orthodoxy, readers should decide for themselves which interpretation coheres with the context of Paul's epistles.

a. See James D. G. Dunn, *The Theology of Paul the Apostle* (Grand Rapids: Eerdmans, 1998), 379–85; Gordon Fee, *Pauline Christology: An Exegetical-Theological Study* (Peabody, MA: Hendrickson, 2007), 223–26; Daniel B. Wallace, *Greek Grammar: Beyond the Basics* (Grand Rapids: Zondervan, 1996), 113–19; Richard B. Hays, *The Faith of Jesus Christ: The Narrative Substructure of Galatians 3:1–4:11*, 2nd ed. (Grand Rapids: Eerdmans, 2002).

Isaiah (e.g., 46:13; 51:5–8) and Psalms (e.g., 65:5; 71:15), which reveal that God's "righteousness" is his "faithfulness" to save his covenant people. As he once saved the Israelites from slavery in Egypt through Moses, so God now saves his people from sin through the death of Jesus Christ, displaying his faithfulness to the covenant with Abraham (Gen. 12; 13; 15; 17). Those who trust in Abraham's God are considered "righteous," meaning they are also "faithful" covenant members who will inherit the renewed cosmos promised to Abraham's offspring (Rom. 4:1–25). Although the land promise was originally confined to Canaan, Paul follows the interpretation of the promise in the Psalms, Prophets, and Second Temple literature, which expand the inheritance beyond the borders of the original promised land to include the entire renewed earth (Ps. 2; Isa. 65–66; Sir. 44; 4 Ezra 7).

Importantly, Paul specifies that one is not brought into the covenant—declared righteous—"by the works of the law" (Rom. 3:20). Some argue that works of the law should be understood as Jewish legalism, which obligates people to keep all the law to be considered righteous. A more contextualized reading of Romans sees works of the law as the boundary markers of Judaism that traditionally distinguished those inside the covenant from those on the outside, such as circumcision, Sabbath observance, and dietary laws. But according to Paul, all that distinguishes God's people is faith in Jesus Christ (4:13, 16). Faith is what makes people members of the covenant and beneficiaries of the saving promises to Abraham.

THE ROLE OF THE SPIRIT (5:1–8:39)

Paul's explanation of the role of the Spirit in the lives of believers and the entire creation (Rom. 5–8) flows out of his discussion of the Abrahamic covenant promises (Rom. 4). According to Paul, righteous covenant members through faith in the Messiah receive the Holy Spirit (5:1–5). Paul's mention of the Spirit being "poured out into our hearts" (5:5) alludes to Joel 2:28–29, where God promises to "pour out" his eschatological Spirit on his people. This is the very Spirit about whom Ezekiel testifies, who will indwell his new covenant people, empowering them to obey God's commands (Ezek. 36:25–27), and will give life to the dead (37:5–6). In short, the Spirit indwells members of the covenant, giving them new life and enabling them to obey their God, just as Israel's Scriptures anticipated.

Romans 8 reintroduces the topic of the Spirit. In so doing, it continues to allude to the context of Ezekiel 36–37, arguing that the Spirit sets believers free "from the law of sin and death" to live "according to the Spirit" (Rom. 8:2, 4). In other words, the Spirit gives believers new life and empowers them to submit to God's law rather than being hostile to it (8:7). This is the same Spirit who will raise believers from the grave and restore the entire creation (8:12–27). This new creation existence, which is possible only through the renewing work of the Spirit, is that for which believers hope and the creation groans, as the entire world feels the effects of living under the curse and corruption of sin (8:18–25). Since Paul discusses the role of the Spirit in Romans

THE SPIRIT

For Paul, the Spirit is indispensable for life and godliness. Without him, humanity is dead and cannot please God. Have you ever pondered the role of the Spirit in your life? Have you thought about how he gives you new life? Have you thought about how he will raise you from the dead? Have you asked him to help you live faithfully?

5:1–5 and again in Romans 8:1–27, these sections serve as the interpretive framework of Romans 5–8. The intervening text of Romans 5:6–7:25 should be read in view of the Spirit's role in bestowing resurrection life and empowerment for godly obedience.

In this intervening text, Paul argues that, as believers have died with Christ through baptism, they shall also be raised to life with him (Rom. 6:1–5). In the meantime, believers' death with Christ signifies that they have died to sin and are "alive to God in Christ Jesus" (6:11). As a result, we should no longer live as if enslaved to sin (6:12–22). Rather, we should live as those who have been brought "from death to life" and use our bodies as an "instrument of righteousness" (6:13) to please God rather than to sin (7:1–25). Recalling the inception of the section in Romans 5 as well as the conclusion in Romans 8, we see that God's people live as faithful covenant members through the indwelling of the Spirit, who empowers obedience and grants life in light of the future resurrection and restoration of the created order (8:18–30).

THE PLACE OF ISRAEL IN SALVATION (9:1–11:36)

Paul has spent the bulk of the letter explaining that Jews and gentiles become faithful covenant members and recipients of a cosmic inheritance through faith in Jesus the Messiah. He has even shown the Spirit's role in giving life to God's people and empowering them to walk in obedience. In all this, we must remember that Paul is a Jew who feels sorrow and anguish for his people (Rom. 9:1–2). His pain is so great that he is willing to be "cursed," which means he is willing to be removed from the covenant people and destined for destruction, all for the sake of his Jewish kin (9:3). Israelites, after all, are the original beneficiaries of God's mercies, such as adoption as God's children, the covenants, the law, and the saving promises (9:4). To them belong the patriarchs—Abraham, Isaac, and Jacob—from whom the Messiah descended (9:5). Yet, Israel's privileged status did not lead to their trust in Jesus as the promised Messiah. Appealing to Isaiah 28:16, Paul says that they

> ## ISRAEL'S HARDENING
>
> God's "hardening" of Israel does not negate their accountability for unbelief. When we consider the allusion to Isaiah 63:15–19, we see that Israel's hardening is the result of their rebellion, their turning away from God. Israel's obstinance will continue until God has mercy on his people—a topic Paul addresses in Romans 11.

> ## ALL ISRAEL WILL BE SAVED
>
> The Pauline phrase "all Israel will be saved" (Rom. 11:26) has stirred no little debate. Some argue that the phrase encapsulates Jew and gentile believers. Others contend that the phrase refers to all ethnic Israelites throughout history; others that it refers to all elect Jews throughout history; still others that it points to the eschatological conversion of many Jews. Before arriving at a conclusion, we must consider that Paul is an ethnic Israelite who is exasperated over the unbelief of his people. We must also consider that Paul emphasizes faith in Christ for righteousness. Our interpretive decisions must cohere with these aspects of Paul's argument in Romans.

stumbled over "a rock that makes them fall" (Rom. 9:33). Consequently, they failed to attain the status of righteousness (9:31–32).

But Israel's failure does not mean that "God's word had failed" (Rom. 9:6). Paul argues that God's people do not have to be ethnically related to Abraham (9:6–7). What matters is that they are children of the promise, like Isaac (9:8–9). In Romans 4:1–25, being children of the promise is linked to exhibiting the saving faith of Abraham, making a person righteous. All such people are included in the spiritual lineage of Abraham, Isaac, and Jacob (9:6–29). Although many Jews remain incredulous, membership in God's covenant people is available to both Jew and gentile (9:24). Many Jews remain outside the covenant because they do not pursue "righteousness that is by faith" (9:30). They rely, instead, on the works associated with old covenant membership, like circumcision, Sabbath observance, and dietary laws, which traditionally separated Jews from gentiles (9:31–32; 10:3).

God's salvation does not require a person to adopt the ethnic markers of the old covenant, for Jesus fulfills the law, making righteousness available to all (Rom. 10:4). Everyone who trusts in Jesus the Messiah will experience God's eschatological salvation and the world promised to Abraham's descendants

(10:5–13). The message that many Jews rejected has resulted in mercy extended to the gentiles (10:14–21).

Despite Israel's persistent unbelief, Paul argues that God has not rejected Israel (Rom. 11:1–6). Even now there is a believing remnant of ethnic Israelites (11:5). The purpose of Israel's hardening is so that salvation can be extended to the gentiles (11:11).

Yet, Israel will not remain incredulous. Paul boldly claims that "all Israel will be saved" (Rom. 11:26), fulfilling the hopes of Isaiah 59:20–21. Paul also says that God has "bound everyone over to disobedience so that he may have mercy on them all" (Rom. 11:32). Whatever we think about these passages, we must acknowledge that God is sovereignly working through history to bring Jew and gentile into the one people of God, who will dwell in the renewed world promised to Abraham.

A CALL TO HOLINESS (12:1–15:33)

We would not blame Paul for ending the letter in chapter 11. After all, he has already written nothing short of a theological manifesto, recapitulating how the promises to Israel are fulfilled in Jesus and extend to people of all nations who trust in Jesus Christ. Yet, he presses on for several chapters to discuss holy living. That Paul spends a sizable portion of the letter on ethics may confuse those who disconnect "right doctrine" from "right living." Paul, however, does not bifurcate doctrine and ethics—he is a Jew who understands that the old covenant anticipated the day when God would empower his people to trust and obey him from the heart (Jer. 31; Ezek. 36:25–27). So he expands on the expectations associated with being a covenant member.

Paul argues that believers are to present themselves as "a living sacrifice, holy and pleasing to God" (Rom. 12:1). The Spirit who indwells new covenant believers enables them to live holy lives by loving others (5:1–5; 8:1–27). Paul makes explicit mention of this hope by quoting Leviticus 19:18: "Love your neighbor as yourself" (Rom. 13:9). The direct quotation of this verse shows that Paul's expectations are analogous to what has always been expected of God's people. Although Israel fell short of holiness, new covenant believers have the example of Jesus, who fulfilled the law by loving others by the power of the Spirit (15:1–7). Believers follow Jesus's loving example when they show genuine love for others (12:9), provide for the needs of the poor and show hospitality (12:13), love their enemies (12:20), submit to authorities (13:1–7), abstain from passing premature judgment on others (14:1–12), and forgo food and drink that may cause weaker believers to stumble in the faith (14:13–23).

Paul rounds out the letter by reaffirming that the promises made to patriarchs like Abraham, Isaac, and Jacob are available to the gentiles through Jesus the Messiah (Rom. 15:8–13). Although centuries of Jews considered gentiles outsiders to the covenantal promises, Paul strings together several quotations from Deuteronomy 32:43, Psalm 117:1, and Isaiah 11:10 to reveal that God has always intended for the gentiles to praise the God who makes them recipients of the saving promises to Abraham. As he mentions in the letter's opening, Paul confirms his mission to the gentiles so that they might become faithful covenant members by the power of the Spirit (Rom. 15:14–21). He is so determined to fulfill his mission that he is willing to go to the westernmost edge of the Roman Empire, Spain (15:23–33).

Greetings and Instructions (16:1–27)

Paul closes the letter with some personal greetings and final instructions to the readers of the letter (Rom. 16:1–23). The greetings are intended for coworkers such as Priscilla and Aquila (16:3) and fellow prisoners Andronicus and Junia (16:7). The Romans are instructed to, among other things, welcome and assist deaconess Phoebe (16:1–2) and be watchful of those who cause divisions among believers (16:17). Paul also includes a doxology to the God who reveals the mystery of Jews and gentiles being brought into the one people of Jesus the Messiah (16:25–27). What a fitting end to Paul's most significant letter.

Canonical Function

Romans is the appropriate starting point for the Pauline corpus. First, it links the book of Acts and the Pauline letter collection. In the final chapter of Acts, Paul announces that the gospel of the kingdom will be announced to nations more receptive than the Jews (Acts 28:28–31). The first chapter in Romans takes up Paul's concern to take the gospel to the gentiles, a theme that he develops throughout the letter and punctuates with a doxology about the mystery of the gospel now made known to the nations (Rom. 16:25–27). The remainder of Paul's letters are written to churches in such places as Corinth, Ephesus, and Colossae, cities in gentile lands.

Second, Romans is the theological framework for the entire Pauline corpus. No other letter more dispassionately explains that Paul's concern for the nations is grounded in the covenant with Abraham. No other letter spends several chapters explaining how God displays his covenant faithfulness through Jesus the Messiah, bringing Jews and gentiles into the one people of God. The message of Romans prepares the reader for the letters from 1 Corinthians to Hebrews, which addresses how Jesus makes people members of God's family who are empowered to love God and others. This "double love" is manifested in a variety of ways throughout the Pauline epistles. Hebrews then encourages believers to continue following Jesus until they receive the eternal inheritance promised to God's people.

Authorship, Dating, and Audience

There is near universal agreement that Paul is the author of Romans. One of the significant disputes about the composition of Romans is whether the book ends at 15:33, 16:24, or 16:27. The majority of manuscripts, however, testify to the inclusion of 15:33–16:27 in the final form of Romans.

Romans was composed during Paul's third missionary journey (Acts 18:23–21:16). Toward the end of his third journey, Paul arrived in Corinth, where he penned the letter to the Romans around AD 54. It is possible that Paul composed Romans after this date, when Jews may have been allowed to return to Rome following Claudius's death in AD 54.[12] If so, then it is possible that Paul composed Romans in the mid- to late 50s.

Little is known about the audience of Romans. Perhaps all we can affirm is that the letter was originally intended for the church in Rome, which Paul neither planted nor visited (Rom. 1:7). Beyond that, scholars speculate about whether the recipients were Jewish or gentile. Given Paul's concern for Jews and gentiles, it is possible that the original audience was composed of both groups. The diatribe in Romans 9–11 makes it feasible that the majority of the audience was gentiles who needed to understand the place of their Jewish brethren in the plan of God. This is a message that still speaks volumes to a church that is increasingly composed of all the nations of the earth.

1 Corinthians

Paul holds the Corinthian church accountable for obeying the God with whom they are in covenant through the saving work of Jesus Christ. Although the embodiment of Jesus is not emphasized in Romans, in 1 Corinthians Paul

---

12. Andreas J. Köstenberger, L. Scott Kellum, and Charles L. Quarles, *The Cradle, the Cross, and the Crown: An Introduction to the New Testament*, 2nd ed. (Nashville: B&H Academic, 2016), 594–95.

stresses that Jesus has a real body, which really did suffer and really was glorified. Platonism likely influenced the Corinthians' low view of Jesus's humanity and their lack of emphasis on loving others in the flesh.

Paul draws on Old Testament quotations and allusions to compel the Corinthians to live holy lives. Although Jesus has nullified the reign of sin and death and has sent his Spirit to empower his people to love one another, "the community still lives between the times, awaiting 'the day of our Lord Jesus Christ' (1:8)."[13] The readers of 1 Corinthians must therefore live out their Spirit-empowered faithfulness in light of the tension between the old age that is already passing away and the new age that has not yet been consummated.

Outline and Overview

First Corinthians can be divided into five sections.[14] Paul opens the letter (1 Cor. 1:1–9) and calls for unity amid divisions among the Corinthians (1:10–4:21). He then calls for the church to abstain from sexual immorality and to avoid lawsuits among believers (5:1–6:20). In the longest section, Paul responds to contested issues in Corinth, such as sexual relations in marriage, food offered to idols, the Lord's Supper, and the resurrection (7:1–15:58). Paul supplies final instructions and closes with a greeting (16:1–24).

OPENING (1:1–9)

Paul opens the letter by addressing his immediate audience: "the church of God in Corinth" (1 Cor. 1:2). He then broadens the letter's scope: "those sanctified in Christ Jesus and called to be his holy people, together with all those everywhere who call on the name of our Lord Jesus Christ" (1:2). Paul prays that the Spirit will sustain his readers until the day Jesus Christ returns to the earth (1:4–9). Readers would be wise to heed the instructions in the letter so that they might be able to stand "blameless on the day of our Lord Jesus Christ" (1:8).

UNITY AMID DIVISIONS (1:10–4:21)

Paul shapes the present section in response to a report from Chloe's people (1 Cor. 1:11). Apparently, the Corinthians are divided over church leaders (1:10). Some claim to follow Paul, others Apollos, others Cephas, still others

---

13. Richard B. Hays, *First Corinthians*, Interpretation: A Bible Commentary for Teaching and Preaching (Louisville: Westminster John Knox, 2011), 10.
14. My outline closely follows Hays, *First Corinthians*, xi–xv.

Christ (1:12). The reality is that the Corinthians should be united in following Jesus Christ (1:13). Paul underscores his point by reminding readers that he was sent to preach the gospel of the crucified Christ, not to make followers (1:14–17).

Paul concedes that this message is foolishness to those perishing—for there is no power or authority in a message about a crucified and humiliated leader (1 Cor. 1:18). But God's wisdom is unlike that of a perishing world, choosing to deliver believers out of the present age through the weakness of crucifixion (1:21). For Paul, the weakness of the cross is the power and wisdom of God (1:22–25).

This is the very message that Paul preached to the Corinthians. He did not depend on what the world considers lofty or impressive (1 Cor. 2:1–2). He relied on the Spirit so that their faith would "not rest on human wisdom, but on God's power" (2:5). The world's wisdom, after all, is in the process of passing away, along with the present age, whereas God's wisdom has been present since the foundation of the world (2:7–9). People can comprehend such teachings only through the Spirit, whom they have received from God (2:10–15).

Unfortunately, Paul cannot address the Corinthians as "people who live by the Spirit." They are "still worldly—mere infants in Christ" (1 Cor. 3:1). The Corinthians do not value the Spirit's emphasis on oneness in Christ. Rather, they esteem the standards of the present age, which leads to divisions over leaders like Paul and Apollos (3:3–4). The Corinthians should not divide over servants whom God used to bring them to faith in Jesus (3:5–6). Paul uses an agricultural metaphor to make his point: "I planted the seed, Apollos watered it, but God has been making it grow" (3:6).

Paul adds that all servants are workers of "God's field" (1 Cor. 3:9). Paul's mention of a field alludes to Isaiah 5:1–7, which identifies Israel as God's cultivated vineyard, and Jeremiah 26:18, which speaks of Zion as a plowed field. Accordingly, Paul and Apollos, who will give an eschatological account for their work, are servants called to tend to God's people (1 Cor. 3:8). This should motivate readers to follow the owner of the vineyard rather than align themselves with the workers.

Paul associates the Corinthians with "God's building" (1 Cor. 3:9), which recalls the temple, where God dwelled in the midst of his people. The Corinthians are the new temple in which the Spirit dwells, built on the foundation of Jesus the Messiah (3:10–17; cf. Ezek. 40–48). As God's dwelling, the Corinthians are called to unified holiness. Paul likens himself to a "wise

CHRISTIAN LEADERS

Are you ever tempted to align yourself with gifted leaders? Does your identification with such people overshadow your devotion to Christ? If you are a Christian leader, are you tempted to exercise your ministerial gifts to draw a group of followers? What would Paul say about the temptations to divide over leaders and to exercise spiritual gifts in divisive ways?

builder" of the temple, for which he laid the foundation of Christ (1 Cor. 3:10). The workers of the temple, like Paul and Apollos, will appear before God to account for the quality of their work (3:10–15). This is all the more reason for readers to align themselves with the eschatological judge rather than the workers.

Paul and Apollos are called to be faithful servants of Christ until he returns (1 Cor. 4:1–2). The Corinthians should withhold judgment on their leaders until Jesus reveals how well they have stewarded the people entrusted to them (4:3–5). Instead, they should focus on maintaining unity (4:6–13). Paul will soon return to Corinth to see how the Corinthians are living out the unity to which they have been called (4:14–20). Paul compares himself to a father who will visit his children, who will determine whether they deserve a rod or gentleness (4:21). In the meantime, Paul calls readers to "imitate" him (4:16). Their obedience should result in increased faithfulness to Jesus Christ and the shunning of behaviors like boasting and divisiveness.

Avoiding Sexual Immorality and Lawsuits (5:1–6:20)

Paul responds to reports of a man involved in a sexually immoral relationship with his mother-in-law (1 Cor. 5:1). He urges the Corinthians to remove the man from their body so that "his spirit may be saved on the day of the Lord" (5:5). The goal of the man's excommunication is to grieve him to the point of repentance and restoration to the community so that he might not be judged at the return of Jesus Christ.

This scene recalls Deuteronomy 19:16–20, where the congregation is gathered to execute judgment on a fellow covenant member (cf. Lev. 24; Num. 15).[15] If the person is convicted of wrongdoing, then the people are to "purge

---

15. Roy E. Ciampa and Brian S. Rosner, "1 Corinthians," in *Commentary on the New Testament Use of the Old Testament*, ed. G. K. Beale and D. A. Carson (Grand Rapids: Baker Academic, 2007), 707.

CORINTHIAN SLOGANS

The Corinthians used "slogans" to justify their unethical behavior. To rectify this problem, Paul quotes their slogans and provides theological correctives. One example is in 1 Corinthians 6:12, where Paul quotes the slogan "I have the right to do anything" and follows with a corrective: "But not everything is beneficial." Can you detect other slogans in 1 Corinthians 6:12–18? Can you identify Paul's theological correctives?

the evil from among you" (Deut. 19:19). The community listens to the judgment with fear and commits to "never again" allow "such an evil thing" to be done in their midst (19:20). As with the instructions to Israel, the concern here is about the holiness of the entire community. Paul is well aware that the people of God are the Spirit-indwelled temple, called to be holy in the present age. So he calls on the Corinthian church to execute judgment on sinful members of the congregation, like the greedy, idolaters, revilers, drunkards, and swindlers (1 Cor. 5:9–13).

Continuing with the theme of unethical conduct, Paul urges the Corinthians to avoid lawsuits among believers (1 Cor. 6:1). Since they will participate in the eschatological judgment, Paul believes that the Corinthians are more than capable of handling trivial matters within the context of the community (6:2–5). He prefers this approach over taking civil matters before unbelievers unqualified for adjudicating eschatological affairs (6:6–8). Such expectations are in keeping with the standards of the holy temple of God rather than those of the present age, which encourage people to exercise their own rights over those of others (6:9–10). Since the Corinthians have been delivered from the present sinful age, they should conduct themselves as the Spirit-indwelled people of God and not be conformed to the standards of the present world (6:11).

Subsequently, Paul returns to the issue of sexual immorality (1 Cor. 6:12–18). Paul disagrees with those who see no harm in visiting prostitutes. He argues that a person's body and soul are united to Christ, making them a member of his temple (6:15–18). As a result, having sex with a prostitute draws the entire body of Christ into the sinful act, polluting the temple of God (6:14–16). Paul urges the Corinthians not to defile the body but to live as Spirit-indwelled people of God who have been redeemed from the present sinful age (6:19–20).

Contested Matters (7:1–15:58)

Paul now responds to a series of issues about which the Corinthians wrote (1 Cor. 7:1). The first is marriage (1 Cor. 7–15). Paul acknowledges that marriage is the proper context for fulfilling sexual desires (7:8–9). Couples should abstain from sexual relations only for an agreed-upon time in order to devote themselves to prayer (7:5). They should resume sexual activity as soon as possible, lest Satan tempt them into sexual immorality (7:5). While marriage is a gift from God, Paul prefers the gift of singleness, which permits believers to dedicate undivided service to the Lord (7:7–8, 25–40).

Paul encourages the Corinthians to preserve their marital unions, even if they are united to unbelievers (1 Cor. 7:10–16). According to Paul, God may use a believer to deliver their household from the present evil age and into his holy temple (7:12–16). If a believer were to flee their unbelieving spouse, there would be no sanctifying presence in the household.

Paul then responds to a related matter, encouraging people to be content with their situation in life (1 Cor. 7:17–24). He applies this expectation to slaves, who are to be unconcerned with their chains, since they are free persons in Christ (7:21–22). Paul, however, understands the complex reality of being a slave—although free from the slavery of sin, they are still in chains. He encourages slaves to take the opportunity to be released from their bonds so that they may live out their freedom in Christ (7:21).

Paul now turns to the matter of food sacrificed to idols (1 Cor. 8:1–11:1). Some believers questioned whether it was appropriate to eat meat sacrificed to an idol and sold in the marketplace. In response, Paul acknowledges that idols are inanimate creations (8:4). He recognizes that "there is no God but one" (8:4). His statement alludes to the Shema in Deuteronomy 6, which confesses the existence of Israel's creator God, who is one and the same with Jesus Christ, "through whom all things came and through whom we live" (1 Cor. 8:6). For Paul, a dead idol is no match for the living God.

Even with this knowledge, Paul understands that some believers are so sensitive to eating meat sacrificed to idols that it risks defiling their conscience (1 Cor. 8:7). He appeals to the principle of love for neighbor to argue that it is best to abstain from eating meat sacrificed to idols in the presence of those with weaker consciences (7:8–13). There is no point in wounding a fellow believer for whom Christ gave his life (8:11).

Paul uses his life as an apostle to illustrate the principle of love for neighbor (1 Cor. 9:1–27). He concedes that he has the right to a spouse and provision, though he has not taken advantage of these privileges for the sake of the gospel (9:1–18). Though he is free in Christ, he has chosen to make himself a slave to others so that they might partake of the blessings of the gospel (9:19–23). Paul's apostolic life demonstrates loving others over taking advantage of one's rights.

As the Corinthians consider Paul's instructions about eating meat sacrificed to idols, they should consider the story of Israel's original wilderness generation (1 Cor. 10:1–5). Looking back on this account, Paul contends that it was Christ who provided nourishment for Israel in the wilderness (10:4). Yet, this generation displeased God and fell dead in the wilderness (10:5). These events are examples for believers in the present age so that they might not succumb to the idolatry of the Israelites and fall dead in the present wilderness of sin (10:11).

Consequently, the Corinthians should make certain that their partaking of meat sacrificed to idols does not provoke the Lord to jealousy, as the wilderness generation provoked the Lord (1 Cor. 10:21–22). Whether they choose to "eat or drink," or in whatever else they do, they are to "do it all for the glory of God" (10:31), always seeking the benefit of others (10:32). The Corinthians should imitate Paul as he imitates Christ—both of whom love others more than themselves (11:1).

Paul then responds to a couple of issues related to corporate gatherings. The first is head coverings (1 Cor. 11:2–16). Paul instructs women to pray with a head covering and men to pray without one (11:3–16). Although head coverings are not transcultural, what transcends time and culture is praying in a manner that honors God (11:3).

The second matter related to corporate gatherings is the Lord's Supper (1 Cor. 11:17–34). The Corinthians were bringing social divisions into their practice of the Supper (11:18). Paul scolds them: "I have no praise for you, for your meetings do more harm than good" (11:17). The Lord's Supper should not accent divisions—it should promote oneness in Jesus Christ. A visible reminder of this reality is partaking of the bread, which symbolizes the broken body of Jesus on the cross, and the cup, which symbolizes the blood of Jesus poured out to initiate a new covenant (11:23–26; cf. Luke 22:19–20).

Paul encourages the Corinthians to examine themselves before partaking of the Lord's Supper to determine whether they are partaking of the meal in a manner that promotes unity or division in the "body" (1 Cor. 11:27–28). Those bringing divisions into the meal should expect to incur judgment, like those who have become weak and ill and even died (11:29–30).

Spiritual gifts are also included in the list of matters over which the Corinthians are divided (1 Cor. 12:1–14:40). Paul explains that the Spirit bestows

SPIRITUAL GIFTS TODAY

Christians debate whether miraculous gifts like healing, tongues, visions, and prophecy are still in existence. Some say that such gifts ceased after the apostolic age. Others say they will continue until the arrival of Jesus Christ. As you consider your own position, think about the following: Does Paul ever say that miraculous gifts will cease in the present age? Do miraculous gifts still benefit the body of Christ? Do you know believers who still exercise miraculous gifts? Have you asked them about their experiences?

a variety of spiritual gifts on believers, like healings, prophecy, tongues, and the interpretation of tongues (12:4–11). The Spirit's bestowal of spiritual gifts alludes to Joel 2:28–32, which anticipates the time when God will empower men and women to prophesy, experience inspired dreams, and see visions. The Corinthians are therefore experiencing the manifestations of the Spirit associated with the arrival of the new age (cf. Gal. 3:5).

The Spirit bestows gifts "for the common good" (1 Cor. 12:7). While the Corinthians value miraculous gifts like tongues, all spiritual gifts are indispensable for the edification of the body (12:21–26; 14:1–19). Paul appeals to the more excellent way of love (13:1–13) to urge the Corinthians to exercise spiritual gifts in ways that edify others (14:1–25). After all, believers should use their gifts for the sake of the body of Christ—never for self-promotion (14:26–40).

Near the end of the letter, Paul corrects the Corinthians' deficient view of the resurrection. The resurrection is so important that he reminds readers that it is at the heart of what he preaches—that Christ died "for our sins," was buried, and rose on the third day "according to the Scriptures" (1 Cor. 15:3–4). One of the primary Scripture passages to which Paul alludes is Isaiah 52–53, which anticipates that a servant will suffer for Israel's sins, after which he will "see his offspring" and "prolong his days" (53:10). Otherwise stated, Isaiah anticipates that a servant will die for Israel's sins and rise from the grave. Paul's reference to Jesus dying and rising "on the third day" (1 Cor. 15:4) alludes to Jonah 1:17, a text that Matthew 12:40 reads typologically: "As Jonah was three days and three nights in the belly of a huge fish, so the Son of Man will be three days and three nights in the heart of the earth." Paul adds that the resurrection of Jesus was followed by appearances to his followers (1 Cor. 15:5–8).

Paul contends that the bodily resurrection of the Messiah is essential to the faith (1 Cor. 15:12–19). He illustrates his point by making a typological connection to Adam: "But Christ has indeed been raised from the dead, the firstfruits of those who have fallen asleep. . . . For as in Adam all die, so in Christ all will be made alive" (15:20, 22). Christ's resurrection empowers humanity's resurrection into the imperishable image of Christ (15:42–58).

CLOSING (16:1–24)

The letter closes with instructions about the collection for believers in Jerusalem (1 Cor. 16:1–4). Paul informs the Corinthians about his plans to visit them (16:5–9) and encourages them to welcome Timothy (16:10) and Apollos (16:12) and to be subject to their leaders (16:15–17). He ends with final greetings for the believers at Corinth (16:19–22).

Canonical Function

The first letter to the Corinthians complements the message of Romans. A sequential reading of these letters enables us to envision how a believer's righteous status (Romans) should be lived out in the context of community (1 Corinthians). Failing to love others makes one guilty of breaking the covenant. In Romans 5–8 and 12–15, faithfulness is empowered by the promised Spirit, fulfilling the expectations of prophets like Ezekiel and Jeremiah. Even in places where 1 Corinthians does not mention the Spirit, we should assume that the Spirit is the one who enables believers to avoid divisions over leaders, to abstain from sexual immorality, to preserve the bonds of marriage, to be free from the shackles of slavery, to promote unity in the Lord's Supper, to use spiritual gifts for the benefit of the body, and to cling to the hope of the resurrection. The work of the Spirit also permeates the second letter to the Corinthians.

Authorship, Dating, and Audience

The opening and closing sections of 1 Corinthians identify Paul as the author (1 Cor. 1:1; 16:21). The theology of the letter coheres with that of other Pauline letters, like Romans and Galatians, emphasizing themes such as the unity of believers, the work of the Spirit, and the centrality of Jesus the Messiah. Scholars are so certain of Paul's authorship of 1 Corinthians that it is considered an undisputed Pauline epistle.

The date of 1 Corinthians is associated with Paul's third missionary journey, when he returns to Ephesus and ministers for about two and a half years.[16]

---

16. G. K. Beale and Benjamin L. Gladd, *The Story Retold: A Biblical-Theological Introduction to the New Testament* (Downers Grove, IL: IVP Academic, 2020), 205; D. A. Carson and

Paul pens 1 Corinthians while a resident in Ephesus, somewhere between AD 52 and 55 (16:8). The original audience of the letter was the church at Corinth—a church rife with factions, immorality, and doctrinal problems. Its inclusion in the canon signifies its relevance for audiences still struggling with sinful issues linked to the old age of sin and death.

2 Corinthians

The first letter to the Corinthians did not have the transformative effect Paul had intended. So he writes a second letter to the same audience in which he exhorts readers to live Spirit-filled lives in light of the final resurrection and the consummation of the eschaton. He also rebuffs the influence of false apostles who have no interest in aiding the Corinthians' growth in holiness. Paul supports his argument by weaving scriptural allusions and quotations throughout the letter. He also makes liberal use of temple imagery. He does all this to underscore that his readers are new covenant believers who are to be holy as they await the return of Jesus Christ.

Scholars argue that 2 Corinthians is a patchwork of several letters. Some divide the letter into two original compositions: (1) chapters 1–9 and (2) chapters 10–13. Others divide the letter into as many as four original compositions: (1) 1:3–2:13, (2) 2:14–7:3, (3) 7:4–9:15, (4) 10:1–13:14.[17] Such divisions are based on shifts in tone and emphasis. Whatever one believes about the compositional history of 2 Corinthians, the manuscript tradition testifies that the letter has always circulated as a unified whole. The total witness of the letter encourages readers to live faithfully in light of the arrival and future consummation of the new age.

Outline and Overview

The following outline of 2 Corinthians follows a fourfold structure.[18] Paul defends his apostolic ministry (2 Cor. 1:1–7:16). He then discusses the collection for the saints in Jerusalem (8:1–9:15) and offers another defense of his

---

Douglas J. Moo, *An Introduction to the New Testament*, 2nd ed. (Grand Rapids: Zondervan, 2005), 420–25.

17. See Trobisch, *Paul's Letter Collection*, 80–86.

18. My outline draws on Guy Prentiss Waters, "1 and 2 Corinthians," in *A Biblical-Theological Introduction to the New Testament: The Gospel Realized*, ed. Michael J. Kruger (Wheaton: Crossway, 2016), 206; Constantine R. Campbell and Jonathan T. Pennington, *Reading the New Testament as Christian Scripture: A Literary, Canonical, and Theological Survey* (Grand Rapids: Baker Academic, 2020), 230.

apostolic ministry—this time in response to so-called super apostles (10:1–12:13). Paul closes the letter with an announcement of his upcoming visit to Corinth and final greetings (12:14–13:14). Although much of the letter focuses on a defense of Paul's ministry, we would be remiss to overlook the clear exhortations to holiness throughout the letter.

PAUL'S DEFENSE OF HIS APOSTOLIC MINISTRY (1:1–7:16)

After an initial greeting, Paul admits facing sufferings in ministry (2 Cor. 1:1–11). Throughout such difficulties, Paul and his associates have relied not on their own strength but "on God, who raises the dead" (1:9). Paul's confidence is similar to that of Joseph, who believed that God is so faithful that his dead bones will be raised to life in the land promised to Abraham's offspring (Gen. 50:22–26).

Paul explains that he did not visit the Corinthians, as he had initially intended, so that he would not cause them additional pain (2 Cor. 1:12–2:4). His explanation is in response to some who claimed that he had vacillated on his initial commitment (1:15–18). He appeals to the work of the Spirit, whom God has placed "in our hearts as a deposit, guaranteeing what is to come" (1:22), which is similar to Ephesians 1:13–14, where he states that believers have been "marked in him with a seal, the promised Holy Spirit, who is a deposit guaranteeing our inheritance." The Spirit who will raise Paul into his inheritance also leads him to make decisions that promote abundant love for the Corinthians, not more pain (2 Cor. 2:4). This is the very same Spirit who leads Paul to places like Macedonia so that he might be "the pleasing aroma of Christ" (2:15).

Wherever he travels, Paul does not carry letters of recommendation to validate his ministry, as some are in the habit of doing (2 Cor. 3:1). His only validation is what the Spirit has enabled him to accomplish among the Corinthians (3:2–3). Paul's Spirit-empowered ministry is associated with the arrival of the new covenant (3:4–6). The old covenant, on the other hand, was associated with Moses's commandments chiseled on stone (3:7–9). What was once considered glorious has given way to the even greater glory of the new covenant—which is associated with the Spirit's power to renew people into the glorious image of the Lord Jesus Christ (3:7–12).

The god of the present age has blinded unbelievers from understanding the glorious gospel of Christ associated with the new covenant (2 Cor. 4:4). Yet, the God who shined his creative light into the primordial darkness has also shined into the darkened hearts of humanity, opening their eyes to understand the glorious gospel (4:6; cf. Gen. 1:4). This is the God in whom Paul trusts to resurrect him and the Corinthians, just as he raised Jesus Christ (2 Cor. 4:7–15). The hope of resurrection is that for which Paul strives, allowing him to endure the difficulties of the present age, knowing that he has an "eternal glory" that awaits him (4:17). Paul acknowledges that the Spirit empowers the resurrection for which he longs (5:1–10; cf. Ezek. 36–37).

Paul persuades the Corinthians to live for the once-crucified-now-resurrected Christ (2 Cor. 5:11–15). For Paul, Christ dying "for all" suggests that people have died to the old age of sin and death and are now new creations (5:14–15). Paul adds that Christ "died for all, that those who live should no longer live for themselves but for him who died for them and was raised again" (5:15). This statement alludes to Isaiah's servant, who died and was raised for Israel (Isa. 52:13–53:12), and Ezekiel's vision of God enabling his people to obey his commandments and decrees (Ezek. 37:24). These prophetic hopes are fulfilled in Jesus Christ, whose Spirit empowers his people to live holy lives associated with the new covenant age.

Paul's ministry revolves around proclaiming the Christ who died for sinners to make them righteous before God (2 Cor. 5:21). Paul suffers all kinds of afflictions for the God who extends grace to all, knowing that the day of salvation is near (6:1–10). He expects that those who have accepted God's gracious gift of salvation will live holy lives, separating themselves from practices that pollute the people of God (6:14–7:1). He is even confident that the Corinthians will live out the obedience that was reported to him (7:2–16).

Collection for the Jerusalem Saints (8:1–9:15)

Paul turns to the topic of the collection for the saints in Jerusalem (2 Cor. 8:1–9:15). He expects that the Corinthians will give cheerfully to struggling brothers and sisters (9:7). In turn, he promises that God will overflow his grace on them (9:6–8). Paul's assurance is based on texts such as Proverbs

Christian leaders may feel pressure to display impressive preaching and teaching skills to justify their ministry. Perhaps we feel pressure from modern "super apostles," whose books and social media accounts provide a steady stream of advice on how to be "successful" in ministry. Based on 2 Corinthians, are these the distinctives of Paul's ministry? If not, how should we shape our ministry so it reflects the values of Paul rather than those of so-called super apostles?

19:17 and 22:9, which underscore that the Lord repays those who give to the poor. For further motivation, Paul uses the example of the Macedonians, who gave generously out of their own poverty to support other believers (2 Cor. 9:1–4). He even uses the example of Jesus Christ, "that though he was rich, yet for your sake he became poor, so that you through his poverty might become rich" (8:9). In all this, Paul is confident that the Corinthians will give generously to the collection (9:5).

Paul undergirds God's concern for the poor by quoting Psalm 112:9: "They have freely scattered their gifts to the poor; their righteousness endures forever" (2 Cor. 9:9). The Corinthians can certainly trust that God will provide for their own needs as they aid the poor saints in Jerusalem (9:10–11). As a result of their generosity, the Jerusalem saints will glorify God (9:13).

ANOTHER DEFENSE OF PAUL'S APOSTOLIC MINISTRY (10:1–12:13)

Paul begins his second defense of his apostolic ministry with a response to those claiming that he is weak in appearance but stern in his letters (2 Cor. 10:1–10). He could certainly be bold in his presence, matching the authority in his correspondences (10:11). Yet, he always takes an appropriate posture for "building up," not "tearing down" (10:8).

Paul then defends himself against so-called super apostles (2 Cor. 11:1–12:13). Although their rhetorical skills are impressive, they promote a different gospel and a different Jesus (11:1–5). Such people are "false apostles, deceitful workers, masquerading as apostles of Christ" (11:13). Paul goes so far as to compare them to Satan's servants, who "masquerade as servants of righteousness" (11:15). Such people do not compare to Paul, whose apostolic ministry is evidenced by the grace of God through Paul's many pains and sufferings (11:16–12:10). The Corinthians themselves were witnesses to Paul performing signs, wonders, and miracles associated with a true apostolic ministry (12:11–13). All this proves that Paul is a true apostle—the so-called super apostles are not.

Paul's Upcoming Visit to Corinth and Final Greetings (12:14–13:14)

Paul closes the letter with the promise of a third visit to Corinth (2 Cor. 12:14). He expresses fear that when he arrives he will find them still living in "impurity, sexual sin and debauchery," which would reveal that they are not living as people indwelled by the Spirit of the new age (12:21). So he intends to come to them in person so that he might deal with them in the power of God (13:1–4). Before he visits, the Corinthians are to examine whether they are truly followers of Christ and affirm Paul as a genuine apostle, as he has proven throughout the letter (13:5–6).

Despite the call to examine their faith, Paul affirms the Corinthians as "brothers and sisters" (2 Cor. 13:11). As such, they should seek restoration, peace, and oneness of mind with one another (13:11). Paul's request is possible only through "the grace of the Lord Jesus Christ, and the love of God, and the fellowship of the Holy Spirit" (13:14).

Canonical Function

Second Corinthians is the final canonical letter to the church in Corinth. Paul composed a painful letter between 1 and 2 Corinthians (2 Cor. 2:3–4). This letter, like the one that preceded 1 Corinthians, did not make it into the canon of Scripture. What we have are two canonical letters to the Corinthians. The second letter continues the need for a Spirit-led life associated with the new covenant age. This involves trusting in Paul's apostolic ministry, rejecting so-called super apostles, and providing for impoverished saints in Jerusalem. The closing, in which Paul reaffirms the need for restoration, peace, and unity (13:11–13), provides an important conclusion to the letters to the Corinthians. These issues were originally raised in 1 Corinthians, where Paul discusses dividing over leaders (1 Cor. 1:10–25) and disunity over the Lord's Supper (11:17–25). On the whole, 1 and 2 Corinthians encourage readers to trust in the God whose Spirit empowers them to seek unity and reconciliation with others until we all attain to the resurrection of the dead (1 Cor. 15:1–58; 2 Cor. 4:7–18).

Authorship, Dating, and Audience

Paul identifies himself as the author of the letter (2 Cor. 1:1). Theological themes like resurrection, the Spirit, and unity cohere with other Pauline letters.

The evidence for Paul's authorship is not seriously contested by the majority of scholars. The only point of contention is the composite nature of the letter. But that is attributable to the process of shaping and composing the letter before it reached its final form.

Second Corinthians was written after 1 Corinthians, which was composed somewhere between AD 52 and 55, and the noncanonical painful letter. He likely wrote 2 Corinthians from Macedonia somewhere in the vicinity of AD 55–56. The audience is the same dysfunctional church to which he addressed 1 Corinthians.

Galatians

Galatians has strong thematic connections with Romans, reintroducing topics such as the story of Abraham, the work of the Spirit, the promised inheritance, righteousness, works of the law, Paul's gentile mission, and Jew-gentile relations. Additionally, Galatians follows the pattern of theological instruction (chaps. 1–4) followed by ethical exhortation (chaps. 5–6) established in Romans. From such connections, we envision that Romans and Galatians are the bookends for an initial Pauline literary grouping consisting of Romans, 1 and 2 Corinthians, and Galatians.[19] The intervening letters to the Corinthians encourage readers to live out the ethics of the new covenant. The following three epistles (Ephesians, Philippians, and Colossians) continue the pattern of theological instruction and ethical exhortation linked to Romans and Galatians.[20]

In Galatians, Paul uses a masterful combination of scriptural quotations and allusions to achieve his literary purposes. Paul employs quotations when his argument requires more precision, such as using Genesis 13:15 and 17:8 to identify Jesus as the true offspring of Abraham (Gal. 3:16). As he weaves Israel's Scriptures into his letters, Paul aims to show that faith in Christ makes Jews and gentiles fellow children of Abraham and recipients of the salvific promises. Nothing else is required to be beneficiaries of all God promised his people.

Outline and Overview

Galatians can be divided into five main sections. Following an initial greeting (Gal. 1:1–5), Paul describes his calling to preach the gospel among the gen-

19. Emerson (*Christ and the New Creation*, 65–94) and Trobisch (*Paul's Letter Collection*, 55–96) also claim Romans, 1 and 2 Corinthians, and Galatians are a literary grouping within the Pauline corpus.
20. Also Emerson, *Christ and the New Creation*, 91–93.

tiles (1:6–2:10). He argues that Jewish believers should not separate themselves from gentiles who trust in the same Messiah (2:11–21). He then identifies the genuine children of Abraham and heirs of the salvific promises (3:1–4:7) and tries to persuade the Galatians to avoid returning to slavery under the law (4:8–31). Last, Paul compels the Galatians to live as those whom the Spirit has freed from slavery and made heirs of a new creation (5:1–6:18).

Initial Greeting (1:1–5)

Paul introduces himself as an apostle of the resurrected Christ (Gal. 1:1–2). He offers the Galatians "grace and peace" from the Father and "the Lord Jesus Christ, who gave himself for our sins to rescue us from the present evil age" (1:3–4). This statement expresses the cosmic nature of their salvation through Jesus Christ.

Paul's Apostolic Calling (1:6–2:10)

Given the magnitude of their deliverance, Paul is disturbed at the prospect of the Galatians turning to "a different gospel" (Gal. 1:6). Paul is so upset that he wishes those preaching a false gospel would be under a "curse"—which is shorthand for wishing they would be cut off from the covenant community and devoted to eschatological destruction (1:8–9). Chapters 3–6 reveal that the false gospel in Galatia requires gentiles to adopt Jewish distinctives to be considered faithful covenant members.

Paul's calling to preach the gospel among the gentiles recalls Jeremiah's, who was also separated before birth to be a prophet among the nations (Gal. 1:11–17; cf. Jer. 1:5). Paul's calling was approved by pillar apostles James, Peter, and John, who agreed that he was called to take the gospel to the uncircumcised gentiles. The pillar apostles required only that Paul remember the poor (Gal. 2:10; cf. Acts 11:28–30; Rom. 16; 2 Cor. 8–9).

Separating from Gentiles (2:11–21)

Paul tells us that Peter separated himself from eating with Jewish believers, even persuading Barnabas to participate in the hypocrisy (Gal. 2:11–14). Peter began the practice when Jewish believers came from James, who expected that Jews would avoid eating with gentiles, as was the custom for old covenant believers (2:12). Paul strongly rejects this practice. For him, the gentiles had been declared righteous, making them members of the same covenant through Jesus Christ (2:15–16). Works of the law that once separated Jews and

INCLUSION IN THE FAMILY OF GOD

Are there any distinguishing marks, other than faith in Christ, that we impose on other believers, like Jewish believers were imposing on gentile converts, to consider them genuine members of God's family? Do we expect Christians to adopt certain social positions? Do we expect them to be members of a certain political party? Do we expect them to approve of one style of preaching or approach to Christian counseling? What do you think Paul would say about the "boundary markers" we impose on others?

gentiles, like circumcision and food laws, have no bearing on who is welcomed into the family of God (2:16). The only boundary marker that matters is the crucified flesh of Jesus (2:20).

True Children and Heirs (3:1–4:7)

Paul is so upset with his readers that he calls them "foolish Galatians!" (Gal. 3:1). He follows by showing them the folly of adopting works of the law (3:2–14). He stresses that works like circumcision do not bring the Galatians into the people of God—only faith in the God who bestows his Spirit on his people (3:5). Paul quotes Genesis 15:6 to show that Abraham was declared righteous through faith in the God who brings Jews and gentiles into the same family (Gal. 3:6–9). He also quotes Genesis 12:3 and 18:18 to show that God always intended to incorporate the nations into the family of Abraham: "All nations will be blessed through you" (Gal. 3:8).

Paul takes his argument to its logical conclusion, quoting Deuteronomy 27:26 to contend that relying on works of the law like circumcision obligates a person to do "everything written in the Book of the Law" (Gal. 3:10). Since doing all the law requires is impossible, such a person is "under a curse," destined for eschatological destruction (3:10; cf. 1:8–9). Succumbing to works of the law has the unintended effect of casting a person outside the covenant community. The Galatians' only hope is Jesus Christ, who was "hung on a pole" (Deut. 21:23), bearing their curse, so that gentiles like them might receive the promised Spirit (Gal. 3:14; cf. Isa. 44:3).

To illustrate his point, Paul compares an unalterable human covenant to the Abrahamic covenant (Gal. 3:15–18). If a human covenant cannot be changed once it has been ratified, how much more is this the case with the covenant God made with Abraham (3:15)? Paul quotes the words "and to your offspring"

PAUL AND GIFT-GIVING

John Barclay's *Paul and the Gift* situates Paul's understanding of grace within the Jewish and Greco-Roman contexts of gift giving.[a] In so doing, he argues that God extends grace without regard for the worthiness of the recipient. Does Barclay's view of "grace as an incongruous gift" change your understanding of grace? Does it change how you understand your worthiness of God's gracious gift of Jesus Christ (Gal. 4:4–5)?

a. John M. Barclay, *Paul and the Gift* (Grand Rapids: Eerdmans, 2015).

from Genesis 13:15, 17:8, and 24:7 to identify Jesus Christ as the genuine descendant of Abraham and recipient of the promised land inheritance (Gal. 3:16). Texts like Psalm 2 and Isaiah 65–66 expand the promise beyond Canaan to include the entire eschatological world. Romans 4:13 follows this developed understanding of the land promise, showing that Abraham and his offspring will inherit the entire cosmos. As a result, Jesus is the offspring of Abraham who will receive the entire world as his eschatological inheritance. All who trust in Jesus Christ are also Abraham's children, who receive the promised Spirit and are fellow heirs of the future world (Gal. 3:22, 27, 29; 4:6–7). No boundary markers are required to be considered God's people and recipients of all God promised to Abraham and his offspring.

AVOIDING A RETURN TO SLAVERY (4:8–31)

Paul questions why the Galatians would desire to return to being enslaved to false gods (Gal. 4:9–10). The Galatians are even keeping Jewish calendrical requirements associated with the old age of slavery under the law (4:10). Paul begs them to follow his example as one who understands that the arrival of Jesus Christ means they are no longer required to submit to such practices (4:12).

Paul knows that influential Jewish teachers desire to win over the Galatians (Gal. 4:17). He hopes they will reject the teachers' persuasive tactics and follow his example (4:18). Paul will continue to experience anguish and distress, just like a mother experiencing birth pains, until the Galatians mature into the image of Christ (4:19).[21] His use of birth imagery recalls Isaiah 42:14 and

---

21. Thomas R. Schreiner, *Galatians*, Zondervan Exegetical Commentary on the New Testament 9 (Grand Rapids: Zondervan, 2010), 289.

45:10, which illustrate God's tortured concern for his people.[22] Paul's use of such imagery displays his anguish for the Galatians' spiritual well-being. Though he would rather speak tenderly, just like a mother, the severity of the situation means that he must use a strong tone (Gal. 4:18–20).

Paul draws on the Hagar and Sarah story to make a typological illustration (Gal. 4:21–31). He likens those desiring to return to the law to Hagar and her children, who are in slavery (4:24–25). Sarah and her offspring, however, are the free children of the promise, like Isaac (4:23). Paul identifies himself and the Galatians as the children of the free woman who will be delivered out of the barrenness of exile to inherit the eschatological land promised to Abraham (4:26–28, 31). As Ishmael ("the son born according to the flesh") persecuted Isaac, so the Jewish teachers persecute the Galatians, the true children of promise (4:29). The Galatians should cast out the children of the slave women who are not recipients of the promises, just as Abraham cast out Hagar and Ishmael (4:30–31; cf. Gen. 21:10).

Living as Free Heirs (5:1–6:18)

Paul transitions to a block of ethical instruction based on the reality that the Galatians are the free children of Abraham who have received the promised Spirit. Since they are free, the Galatians should not return to a life of slavery (Gal. 5:1). If they accept the Jewish boundary marker of circumcision, then they must keep the demands of the entire law (5:2–3). Their bondage to the law's requirements would result in their being separated from Christ (5:4). Paul exhorts the Galatians to rely on the power of the Spirit to eagerly await "the righteousness for which we hope," when God will deliver his people into their cosmic inheritance (5:5).

In the meantime, Paul exhorts them to "love their neighbor," fulfilling the intent of the law (Gal. 5:14; cf. Lev. 19:18). In seeking to love others, they should follow the leading of the Spirit—who produces the fruit of love, joy, peace, patience, kindness, goodness, faithfulness, gentleness, and self-control associated with life in a new creation—not the desires of the flesh, like sexual immorality, drunkenness, strife, jealousy, dissension, and envy associated with the age of slavery (Gal. 5:16–26). Simply put, the Galatians should sow "to please the Spirit" so that they might "reap eternal life" (6:8). If they persist in doing good, they will assure themselves of an eternal reward (6:9–10).

---

22. Susan Grove Eastman, *Recovering Paul's Mother Tongue: Language and Theology in Galatians* (Grand Rapids: Eerdmans, 2007), 97–126.

Paul has spent much of the letter opposing Jewish believers who compel gentiles to adopt boundary markers like circumcision. So it is appropriate for him to conclude the letter by emphasizing that the only distinguishing mark that matters is the crucified flesh of Christ (Gal. 6:14). Circumcision is a relic of the old creation, and it has no value in the new creation (6:15). Paul wishes peace upon all who live by this standard (6:16).

Canonical Function

Galatians closes the initial grouping of Pauline letters consisting of Romans, 1 and 2 Corinthians, and Galatians. The bookends of this unit, Romans and Galatians, follow a theological instruction–ethical exhortation pattern. Galatians exhorts readers to live out their righteous status as free sons and daughters of Abraham who will dwell in the new creation and to avoid adopting the mark of circumcision associated with the old age of slavery. As sons and daughters of Abraham and fellow heirs with Christ, we should rely on the Spirit to compel us to boast only in the crucified Christ and to love our neighbor. No identifiable markers associated with the passing age result in receiving an eschatological inheritance.

The pattern of theological instruction and ethical exhortation established in the initial Pauline letter grouping continues into Ephesians, Philippians, and Colossians. Each letter will express its own theological and ethical concerns.

Authorship, Dating, and Audience

There is little doubt that Paul wrote the letter to the Galatians. The letter identifies him as the author (Gal. 1:1) and records genuine events about his calling and mission to the gentiles (1:12–24; 2:1–14). Paul even identifies himself as the one writing "with [his] own hand" (6:10). Galatians is another undisputed Pauline epistle.

The date of Galatians depends on whether the letter is addressed to a North Galatian or a South Galatian audience. The North Galatian theory claims that Paul writes to the churches he visited in Acts 16:1–5 and on his third missionary journey in Acts 18:23 (AD 49–51).[23] The South Galatian theory claims that Paul writes to the churches he visited on his first missionary journey in Acts 13:1–14:28 (AD 45–47). The North Galatian theory date would be in the 50s and the South Galatian date in the late 40s. Both views are possible. Neither significantly changes the interpretation of Galatians.

---

23. Schreiner, *Galatians*, 24–29; Beale and Gladd, *Story Retold*, 246.

◼ Ephesians

Ephesians has a customary title associated with the Pauline corpus (*Pros Ephesious*, "to the Ephesians"). Several early manuscripts, however, like Papyrus 46 ($\mathfrak{P}^{46}$), Sinaiticus (ℵ), and Vaticanus (B), do not include the words *en Ephesō* ("in Ephesus," 1:1), giving the impression of a circular letter. The words *en Ephesō* are included in fifth-century manuscripts Alexandrinus (A) and Bezae (D) and the majority of later witnesses (e.g., F, G). Although a valid case can be made for either reading, the manuscript tradition overwhelmingly includes the customary title *Pros Ephesious* and the words *en Ephesō*.[24] As a result, we should assume that the letter was originally addressed to the Ephesian church.

The letter takes up prior themes, like the role of the Spirit and Jew-gentile unity, while also taking on new ones, such as spiritual warfare and household conduct. Overall, the letter encourages readers to live out their Spirit-empowered unity in Christ. The Spirit who empowers believers also assures them of a future inheritance. Paul supports his argument by relying on choice quotations from and various allusions to the Old Testament.

Outline and Overview

Ephesians can be divided into two major sections. The first section expounds on Jew-gentile unity in Christ (Eph. 1:1–3:21). The second section exhorts believers to live out their unity by the power of the Spirit (4:1–6:24). All this is possible through Jesus Christ, who abolishes the enmity that existed between God and humanity.

UNITY IN CHRIST (1:1–3:21)

After an initial greeting (Eph. 1:1–2), Paul contends that God has adopted believers into the family of God through Jesus Christ (1:3–6). When we consider the allusions to texts like Genesis 12, 15, and 18, we envision that believers have been brought into the family of Abraham, making them heirs of the promises God made to his people in the Old Testament. Paul adds that it is through Jesus Christ that God has revealed his "mysterious" desire to reconcile all things in heaven and earth to himself (Eph. 1:7–10). God's goal is to bring the entire created order back into a right relationship with him, just like it was in the original garden of Eden.

---

24. Marcion titles the letter "to the Laodiceans."

Furthermore, God's people have the hope of an inheritance through Jesus Christ (Eph. 1:11). Although the inheritance is undefined, we should recall earlier discussions in Romans 4 and Galatians 3, where Paul envisions that the land promised to Abraham's offspring is expanded to include the entire renewed creation (Ps. 2; Isa. 65–66). There is no reason to think that Paul departs from this understanding of the inheritance in Ephesians. Though believers have not yet received their eschatological inheritance, the Spirit will see to it that they receive what has been promised to them when all things are reconciled to God in Christ (Eph. 1:13–14).

The resurrection of Christ brings about the reconciliation of the cosmos and establishes his authority over the entire spiritual realm (Eph. 1:20–21). Paul quotes Psalm 8:6 ("put everything under their feet") to extend Christ's authority over the church (Eph. 1:22–23). While humans lived in rebellion and were dead in their sins, God poured out his grace, making them alive in Christ so that they might live as new creations (2:1–10). He made alive both Jews and gentiles, who once lived in enmity but are now one new humanity through Jesus Christ (2:11–16). Both groups are brought into the people of God and indwelled with the Spirit, who facilitates their growth in holiness until they inherit the new creation (2:17–22).

Although the plan was hidden from prior generations, the Spirit has now revealed that Jesus Christ makes gentiles members of the people of God and coheirs of the promises made to Abraham (Eph. 3:1–6). As a result, Jews and gentiles are members of the family of God and equal participants in the saving promises. God gave Paul the grace to preach this gospel to the gentiles so that all may know the plan of God once hidden but now revealed through Jesus Christ (3:7–13).

LIVING AS ONE NEW HUMANITY IN CHRIST (4:1–6:24)

Paul encourages readers to "make every effort to keep the unity of the Spirit through the bond of peace" (Eph. 4:3). Yet, unity does not suggest that God's people are the same. Paul concedes that Christ extends his grace to his people in diverse ways, appointing some to be apostles, others prophets and evangelists, still others pastors and teachers (4:7–11). Such manifestations of grace are extended to believers for the maturity of the one body of Christ (4:12–16).

Paul exhorts readers to avoid sinning against fellow believers by stealing, using foul language, being angry, committing sexual immorality, and being greedy (Eph. 4:17–5:5). Such acts are not fitting for those who will dwell in the cosmic kingdom over which Jesus will reign (5:5). Instead, believers should be

HOUSEHOLD CODES

Paul employs household codes in Ephesians 5–6 and Colossians 3. Household codes were common in Greco-Roman literature like Aristotle's *Politics* and Plato's *Laws*, which discuss proper conduct in relationships between husbands and wives, fathers and children, and masters and slaves. Such authors expect that wives, children, and slaves will submit to their respective authorities for the good of the state. Paul, on the other hand, expects submission for the sake of Christ. Since the new age has arrived, Paul also holds that believers should work toward the elimination of the sinful dynamics of the passing age, like slave/master relationships (1 Cor. 7:21–24; Philemon). As a result, we should read Paul's household codes in ways consistent with the submission to Christ expected of those who belong to a new age.

kind to one another, compassionate, and forgiving (4:17–32). Believers should also conduct themselves appropriately in their various household relationships, such as between wives and husbands, children and parents, and slaves and masters (5:22–6:9). All such relationships should honor their ultimate authority, Jesus Christ (5:22). Paul expects that believers will live out their Spirit-led unity in anticipation of the reception of their cosmic inheritance.

Paul understands that the forces of darkness oppose Christ-honoring unity among believers (Eph. 6:12). He alludes to divine armor imagery in Isaiah 59 to encourage believers to stand against the powers of darkness by putting on the belt of truth, the breastplate of righteousness, the sandals of peace, the shield of faith, the helmet of salvation, and the sword of the Spirit (Eph. 6:13–17). Such precautions will embolden Paul's readers to live out their status as fellow children of God and coheirs of all God promised his people.

Canonical Function

Ephesians follows the pattern of theological instruction and ethical exhortation. We see theological instruction in Paul's argument that Jews and gentiles are heirs of all that God promised to Abraham—which was God's plan from the beginning and is now revealed in Jesus Christ. We see ethical exhortation in Paul's encouragement to live out Spirit-led unity despite opposition from the forces of darkness. The unity among diverse believers who worship the same Lord Jesus is the very thing God promised to Abraham: "Through your offspring all nations on earth will be blessed" (Gen. 22:18). Though Ephesians does not identify the offspring of Abraham, the earlier letter to the Galatians identifies this individual as Jesus Christ, through whom Jews and gentiles are made fellow heirs of the coming world (Gal. 3:16; cf. Rom. 4:13).

Authorship, Dating, and Audience

The majority of scholars doubt the authorship of Ephesians. Although the letter attests to Pauline authorship (Eph. 1:1; 3:1), many scholars attribute the letter to a follower of Paul. They argue that the style, language, and themes in Ephesians differ from those in Paul's undisputed letters. A close look at Ephesians reveals insignificant style and language differences compared to Romans and Galatians. Although Ephesians includes themes such as spiritual warfare and Christ's supremacy over the spiritual realm, it also includes themes found in undisputed Pauline epistles, such as the inheritance, the Spirit, and Jew-gentile relations. Overall, Ephesians has enough commonality with Paul's universally accepted letters to be considered an authentic epistle.

The date for Ephesians depends on whether Paul wrote the letter while imprisoned in Rome or Caesarea.[25] If composed in Rome, Ephesians could be dated to around AD 61–62. If composed in Caesarea, it could be dated to around AD 59–60. Ephesians could also be dated to the mid-50s if composed in Ephesus or Corinth. These possibilities suggest that we should be open to a date range anywhere from the mid-50s to the early 60s AD for a letter written to an ecclesial audience in Ephesus.

Philippians

Philippians is positioned after Galatians and Ephesians. Unlike these letters, which employ a mixture of Old Testament quotations and allusions, Philippians almost exclusively uses allusions, which encourage readers to live in light of the gospel of Jesus Christ. Unlike in Galatians, in Philippians Paul's tone is joyful and encouraging; he calls readers partners "in God's grace with me" and expresses his longing for them "with the affection of Christ Jesus" (Phil. 1:7–8). Paul also encourages his audience to "rejoice in the Lord" (3:1) and shares that he "rejoiced greatly in the Lord" because they "renewed [their concern]" for him (4:10). Paul's joyful tone in Philippians frames his theological instruction and ethical expectations in ways we have yet to see in the Pauline corpus.

25. Following Carson and Moo, *Introduction to the New Testament*, 506–7.

Outline and Overview

After a customary greeting (Phil. 1:1–2), Paul explains the gospel for which he suffers (1:3–30). He then encourages readers to live in step with the gospel of Christ (2:1–30). He subsequently exhorts them to guard themselves against false teachers and strain toward the goal of attaining the resurrection of the dead (3:1–4:1). Paul closes with final exhortations, prayers, and greetings (4:2–22).

GREETING AND PAUL'S GOSPEL (1:1–30)

The greeting identifies Paul and Timothy as servants of Christ Jesus (Phil. 1:1). The theme of service sets the tone for Paul's later discussion about Jesus Christ, who is the model of humble service for all believers (2:1–11).

Paul thanks God for the Philippians' partnership in the gospel (Phil. 1:3–5), knowing "that he who began a good work in you will carry it on to completion until the day of Christ Jesus" (1:6). The mention of the one "who began a good work" alludes to the Spirit in Ezekiel 36–37, who enables people to walk in newness of life. The Spirit will continue to work in the lives of believers until Jesus raises them from the grave. Until then, Paul wishes that the Philippians' "love may abound more and more in knowledge and depth of insight, so that you may be able to discern what is best and may be pure and blameless for the day of Christ" (Phil. 1:9–10).

In Paul's case, whatever suffering he endures is for the sake of the advancement of the gospel (Phil. 1:12–14). Even those who desire to cause him difficulty by preaching the gospel out of selfish ambition serve to advance the good news (1:17–18). No matter what he endures, Paul seeks to honor the Lord Jesus (1:20). Though he would rather be with the Lord, he believes that he will continue living so that he might see the spiritual growth of the Philippians (1:21–26). Until Jesus returns, Paul expects the Philippians to live in a manner worthy of the gospel, which includes suffering for the sake of Christ (1:27–30).

LIVING IN LIGHT OF THE GOSPEL (2:1–30)

Paul appeals to the "encouragement from being united with Christ" to encourage the Philippians to be "like-minded, having the same love, being one in spirit and of one mind" (Phil. 2:1–2). The Philippians should carry out Paul's expectations by considering others greater than themselves and considering the interests of others (2:3–4). They have the example of Christ, who had

APPLICATION OF THE *KENŌSIS*

The "emptying of Jesus"—what is often called the *kenōsis*—is the prime example of Christian conduct and humility. If the Lord of the universe was willing to humble himself on a cross, then we should be willing to humble ourselves for the sake of others. Who are some people you have refused to serve, perhaps because you esteem yourself above them? What are some ways you can humble yourself to serve them, just as Jesus has served us?

every right to exercise his divine privileges but chose to humble himself by suffering on the cross (2:5–8). Paul's illustration alludes to Isaiah's servant, who suffers for the transgressions of the people (Isa. 52–53). Jesus takes on the role of Isaiah's suffering servant. In so doing, Jesus does not "empty" himself of his divinity but deprives himself of any privileges associated with his sovereign rule, like refusing to suffer on a cross. Christ's humble service results in God exalting him "above every name" so that "at the name of Jesus every knee should bow, in heaven and on earth and under the earth, and every tongue acknowledge that Jesus Christ is Lord" (Phil. 2:9–11). Paul's reference to "every knee bowing" and "every tongue acknowledging" recalls the eschatological context of Isaiah 45:23, where such allegiance is directed to God. Paul's application of this text identifies Jesus as the God to whom all of humanity will swear allegiance.

If Christ deprived himself of his divine prerogatives, then the Philippians can humble themselves to serve their brothers and sisters. They should be willing to "do everything without grumbling or arguing," distinguishing themselves as children of God in the midst of a "crooked generation" (Phil. 2:14–15). Timothy and Epaphroditus demonstrated Christlike humility in their service to Paul and others (2:19–28). Paul expects that the Philippians will honor all such exemplary people (2:29–30).

EXHORTATION (3:1–4:1)

The Philippians should guard themselves against those compelling gentile believers to undergo circumcision (Phil. 3:2). Paul assures them that they have no need for circumcision, because they have the Spirit, who designates them as the people of God (3:3). He argues similarly in Galatians, where Jews were compelling gentile believers to adopt circumcision to be considered genuine covenant members. The Philippians have no reason to yield to the same pressure.

Of all people, Paul has grounds to trust in the external markers of Judaism: he was circumcised on the eighth day and is an ethnic Israelite and a member of the tribe of Benjamin (Phil. 3:4–5). He has all the distinguishing marks of a faithful covenant member. But he regards knowing Christ as superior to anything in which he once trusted to identify him as a genuine member of God's people (3:8). His goal is to attain the resurrection of the dead (3:8–11).

Paul concedes that he has not achieved the perfected status associated with the resurrection (Phil. 3:12). He invites readers to press on with him, rejecting those who would desire for them to put on the fleshly marks of Judaism (3:12–21), until Jesus Christ returns to transform their "lowly bodies so that they will be like his glorious body" (3:21). He encourages them to "stand firm in the Lord" until that day (4:1).

Final Exhortations, Prayers, and Greetings (4:2–22)

Paul's final exhortations include a call to assist gospel laborers Euodia and Syntyche in putting aside their differences (Phil. 4:2–3). He urges the Philippians to rejoice in the Lord, to present their requests to God, and to allow the peace of Jesus to guard their hearts (4:4–7). He also urges them to ponder and practice what is honorable (4:8–9). He concludes the letter by expressing his appreciation for the Philippians' partnership in the gospel and final greetings from fellow believers (4:14–23).

Canonical Function

Philippians also follows the pattern of theological instruction and ethical exhortation. The theological instruction is similar to that in Romans 3–4 and Galatians 3. It explains that Jesús Christ brings Jews and gentiles into the same family without their having to adopt the ethnic boundary markers of Judaism. The ethical exhortation, which encourages readers to love their neighbor, is similar to that in Romans 5–8 and 12–15 and Galatians 5–6. Overall, Philippians explains that Jesus's humble example is the theological basis for how readers should regard themselves as servants of others as they await their resurrection into the image of Jesus Christ (cf. Rom. 8:12–29).

Authorship, Dating, and Audience

Philippians bears all the marks of Pauline authorship. The letter identifies Paul as the author (Phil. 1:1) and records his personal exhortations (4:2–9) and his personal struggles in ministry (1:12–26; 4:10–13). Philippians has similarities with other authentic letters of Paul, which speak of Jew-gentile relations, the hope of resurrection, and Spirit-empowered ethics.

The date of Philippians is associated with Paul's imprisonment in Rome, Caesarea, or Ephesus. Of these options, the letter shows evidence of being written in Rome, for Paul makes mention of the palace guard (Phil. 1:13) and Caesar's household (4:22). As a result, the epistle may be dated to Paul's Roman imprisonment in the early 60s.

The historical audience is the church in Philippi, whom Paul first encountered on his second missionary journey (Acts 16:12–40). The church that had been a consistent partner in Paul's gospel ministry (Phil. 1:5) is now encouraged to overcome false teaching (3:2–11) and division (4:2) by following the servant-like example of Jesus Christ.

Colossians

Colossians is the final Pauline letter that follows a theological instruction and ethical exhortation pattern. Aside from the overall structure, the letter shares similarities with Ephesians, which argues for the supremacy of Jesus Christ and includes instructions on household relationships. The letter also shares similarities with Galatians, 1 and 2 Corinthians, and Philippians, which testify to Paul's sufferings in ministry. Individually, Colossians makes a strong case for the cosmic nature of Christ's atonement, resulting in his victory over the spiritual forces of the universe and his reconciliation of all things in heaven and earth. As the beneficiaries of the atonement, the Colossians are to walk in victory over the spiritual powers over which Christ has triumphed.

That Colossians and Philemon were written in the same vicinity and around the same time has led scholars to address these letters collectively. Since we are following the ordering of the New Testament canon, we will discuss Philemon after Titus and before Hebrews. The sequence of the canon takes hermeneutical priority over the historical composition of documents.

Outline and Overview

Paul explains the supremacy of Jesus Christ over all things (Col. 1:1–2:5). He then exhorts the Colossians to live as those whom the sovereign Christ has raised to life (2:6–4:6). Paul closes the letter with final requests and greetings (4:7–18).

THE SUPREMACY OF CHRIST (1:1–2:5)

Paul greets the Colossians and shares his appreciation for their faithfulness to Christ Jesus (Col. 1:1–8). He prays that they will continue to be filled with "wisdom and understanding" so that they might continue living worthy of the Lord, "bearing fruit" and "growing in the knowledge of God" (1:9–10). Their goal should be to receive the inheritance that has been stored up in the heavens (1:5, 12). As in other Pauline letters, the inheritance theme recalls the Abrahamic land promise, which has been expanded to include the entire renewed earth (Ps. 2; Isa. 65–66; Rom. 4:13; 8:12–25). The new earth will be revealed when God restores all things (Rev. 21–22). Only then will the Colossians' status as members of the kingdom of God's Son, Jesus Christ, become a reality on the earth (Col. 1:13–14).

The Christ who delivers his people from darkness is the creator of and supreme authority over all things in heaven and on earth, including heavenly rulers and authorities (Col. 1:15–17). His authority also extends over the church (1:18). Jesus's preeminence is rooted in his being the first person to conquer the grave and in his reconciling all things to himself through his blood (1:18–20).

Paul prays that the Colossians will live holy lives so as to be blameless when Christ returns to make all things new (Col. 1:21–23). Paul is a minister of this future hope, which is also extended to gentiles (1:24–2:5). He endures sufferings so that people will come to know the "mystery" that was once hidden but is now revealed through the work of Christ: that the blessings of salvation promised to Abraham are extended to gentiles (1:24–26; cf. Gen. 12; 15; 17).

LIVE AS NEW CREATIONS (2:6–4:6)

After expounding on the supremacy of Christ, Paul focuses the remainder of the letter on ethical exhortation. Colossians 2:6 sets the tone: "Just as you received Christ Jesus as Lord, continue to live your lives in him." The Colossians should avoid being taken captive by the "hollow and deceptive philosophy" of the principalities and powers of the present age (2:8). Jesus, after all, defeated all spiritual powers through his work on the cross: "Having disarmed the powers and authorities, he made a public spectacle of them" (2:15). Consequently, the Colossians should not subject themselves to practices associated with the old age, like not handling, tasting, or touching certain foods or drinks (2:16–23). Such practices were always intended as types or shadows, which Christ has fulfilled (2:17). The Colossians should hold fast to Christ, leading to their growth in holiness (2:18–19).

THE COLOSSIAN HERESY

In Colossians 2, Paul warns against being deceived by religious practices that combine Jewish and pagan elements, what scholars call the "Colossian heresy." We have no real description of the heresy beyond what Paul describes in the letter. We are left to assume that the Colossians may have been worshiping angelic beings and practicing asceticism.

Since believers have been raised with Christ, they should set their minds on things that will characterize life when he makes all things new (Col. 3:1–4). They should practice, for instance, kindness, humility, patience, and forgiveness rather than sexual immorality, covetousness, and idolatry, which are worthy of God's coming wrath (3:5–14). Practicing such virtues reveals that the peace of Christ rules over them (3:15).

Paul also expects that the Colossians will honor Christ in their household relationships. As in Ephesians 5–6, Paul employs a household code to underscore that relationships between husbands and wives, children and parents, and slaves and master should glorify the Lord (Col. 3:18–4:1). Living according to the expectations of the Lord Jesus, rather than those of the principalities and powers of the passing age, testifies to life in the coming age.

FINAL REQUESTS AND GREETINGS (4:7–18)

Paul requests prayers for his efforts to share "the mystery" of the hope Jews and gentiles have in Christ and for the Colossians to live wisely before those outside the community of faith (Col. 4:2–6). He closes the letter with final greetings from fellow believers such as Aristarchus, Epaphras, and Luke the beloved physician (4:7–18).

Canonical Function

Colossians challenges readers to live in light of the supremacy of Jesus Christ. Since his death results in the triumph over the powers of the old age, believers should live as those under the lordship of Jesus. They should honor Jesus in all things, refusing to submit to the expectations of conquered spiritual authorities. They should also refuse to submit to relationship expectations of the passing age, which include unqualified submission to human authorities. They must remember that their submission is always directed at Christ, who calls them to practices that promote the spiritual maturity and well-being of others. In honoring Christ, they exhibit the values of a new creation.

Authorship, Dating, and Audience

The majority of scholars claim that Paul was not the author of Colossians. Although the letter assumes Pauline authorship (Col. 1:1, 23; 4:18), many scholars believe that someone wrote the letter under the name of Paul. They argue that the letter's style and theology differ so significantly from other Pauline epistles that someone other than Paul had to have written it.

A closer look at Colossians reveals that the language is not significantly different from authentic epistles like Galatians and Philippians. Differences of style may be attributed to unique situations that required different vocabulary and syntax. There is also the possibility that Paul employed a secretary for most (if not all) of his works (cf. Rom. 16:22). What's more, Colossians discusses theological themes, like the inheritance, the supremacy of Christ, and Jew-gentile unity, found in other Pauline epistles. Consequently, we do not have enough evidence to overturn Pauline authorship of Colossians.

Colossians was written while Paul was under house arrest in Rome. Thus, we may date the letter somewhere in the early 60s (Acts 28:30–31; Col. 4:18). The church in Colossae was the original audience (Col. 1:2). Although we know little about the historical audience, we do know that, like all the Pauline epistles, the inclusion of Colossians in the canon signifies its relevance for all believers.

1 Thessalonians

First Thessalonians initiates a thematic shift in the Pauline epistles. Whereas prior epistles call for ethical living in light of theological instruction about Jesus Christ, 1 and 2 Thessalonians call readers to live wisely in view of his imminent return.[26] The imminent return of Christ should motivate readers to obey the Spirit's prompting to love God and others rather than the sinful desires associated with the old age. It should also motivate readers to resist false teachings, knowing that Jesus could return at any moment. Paul draws on Old Testament passages to underscore his point about the Lord's return.

26. See Childs, *Church's Guide for Reading Paul*, 207–9; Emerson, *Christ and the New Creation*, 95–100.

Outline and Overview

After an initial greeting (1 Thess. 1:1), Paul thanks the Thessalonians for their labor and love in the Lord Jesus Christ (1:2–10). He reminds them of his faithful proclamation of the gospel of God (2:1–16). He expresses his longing to see them again (2:17–3:13). In the most prominent section, he exhorts the Thessalonians to live holy lives in light of the imminent return of Jesus Christ (4:1–5:11). Paul closes with final instructions and a prayer (5:12–28).

THANKSGIVING (1:1–10)

Paul greets the Thessalonians "in God the Father and the Lord Jesus Christ" (1 Thess. 1:1) and thanks them for their faithful example to the believers in Macedonia, Achaia, and beyond (1:2–7). The Thessalonians turned away from idols to serve "the living and true God," awaiting the return of his "Son from heaven, whom he raised from the dead—Jesus, who rescues us from the coming wrath" (1:9–10). The return of Christ and the coming judgment are what should motivate the Thessalonians' present behavior.

PAUL'S FAITHFUL GOSPEL PROCLAMATION (2:1–16)

Paul and his associates shared the gospel among the Thessalonians in a manner that sought to please God and not people (1 Thess. 2:1–6). They were gentle with the Thessalonians, like a nursing mother, sharing with them the gospel as well as their very lives (2:7–8). They encouraged and exhorted the Thessalonians to live in a manner worthy of the God who called them into his glorious kingdom (2:9–12). Although the Thessalonians suffered persecution on account of the gospel, Paul commends them for accepting the word they heard from him and his associates as the very word of God (2:13–16).

PAUL'S LONGING FOR THE THESSALONIANS (2:17–3:13)

Despite being hindered from visiting them, Paul longs to see the Thessalonians in person (1 Thess. 2:17). He takes pride in them being "our hope, our joy, or the crown in which we will glory" on the day Jesus returns to judge the world (2:19). Yet, he could not stand to be ignorant about their welfare, so he sent Timothy to encourage them in their afflictions and to learn about their faithfulness (3:1–5). Upon his return, Timothy reported their evident faith, love, and mutual desire to see Paul (3:6–10). In return, Paul prays to see the Thessalonians again and for the Lord to increase their love for one another so that they might be "blameless and holy" when Jesus returns with all his saints (3:11–13).

EXHORTATION TO CONTINUE LIVING HOLY LIVES IN Light OF CHRIST'S RETURN (4:1–5:11)

Paul exhorts the Thessalonians to continue living godly lives so that they are sanctified. He exhorts them to avoid vices like sexual immorality, handle their bodies in holy and honorable ways, not be driven by sinful passions, and not wrong their brothers and sisters in Christ (1 Thess. 4:1–5). Paul's call to holiness alludes to Leviticus 11:44, where Yahweh calls Israel to "consecrate yourselves and be holy, because I am holy."

Whoever ignores Paul's command disregards "the very God who gives you his holy Spirit" (1 Thess. 4:8). Paul's statement recalls Ezekiel 36:25–27, which anticipates the age when the Spirit would enable God's people to obey God's commandments. Since the Thessalonians are living in the days of fulfillment, rebuffing the call to holiness is a rejection of the very God whose Spirit compels them to love him and others. But since they know how to love one another—for they have been "taught by God," fulfilling expectations in Isaiah 54:13 and Jeremiah 31:33–34—Paul is confident that they will continue doing so "more and more" (1 Thess. 4:9–12).

So that they might not be uninformed about the nature of the return of Jesus, Paul assures them that Jesus will return and raise deceased believers (1 Thess. 4:13–14). Alluding to Daniel's vision of the son of man, who comes "with the clouds of heaven" (Dan. 7:13), Paul promises that Jesus will raise believers—the dead and those still alive—to meet the Lord in a triumphal procession that will result in their return to dwell with the Lord on the earth (1 Thess. 4:15–18). Allusions to Daniel 7:13–14 and 12:2–3 reveal that the Lord's return coincides with the resurrection of the dead, the final judgment, and the establishment of an eternal kingdom for the nations of the earth. Paul reassures the Thessalonians that such events are still forthcoming.

Paul reminds the Thessalonians that the "day of the Lord will come like a thief in the night" (1 Thess. 5:2), which strongly recalls Jesus's recorded words in Matthew 24:36 and 24:42–44. Since Jesus will return unannounced, believers should be "awake" so that they are not caught off guard (1 Thess. 5:3–7). They should prepare themselves by "putting on faith and love as a breastplate, and the hope of salvation as a helmet" (5:8; cf. Isa. 59). God has destined them to obtain final salvation through Jesus Christ so that they might live with him

MEETING THE LORD IN THE AIR

Many argue that "meeting the Lord in the air" is a reference to believers being raptured from the earth before the great tribulation (1 Thess. 4:17). The context of 1 Thessalonians 4:13–18 appears to describe believers being called up into the heavenlies before the return of Jesus Christ, only to return in a royal procession to establish his reign as king. The entire scene recalls how a Roman ruler would be welcomed by his supporters before entering a city.

ESCHATOLOGICAL HOPE

Are you encouraged by Paul's emphasis on the return of Jesus Christ? Does knowing that Jesus could return at any moment motivate you to live a holy life? How does the return of Jesus influence your evangelism efforts? How does it influence your discipleship efforts?

when he returns (1 Thess. 5:9–10). This eschatological hope should motivate the Thessalonians to encourage one another in the faith (5:11).

FINAL INSTRUCTIONS AND PRAYER (5:12–28)

Paul's final instructions encourage readers to esteem their spiritual leaders, admonish the idle, encourage the fainthearted, help the weak, and be patient with everyone (1 Thess. 5:12–14). He urges them to do good to others, rejoice always, pray without ceasing, and give thanks in all circumstances (5:15–18). They should cling to what is good and abstain from evil (5:20–22). As he closes, Paul prays that God will sanctify them and keep them blameless until the arrival of the Lord Jesus Christ (5:23–24).

Canonical Function

The prior epistles to the Ephesians, Philippians, and Colossians ground their exhortations to live holy lives in the identity of Jesus. Yet, they lack eschatological urgency. When we encounter 1 Thessalonians, we envision that believers are to grow in holiness because Jesus could return at any moment to establish his reign on the earth and judge the dead. Knowing that we will soon stand before the throne of Jesus is more than enough motivation for holy living. Simply put, 1 Thessalonians supplies the eschatological urgency lacking in prior Pauline letters.

Authorship, Dating, and Audience

There is little doubt that Paul is the author of 1 Thessalonians. The letter identifies Paul as the author (1 Thess. 1:1), and a sizable portion of the letter contains personal details about his ministry (2:1–3:13). The letter may be dated to the early 50s, while Paul was in Corinth after being driven from Thessalonica. From Corinth, he writes two letters to his ecclesial audience in Thessalonica.

2 Thessalonians

Second Thessalonians is only three chapters in length—but packs a strong eschatological punch. The entire letter anticipates Jesus's return to judge the wicked and save the faithful. As in 1 Thessalonians, Paul employs timely Old Testament allusions to explain the events related to the return of Jesus Christ. Paul encourages the Thessalonians to be ready for the arrival of Jesus by standing firm in what they have been taught, anticipating the man of lawlessness, and avoiding idleness.

Outline and Overview

Second Thessalonians has several distinguishable sections. After a customary greeting and a word of thanksgiving (2 Thess. 1:1–4), Paul elaborates on the eschatological judgment associated with Christ's second coming (1:5–12). He explains the events related to the revelation of the man of lawlessness (2:1–12) and urges the Thessalonians to stand firm in the faith (2:13–17). He closes the letter by urging the Thessalonians to live in light of the promised return of Jesus Christ (3:1–18).

GREETING, WORD OF THANKSGIVING, AND THE JUDGMENT AT CHRIST'S SECOND COMING (1:1–12)

Second Thessalonians opens with a greeting from Paul and his ministry associates Silas and Timothy (2 Thess. 1:1). Paul thanks God for the Thessalonians' growth in the faith and their increasing love for one another (1:3–4). He assures the Thessalonians that their perseverance amid sufferings will make them worthy of the kingdom of God at the return of Jesus Christ (1:5–12). The return of Jesus, however, is like a double-edged sword, bringing relief to those suffering for the faith and punishment to those who do not worship the true God (1:7–9). This event will cause believers to marvel at the glory of the God who brings justice to the earth (1:10). Paul prays that God will empower the Thessalonians to continue living faithfully so that the name of Jesus will be magnified throughout the world (1:11–12).

THE MAN OF LAWLESSNESS (2:1–12)

The Thessalonians should not be deceived into believing that the day of the Lord has already taken place (2 Thess. 2:1–2). Paul insists that before the Lord's return there will be a rebellion associated with the "man of lawlessness . . . the man doomed to destruction" (2:3). Paul's argument is based on the Septuagint versions of Psalm 88:23 and Isaiah 57:3, which speak of an enemy called "the son of lawlessness."[27] It also relies on the Septuagint version of Isaiah 57:4, which anticipates a "child of destruction, a lawless seed."[28] This imagery comes together in Paul's statement about "the man of lawlessness . . . the man doomed to destruction" to warn the Thessalonians about the figure who must appear before the second coming of Christ.

Paul then draws on imagery from Daniel 11:36 to argue that this eschatological figure will exalt himself above any god or object of worship, even setting "himself up in God's temple, proclaiming himself to be God" (2 Thess. 2:4). These words recall Antiochus Epiphanes's abomination of the temple in 167 BC and Caligula setting up a statue of himself in the temple in AD 40. Such events are shadows of the man of lawlessness, who will exalt himself over God's temple, which is the spiritual church of Christ (cf. 1 Cor. 6:18–19; 1 Thess. 4:3–8; Rev. 3:12; 11:1).[29] This figure will soon be released to deceive the people of the earth (2 Thess. 2:5–8).

When he returns, the Lord will destroy the man of lawlessness. Until then, Satan labors together with this figure to deceive people through false signs and wonders (2 Thess. 2:9–12). The Thessalonians should not be deceived— they should wait for the arrival of the Lord, who will crush Satan and the man of lawlessness.

STAND FIRM (2:13–17)

Paul reminds the Thessalonians that they have been chosen for salvation so that they will be sanctified by the work of the Spirit and conformed into

---

27. Jeffrey A. D. Weima, "1–2 Thessalonians," in Beale and Carson, *Commentary on the New Testament Use of the Old Testament*, 887.

28. My translation is from the LXX version of Isaiah 57:4. See the discussion in Weima, "1–2 Thessalonians," 887.

29. See the helpful discussion in G. K. Beale, *1 and 2 Thessalonians*, The IVP New Testament Commentary Series (Downers Grove, IL: InterVarsity, 2003), 203–11.

THE RETURN OF CHRIST

Believers should not speculate about the return of Jesus Christ. Nor should they fear his return. From 1 and 2 Thessalonians, we gather that believers are simply called to be ready, knowing that Jesus could appear from the heavens at any moment. Paul even warns about a visible figure (the man of lawlessness) who will impersonate Jesus, establishing himself over the church and performing signs and wonders like the ones Jesus performed while on the earth. Believers should avoid being deceived by this figure and live godly lives as they await the return of the true Lord, who will judge the wicked and save the faithful.

the glorious image of Jesus Christ (2 Thess. 2:13–14). God's sanctifying work should embolden the Thessalonians to stand firm in what they have been taught and not be persuaded by false teachings associated with Satan and the man of lawlessness (2:15). Paul prays that Jesus Christ and God the Father will comfort and strengthen his readers (2:16–17).

LIVING IN LIGHT OF THE SECOND COMING (3:1–18)

Paul urges the Thessalonians to pray that the word of the Lord will advance and will be honored through him and his colleagues (2 Thess. 3:1). Paul also urges them to pray that he and his associates will be delivered from wicked people (3:2). Paul is confident that they will do what he asks and prays that they will love God and remain faithful to Christ (3:4–5).

Paul encourages the Thessalonians to avoid idleness (2 Thess. 3:11–12). It is likely some believed that the day of the Lord had arrived, so there was no need to work. It is also possible that some focused so much on the return of Jesus that they devoted themselves to only spiritual matters. The problem is so egregious that the Thessalonians should disassociate themselves from those living in idleness (3:6, 13–15). Idleness runs contrary to the example of Paul and his associates, who work tirelessly so as not to burden anyone (3:7–8). Paul expects that the Thessalonians will work diligently as they await the return of Jesus Christ. He closes the letter with final words of grace and peace and some final greetings (3:16–18).

Canonical Function

The emphasis on the day of the Lord in 1 Thessalonians is only heightened in 2 Thessalonians, assuring readers of the future return of Jesus Christ.

Believers should live faithfully until Jesus appears. This includes holding fast to Christian teaching and avoiding idleness. The reality is that no one knows when Jesus is returning, so we should live as if he will return at any moment (1 Thess. 5:2–4). Jesus's return will be preceded by Satan and the man of lawlessness attempting to turn people away from worshiping Jesus Christ. Though resisting these evil figures will come with a cost, it will be much more painful to stand before Jesus Christ, who will put all false gods and evil forces in their rightful place of torment.

Authorship, Dating, and Audience

Second Thessalonians identifies Paul as the author (2 Thess. 1:1; 3:17). Since he composes the letter shortly after 1 Thessalonians, a reasonable date for 2 Thessalonians is somewhere in the vicinity of AD 50–51. Paul writes to the same audience as in 1 Thessalonians. The Thessalonians are still dealing with issues related to the return of Jesus Christ. The message of 2 Thessalonians will benefit believers until the second coming of Jesus.

▉ The Pastoral Epistles

The Pastoral epistles are addressed to Timothy (*Pros Timotheon A* and *B*) and Titus (*Pros Titon*), Paul's children in the faith. The transition from letters to churches in such places as Ephesus and Colossae to individuals like Timothy and Titus suggests that the Pastorals are a distinct letter collection. We find evidence of a Pastoral epistles collection in canon lists and codices, which always group together 1 and 2 Timothy and Titus. The similar themes in these letters and the consistent use of Old Testament allusions and creedal traditions give readers further warrant for reading 1 and 2 Timothy and Titus as a letter collection.[30]

The proximity of 1 and 2 Thessalonians to the Pastoral epistles suggests that the eschatological expectations of the former should be carried over into the latter. Childs argues, "It would be a serious error to claim that eschatology, indeed even apocalyptic themes, has been completely lost in the pastorals."[31] He contends that statements like "the appearing of our Lord Jesus Christ" (1 Tim. 6:14), "the blessed hope—the appearing of the glory of our great

---

30. See Ray Van Neste, *Cohesion and Structure in the Pastoral Epistles*, Journal for the Study of the New Testament Supplement Series 280 (London: T&T Clark International, 2004), 1–17.

31. Childs, *Church's Guide for Reading Paul*, 215.

God and Savior, Jesus Christ" (Titus 2:13), "until that day" (2 Tim. 1:12), and "in this present age" (Titus 2:12) reinforce the eschatological nature of the Pastoral epistles.[32] The eschatological emphasis of 1 and 2 Thessalonians is alive and well in 1 and 2 Timothy and Titus.

Since 1 and 2 Timothy and Titus are organized into a distinct collection, we will review the contents of each letter under the auspices of the Pastoral epistles. The arrangement of these letters into a collection also warrants a collective treatment of their canonical function, along with matters of authorship, dating, and audience, at the conclusion of the section.

1 Timothy

Paul writes a personal letter to Timothy, addressing matters about which Timothy requires pastoral instruction.[33] Paul opens with a greeting, a warning about false teachers, and a reminder about the mercy of Christ Jesus (1 Tim. 1:1–20). He then supplies guidelines about matters related to ecclesial order and qualifications for church leaders (2:1–4:16). He follows with instructions about honoring church members, like widows and the overseers (5:1–6:2). Paul closes the letter with a final warning about false teachers and gives advice about how to encourage the wealthy (6:3–21).

GREETING, FALSE TEACHERS, AND THE MERCY OF GOD (1:1–20)

Paul greets Timothy as "my true son in the faith" (1 Tim. 2:1) and urges him to remain in Ephesus to oppose false teachers who misuse the Mosaic law (1:3–7). The mishandling of the law by false teachers does not negate its goodness, for the law serves to highlight sinful practices like sexual immorality, same-sex activity, capturing and selling people into slavery, and lying (1:9–11). Such practices are contrary to "sound doctrine that conforms to the gospel concerning the glory of the blessed God" (1:10–11).

Though Paul was formerly a blasphemer and a persecutor of Christians, God extended mercy and grace to him through Jesus Christ (1 Tim. 1:12–14). Paul even calls himself "the worst" of all sinners (1:15). If God extended mercy to a sinner like Paul, then he certainly offers it to all who trust in Jesus for eternal life (1:16). Whereas some have wrecked their faith, Paul continues being faithful to Jesus and maintaining a good conscience (1:18–20).

---

32. Childs, *Church's Guide for Reading Paul*, 215. Emerson also notes Childs's comments. Emerson, *Christ and the New Creation*, 103.

33. My structure follows Campbell and Pennington, *Reading the New Testament*, 291.

Ecclesial Order and Qualifications for Church Leaders (2:1–4:16)

Paul turns to matters related to ecclesial order and oversight. He begins by encouraging prayers for all people, including royalty and those in high positions, so that believers may live peaceful and quiet lives (1 Tim. 2:1–2). Such prayers are pleasing to God, "who wants all people to be saved and to come to a knowledge of the truth" (2:4). Paul follows with a creedal statement affirming that "there is one God and one mediator between God and mankind, the man Jesus Christ, who gave himself as a ransom for all people" (2:5–6). This statement alludes to Deuteronomy 6:4, which affirms that there is only one God, and Psalm 25, which asserts God as savior. This is the very message that Paul was appointed to preach to the gentiles, those once considered outside the boundaries of the saving promises of God (1 Tim. 2:7). The work of Jesus eliminates all such narrow perspectives on God's salvation.

Paul then encourages men to pray without anger and quarreling (1 Tim. 2:8). He instructs women to wear what is fitting for godliness and to abstain from interrupting the worship service (2:9–12). Paul also says that "women will be saved through childbearing" (2:15). Some argue that this statement refers to a woman's role as a wife and mother, others claim that it affirms that God will protect women through the act of childbearing, and still others maintain that it recalls the promise in Genesis 3:15: that salvation will come through a woman's descendant who will crush the head of the serpentine figure known as Satan. The final option coheres with the story of Jesus's victory over Satan on the cross and gives women the distinction of being the beneficiaries of salvation through the savior born to Mary.

Paul then shifts his attention to advice about overseers and deacons. He argues that an overseer should live an exemplary lifestyle, practice hospitality, be able to teach, manage their household, and be mature in faith (1 Tim. 3:1–7). Deacons must have similar qualities, the only exception being the ability to teach (3:8–13). Paul addresses such matters so that people will know how to conduct themselves in the household of God (3:15).

Paul reminds Timothy about the reality of false teachers in the present age (1 Tim. 4:1–5). Paul does not mince words about such teachers, accusing them of devotion to "deceiving spirits and things taught by demons" (4:1). Timothy is responsible for pointing out such false teachings so that he might be a "good minister of Christ Jesus," showing the fruit of being trained in Christian doctrine (4:6). In so doing, he extends the hope of future salvation

THE *PROTOEVANGELIUM*

For centuries, Christian interpreters like Justin Martyr (ca. AD 160) and Irenaeus (ca. AD 180), have argued that Genesis 3:15 is the *protoevangelium*, the "first announcement of the gospel." The argument is that the promise of a woman's offspring who will crush the serpent is the first messianic promise in the Old Testament. Jesus fulfills the promise by crushing the power of Satan on the cross. Paul's mention of women being saved through childbirth may very well recall this hope.

OVERSEERS AND DEACONS

Christians differ on the gender qualifications for overseers and deacons. Some argue that the roles of overseer and deacon are reserved for men. Others contend that the role of overseer is reserved for men but the role of deacon is open to men and women. Still others hold that the roles of overseer and deacon are open to both men and women. One's position should rest on the following: (1) an examination of Paul's instructions in their historical context; and (2) an interpretation of Paul's instructions in light of the arrival of the new age in Christ and the redemptive movement of all things toward their consummation in a new creation. In short, we should wrestle with Paul's historical qualifications for overseers and deacons in view of the eschatological trajectory of Scripture.

for himself and his congregation (4:7–16). Timothy should be an example to the flock, despite his young age (4:12).

HONORING CHURCH MEMBERS (5:1–6:2)

Timothy should honor church members, treating older men as fathers, younger men as brothers, older women as mothers, and younger women as sisters (1 Tim. 5:1–2). He should also care for widows, unless they have family members who can support them (5:9–16). Younger widows should pursue marriage rather than draw support from the church (5:11–16). The church's resources should be used only to support needy widows (5:16). Paul's instructions are consistent with the expectation that God's people will provide for destitute widows (Exod. 22:22–23; Deut. 14:28–29; 15:7–11). Such generosity bestows honor on widows who would otherwise be left poor and needy.

Overseers who labor well are worthy of double honor, especially those who teach and preach regularly (1 Tim. 5:17). Paul quotes two texts to

PAUL'S QUOTATION OF LUKE 10:7

Up to this point, Paul has mainly quoted from the Old Testament. But now he quotes the sentence "the worker deserves his wages" found in Luke 10:7. How would Paul have quoted from a Gospel composed around the same time as the Pastorals, somewhere in the AD 60s? There are three solutions. First, Paul quoted from Luke's recently composed Gospel. Second, Luke was Paul's scribe and found an appropriate place to insert a quotation from his Gospel. Third, Luke and Paul drew from common Christian tradition, which explains the nearly identical quotation in their writings. While the origin of the quotation is uncertain, we can rest assured that both Luke 10:7 and 1 Timothy 5:18 are found in the final forms of their respective documents, making them authoritative Scripture.

support his point. The first is a recontextualized quotation of the Septuagint version of Deuteronomy 25:4: "Do not muzzle an ox while it is treading out the grain" (1 Tim. 5:18). Although Deuteronomy 25:4 includes the Greek word for "ox" (*bous*) as the third word in the clause, Paul moves the word forward to stress the action of the "threshing ox," who represents the "laboring elder."[34] Just as the ox is allowed to benefit from his labor, consuming some of what he threshes, so is the overseer. The second quotation is from Luke 10:7: "The worker deserves his wages" (1 Tim. 5:18). Paul uses this text to underscore that overseers should receive the monetary benefits of their labor. We also hear allusions to priests and Levites, who were allowed to consume portions of the animal sacrifices (Lev. 6:16–18; Num. 18:8–10; Deut. 18:1–2).

Timothy should only consider accusations against overseers on the evidence of two or three witnesses (1 Tim. 5:19). Paul's advice is grounded in Deuteronomy 19:15: "A matter must be established by the testimony of two or three witnesses." Since leaders are susceptible to false accusations, it is an honorable practice to consider an accusation only after it has been corroborated by multiple witnesses. If the accusation is legitimate, an overseer's visible leadership position requires public correction (1 Tim. 5:19–20). The potential for public disrepute is why overseers should not be appointed haphazardly. Timothy should take time observing a person's life, character, and spiritual maturity before entrusting them with church oversight (5:22–25).

34. Philip H. Towner, "1–2 Timothy and Titus," in Beale and Carson, *Commentary on the New Testament Use of the Old Testament*, 899.

FINAL EXHORTATIONS (6:3–21)

Paul closes the letter with some final exhortations. The first is a reminder about the dangers of false teaching (1 Tim. 6:3–5). He also urges Timothy to pursue godliness without the expectation of monetary gain (6:6–10). Timothy should be content with a holy life, trusting that the Lord will provide for his needs (6:6–8). Paul also compels Timothy to hold fast to the good confession about Jesus Christ and to keep the love commandment until the appearance of Jesus Christ (6:11–16). Timothy should encourage the wealthy to trust in God and be rich in good works toward others, providing of their surplus to help the poor among them (6:17–19). After all, wealth in the present age does not guarantee prosperity in the coming one (6:17). By instructing the wealthy on how to leverage their riches, Timothy assures them of a flourishing life in the coming age (6:19).

In the final verses, Paul encourages Timothy to guard what has been entrusted to his care, which is none other than the gospel of Jesus Christ (1 Tim. 6:20). He also urges him to avoid irreverent speech and teachings that have turned people from the faith (6:20–21). Paul extends a final word of grace to his child in the faith (6:21).

2 Timothy

Paul organizes his second letter to Timothy around topics of pastoral instruction. After a greeting, he opens the letter by urging Timothy to fan into flame the gift of God and to guard the good deposit entrusted to him (2 Tim. 1:1–18). He then exhorts Timothy to be a good soldier of Christ Jesus (2:1–13) and a worker approved by God (2:14–3:9). Paul reminds Timothy to live a godly life and to be ready to preach the word in any season of life (3:10–4:8). Paul closes the letter with final instructions and personal greetings (4:9–22).

THE GIFT OF GOD AND THE GOOD DEPOSIT (1:1–18)

Paul expresses his desire to see his spiritual child Timothy, who follows in the faithful footsteps of his grandmother Lois and his mother, Eunice (2 Tim. 1:3–6). Timothy's godly heritage is the reason why he should "fan into flame the gift of God," which he received "through the laying on of my hands" (1:6). This scene recalls Paul and the Ephesian elders laying hands on Timothy, confirming the young minister's gift of instructing others in the faith (1 Tim. 4:13–14). Timothy's young age made him shy of boldly exercising his spiritual gift, so Paul reminds him that God has given him a spirit of "power, love and self-discipline" (2 Tim. 1:7).

Paul also encourages Timothy to guard "the good deposit" of the gospel entrusted to him (2 Tim. 1:14). The gospel is worthy of Timothy's devotion (1:8–12). Paul calls Timothy to join him in suffering for the God who has saved believers from the present age and has called them into a holy vocation (1:8–10).

A Good Soldier of Christ Jesus (2:1–13)

Paul encourages Timothy to suffer as "a good soldier of Christ Jesus" (2 Tim. 2:3). Paul draws on soldier, athlete, and farmer imagery to stress the importance of the diligent labor required of one employed in the service of Christ (2:3–6). Christ's soldier should remember that Jesus is "raised from the dead, descended from David," which is in keeping with Paul's gospel (2:8). The risen Jesus is Isaiah's victorious servant (Isa. 53:10–11) and the promised Davidic king (2 Sam. 7; 1 Chron. 17), for whom Paul suffers so that others might obtain the salvation for which they have been chosen (2 Tim. 2:9–10). Paul affirms Jesus Christ's faithfulness to raise believers from the grave. If they endure, they will reign with him in the eternal kingdom (2:11–13).

An Approved Worker (2:14–3:9)

Timothy should strive to present himself to God as an approved worker, rightly teaching the word of truth (2 Tim. 2:15). He ought to do so despite those spreading false teaching, saying that the resurrection has already taken place (2:16–18). Despite false teaching about the resurrection, Paul assures Timothy that the Lord knows those who belong to him (2:19). God will preserve the genuine faith of his people, despite the prevalence of false teachers.

Timothy should correct false teachers with gentleness, knowing that God may use him to deliver them from the power of the devil (2 Tim. 2:24–26). But he should understand that ungodliness and opposition to the truth will persist until the return of Jesus Christ (3:1–8). Ultimately, false teachers' efforts will not succeed (3:9).

A Godly Life and a Prepared Preacher (3:10–4:8)

Timothy has followed Paul's godly example (2 Tim. 3:10–13). Paul urges Timothy to continue in what he has learned and believed (3:14), which is able to make one "wise for salvation through faith in Christ Jesus" (3:15).

CORRECTING FALSE TEACHERS

Correcting false teachers should always be done with gentleness. Our goal should never be to win arguments or to shame others—for all people are made in God's image and worthy of redemption through Jesus Christ. Let's think about it like this: If God's kindness has led us to repentance, then should we not extend the same kindness to others (Rom. 2:4)? Could God not use our kindness to lead the most egregious of false teachers to repentance?

Timothy should be ready to preach the inspired Scriptures in any season of life, knowing that Jesus Christ will hold him accountable when he returns to judge the dead and establish his eternal kingdom (4:1–5). While Timothy's ministry is just beginning, Paul's is coming to an end—he has fought the good fight, finished the race, and kept the faith (4:6–7). Soon he will meet the Lord at his coming, and he will be rewarded with the crown of righteousness (4:8).

FINAL INSTRUCTIONS AND PERSONAL GREETINGS (4:9–22)

Paul encourages Timothy to visit him soon—for only Luke is with him (2 Tim. 4:9–11). He urges Timothy to bring Mark with him, along with his cloak and scrolls, especially the parchments (4:11, 13). Although some have caused him harm, Paul is confident that the Lord will deliver him into his kingdom (4:14–18). Paul closes the letter with personal greetings from coworkers like Priscilla and Aquila (4:19–22).

Titus

Paul's letter to Titus follows the topical organizational pattern associated with the Pastoral epistles. After a greeting, Paul begins the letter by exhorting Titus to appoint qualified overseers in the Cretan churches (Titus 1:1–16). Paul then instructs Titus to teach sound doctrine (2:1–15) and to encourage the churches of Crete to devote themselves to good works (3:1–15).

GREETING AND QUALIFIED OVERSEERS (1:1–16)

Paul addresses Titus as he does Timothy, as "my true son" in the faith (Titus 1:4). He also supplies Titus with a list of qualifications for ecclesial overseers, such as exemplifying a godly lifestyle and teaching sound doctrine

(1:5–9; cf. 1 Tim. 3:1–7). Titus should appoint godly overseers who will counter the influence of false teachers (Titus 1:9). Paul is particularly concerned about the influence of the circumcision party, those who compel gentiles to take on the external markers of Judaism to be considered genuine covenant members (1:10). Their teaching is upsetting entire families of believers (1:11). Paul commands Timothy to silence and rebuke all such people (1:11, 13; cf. 1 Tim. 1:3–11; 4:1–5; 6:3–10; 2 Tim. 3:1–9).

Teaching Sound Doctrine (2:1–15)

Paul urges Titus to teach sound doctrine (Titus 2:1). Titus's instruction should address the needs of older men and women, younger men, and slaves in the churches of Crete (2:2–10). His teaching should be reflected in a life characterized by good works so as not to give opponents grounds for slander (2:7–8). Overall, Titus's emphasis on sound doctrine should result in the flock's growth in godliness as they await the return of Jesus (2:11–15; cf. 1 Tim. 4:6–16; 2 Tim. 4:1–8).

Devoted to Good Works (3:1–15)

Titus should also encourage the churches to devote themselves to good works (Titus 3:1). Particularly, he should remind them to submit to their authorities, to avoid godless speech, to be gentle, and to show courtesy (3:1–2, 14). Though members of the churches once lived a godless existence, Jesus has saved them and poured out his Spirit on them, empowering them to live as those who possess eternal life in the new age (3:4–8; cf. Ezek. 36–37). By insisting on such things, Titus assures his people of growing in good works as they await the return of Jesus (Titus 3:8).

Canonical Function

The Pastoral epistles are a unit within the Pauline corpus. Following the eschatological emphasis of 1 and 2 Thessalonians, Paul's letters to Timothy and Titus supply his spiritual children with pastoral wisdom on matters such as appointing qualified overseers, warnings against false teachers, and the importance of teaching and living sound doctrine until the return of Jesus Christ. Although the Pastorals were originally intended for Timothy and Titus, their inclusion in the Pauline corpus signifies that all readers of Scripture should adhere to Paul's instructions, especially those who aspire to minister to God's people. And since we are closer to the day of the Lord than when Paul wrote

1 and 2 Timothy and Titus, we have all the more reason to obey the advice contained in these letters, knowing that Jesus will soon return to save his people and judge the wicked.

Authorship, Dating, and Audience

Nineteenth-century scholars introduced doubts about the authorship of the Pastoral epistles, claiming that someone wrote them under Paul's name. The vocabulary and syntax of 1 and 2 Timothy and Titus do differ from those in letters like Romans and Galatians but only because Paul tailors them to suit the needs and circumstances of Timothy and Titus. Vocabulary and syntax differences may also be due to Paul's use of a scribe. The theology of the Pastoral epistles is not radically different from that of Pauline letters like 1 and 2 Thessalonians, which stress sound teaching until the return of Jesus Christ and warn readers about false teachers. Still another problem, however, is that the Pastorals make no mention of Paul being released from house arrest in Rome (Acts 28). Since Acts is not a complete record of Paul's life, it is possible that he was released from prison, enabling him to write and minister freely. All in all, the objections are not convincing enough to overturn centuries of assumptions about the Pauline authorship of 1 and 2 Timothy and Titus.

Though Acts makes no mention of Paul's release from prison, it is likely that he pens the Pastoral epistles shortly after his release in AD 62. A possible date range for these letters is AD 63–65. Paul's initial audience is Timothy and Titus, his spiritual children in the faith. The letters continue speaking to leaders in the church of Jesus Christ and those to whom they minister.

Philemon

Philemon is the shortest Pauline epistle. Like the Pastoral epistles, Philemon is addressed to an individual recipient. Although Paul writes the letter from the same location and approximate time as Colossians, a canonical reading requires that we examine Philemon after the Pastoral epistles. In its canonical position, Philemon is grounded in the theology of prior letters like Romans and Galatians, which stress that Jesus has delivered people from slavery to sin and has made them equal participants in the family of God. Philemon should regard his relationship with Onesimus not according to the standards of the old age but according to the age that frees people of the bonds of a slave/master dynamic.

Outline and Overview

The letter to Philemon has two major sections. The first section identifies Philemon as a member of the family of Jesus Christ (Philem. 1–7). The second section is an appeal to Philemon on behalf of Onesimus (Philem. 8–25). The entire letter should be read in light of the arrival of the eschaton, which obliterates relational dynamics associated with the age of sin.

PHILEMON, A BROTHER IN CHRIST (VV. 1–7)

Paul greets Philemon as a partner in the faith (Philem. 1). Paul also affirms Philemon's faithfulness to Jesus and his love for the saints (Philem. 4–6). Paul even says that he derived much joy and comfort from Philemon because of his love for other believers (Philem. 7). From what we gather, Philemon is a faithful brother who has brought spiritual benefit to members of God's family.

A PLEA FOR ONESIMUS, A FELLOW BROTHER IN CHRIST (VV. 8–25)

Paul now makes a plea for a particular member of God's family: Onesimus (Philem. 8–10). Onesimus became Paul's spiritual child during his Roman imprisonment (Philem. 10). Paul acknowledges Onesimus's helpfulness in ministry and says he is sending him back to Philemon (Philem. 11–12). We should not assume that Paul is returning Onesimus to his master. Why would Paul return a believer to an institution associated with the old age of sin? Wouldn't that contradict his argument in 1 Corinthians 7:21, where he urges slaves to seize their freedom?

Philemon and Onesimus are now brothers in Christ, making them equal members of God's family. As a result, Paul compels Philemon to receive Onesimus "no longer as a slave, but better than a slave, as a dear brother. He is very dear to me but even dearer to you, both as a fellow man and as a brother in the Lord" (Philem. 16). For Paul, their new familial status overrides their former slave/master dynamic. Philemon is therefore compelled to receive Onesimus as he would Paul—as a brother in Christ (Philem. 17). Doing so will bring much spiritual refreshment to Paul (Philem. 20). If Philemon ignores Paul's instructions, he should know that Paul intends to make an extended visit to see to it that Onesimus is treated as one who has been delivered from the bonds of the old age (Philem. 21–22).

Canonical Function

When we read Philemon in light of Paul's prior letters, we envision that freedom from the power of sin also extends to Onesimus. That is why Philemon

READING PHILEMON IN THE PRE-CIVIL WAR AMERICAN SOUTH

Lisa Bowens's *African American Readings of Paul* demonstrates how citizens of the pre–Civil War American South used the letter to Philemon to support returning runaway slaves to their masters.[a] Frederick Douglass and other abolitionists fought against the sinful weaponization of Philemon. They argued that slavery is not a divinely ordained institution. Nor does Paul say that Onesimus is a runaway slave who should be returned to his master. Paul clearly says that Philemon should receive Onesimus as a brother in Christ, not as a slave.

a. Lisa M. Bowens, *African American Readings of Paul: Reception, Resistance, and Transformation* (Grand Rapids: Eerdmans, 2020), 113–24.

should no longer consider Onesimus a slave—he is a free brother in Christ, no longer bound to an institution birthed out of the age of sin. Consequently, appealing to Philemon to support the practice of slavery misses the point of the letter. The letter is not about returning Onesimus to his bonds but about making sure he is freed from them. Philemon is a blueprint for how believers should work for the deliverance of all people from the lingering effects of sin's rule over the earth.

Authorship, Dating, and Audience

Philemon was authored by the apostle Paul (Philem. 1). The letter may be dated to Paul's imprisonment in Rome around AD 61–62. Along with Philemon, the letter's audience includes Apphia, Archippus, and the church that meets at Philemon's house (Philem. 1–2).

■ Hebrews

The letter to the Hebrews is brimming with Old Testament quotations and allusions, showing the supremacy of Jesus over all things. While this significant letter is undoubtedly canonical, most scholars hold to its anonymous authorship. Origen famously quipped, "But who wrote the Epistle in truth, God knows."[35]

Doubts about Hebrews' authorship have not precluded its inclusion in the Pauline letter collection.[36] Late second-century manuscript Papyrus 46

35. Origen, *Homilies* 6.25.11–14.
36. See Trobisch, *Paul's Letter Collection*, 19–22.

($\mathfrak{P}^{46}$) includes Hebrews between Romans and 1 Corinthians. Fourth- and fifth-century codices Sinaiticus ($\aleph$), Alexandrinus (A), Vaticanus (B), and Ephraemi Rescriptus (C) insert Hebrews between 2 Thessalonians and 1 Timothy. The fifth- or sixth-century Codex Claromontanus (Dp) and later Byzantine versions place Hebrews after Philemon. Hebrews even follows the pattern of titles common to the Pauline epistles ("to the Hebrews"). Such observations provide sufficient warrant for interpreting Hebrews within the Pauline letter collection. In its current location, Hebrews functions as an appropriate conclusion to the Pauline corpus before one encounters the Catholic epistles.

Outline and Overview

The content of Hebrews is organized so as to persuade believers about the supremacy of Jesus. The letter immediately establishes Jesus's superiority over all things (Heb. 1:1–4). Hebrews then shows Jesus's supremacy over angels (1:5–2:18), Moses (3:1–4:13), and the priesthood (4:14–7:28). The letter moves into a discussion about Jesus as the high priest of a better covenant (8:1–13) and a better sanctuary (9:1–10:39). Hebrews then includes a section of examples of faithful old covenant figures who anticipated the inheritance of an eternal city (11:1–40). The letter crescendos with an exhortation to follow Jesus into the heavenly city (12:1–13:25).

THE COSMIC SUPREMACY OF JESUS (1:1–4)

Hebrews asserts that Jesus is the heir of all he created (Heb. 1:2). This declaration recalls earlier writers like John and Paul, who argue that Jesus created all things (John 1:1–5; Col. 1:15–17). Hebrews specifies that the Father has granted the Son the entire creation as his inheritance, recalling the similar affirmation in Psalm 2 (Heb. 1:2). After dying for the sins of the world, cleansing all he created, the Son took his rightful position as the king over the cosmos (1:3–4). This section anticipates the conclusion of the letter, which claims that believers seek a lasting city (13:14). The opening of Hebrews allows readers to envision that the lasting city is one and the same with the creation that Jesus cleansed with his blood.

JESUS'S SUPREMACY OVER ANGELS (1:5–2:18)

The author draws on Psalm 102:25–27 to argue that God has subjected the coming world to Jesus rather than angels (Heb. 2:5–8). Although we do not yet see the entire world subjected to Jesus, he has already been crowned with

PROMISED REST FOR CHRISTIANS

The promised rest in Hebrews is the same as the promised inheritance in the Pauline epistles—the new creation over which Jesus will reign (Rom. 4; 8; Gal. 3–4; Eph. 1). When you think about eternity, do you think about rest in heaven? Or do you envision rest in a new creation? Which do you think Paul and the author of Hebrews envision?

glory and honor through his death, bringing people salvation and sanctification (2:8–10). Jesus's death also delivers people from the power of Satan and enables him to come to the aid of those who are tempted (2:14–18). Jesus gives no such help to angels (2:16). That angels require help, whereas Jesus is sovereign, reveals Jesus's supremacy over the angelic realm.

JESUS'S SUPREMACY OVER MOSES (3:1–4:13)

The letter contends that Jesus was faithful to the one who appointed him as redeemer of the cosmos (Heb. 3:2). Although Moses was a faithful servant, Jesus has received a greater glory than Moses, being the faithful builder of the Father's household (3:3–6). Believers are members of the household of God if they hold fast to Jesus, whom the Father has appointed over the people of God (3:6). Although the rebellious wilderness generation never inherited Canaan, falling dead without ever entering the land, those who maintain their confidence in Christ will enter their promised rest in a land far better than the one Joshua led Israel into (3:7–4:13).

JESUS'S SUPREMACY OVER THE PRIESTHOOD (4:14–7:28)

Believers should hold fast to their confession about Jesus, the great high priest who sympathizes with our weaknesses (Heb. 4:14–15). God's people should draw near to Jesus, who dispenses mercy and grace in time of need (4:16). Jesus is greater than all the high priests who came before him because God himself appointed him eternal high priest in the perpetual order of Melchizedek (5:1–10; 7:11–28; cf. Ps. 110:4). All other priests were appointed by men and struggled with sin, so they were obligated to offer sacrifices on their behalf (Heb. 5:1–3; 7:26–28). Such was their existence until they died (7:24). Jesus, on the other hand, was granted a perpetual priesthood, never succumbing to temptation and thereby having no need to offer sacrifices on

OUR SYMPATHETIC HIGH PRIEST

Have you ever regarded Jesus as your sympathetic high priest? Have you considered that Jesus was tempted, just like you, though without sin? Have you considered going to him with your struggles and temptations, knowing that he sympathizes with your weaknesses?

his behalf (4:15; 7:24). Undoubtedly, Jesus is the perfect Son of God who serves as the eternal high priest, leaving no doubt about his supremacy over the priests who preceded him.

JESUS AS HIGH PRIEST OF A BETTER COVENANT AND A BETTER SANCTUARY (8:1–10:39)

Jesus the high priest took his royal throne in the presence of God in the heavenlies (Heb. 8:1–2). Jesus makes an offering in the pattern of the old covenant priestly offerings (8:3). What earthly priests offer is associated with old covenant copies and shadows of the heavenly realities linked to the new covenant (8:5–7). The author quotes Jeremiah 31:31–34 to underscore that the new covenant is a better covenant between God and his people, making the former one obsolete (Heb. 8:8–13).

A new covenant necessitates a new sanctuary that fulfills the symbolic regulations of the old covenant tabernacle (Heb. 9:1–10). When Jesus offered his life as an unblemished sacrifice, he became the mediator of a better covenant and the locus of new covenant worship (9:11–10:18). Through Jesus's sacrifice, believers can confidently draw near to him, the new temple, so that they might be cleansed of their sins and receive endurance to persevere in the faith (10:19–39).

EXAMPLES OF FAITHFULNESS (11:1–40)

The author includes a chapter on examples of faithfulness to encourage readers to persevere in the faith so that they might enter the promised city. According to the author, "faith is confidence in what we hope for and assurance about what we do not see" (Heb. 11:1). Believers do not yet see the new creation, the lasting city yet to come. Old Testament believers like Abel, Noah, Abraham, Joseph, Moses, Jacob, and David are examples of faithfulness, all dying without receiving the place for which they longed. Abraham, in particular, was anticipating the city "with foundations, whose architect and builder is God" (11:10). Such faithful saints were strangers and exiles on the present earth, seeking a better homeland (11:13–16). As a result, God has prepared a better city for them—and for all who persevere in the faith (11:16–40).

Final Exhortation—Follow Jesus! (12:1–13:25)

The author urges readers to keep their eyes fixed on Jesus, who completed the race of faith and took his seat at the right hand of God (Heb. 12:1–2). Since the race is long, believers should persevere through life's struggles and difficulties, knowing their sufferings are preparing them for life in an unshakable kingdom in the coming world (12:3–28). As they persevere in following Christ, believers should continue loving one another, knowing they are being sanctified by Christ's blood, which makes them fit for an eternal inheritance (13:1–19).

Canonical Function

Hebrews is included in the Pauline corpus. The letter's placement at the conclusion of the Pauline letter collection serves to encourage believers to follow Jesus into their eternal resting place, the new creation Jesus redeemed with his blood. The author of Hebrews argues that returning to old covenant practices will not result in entrance into the promised inheritance. Only faithfulness to Jesus leads to the place for which believers have always longed. The argument of Hebrews shares similarities with Pauline letters like Romans and Galatians, which encourage believers to trust in Christ for a cosmic inheritance rather than returning to old covenant practices like circumcision and food laws. Such thematic connections provide further warrant for reading Hebrews alongside other Pauline letters.

Hebrews is an appropriate capstone to the Pauline letter collection. As we read recollections of Old Testament passages and the arguments of prior Pauline letters, we are encouraged to persevere in following the Messiah, in whom we have believed and who has made us beneficiaries of a lasting inheritance. The message of Hebrews also prepares readers for the Catholic epistles. As we read about false teachers and persecution, we recall that these realities are associated with the fallen world, through which we must sojourn to inherit a new creation.

Authorship, Dating, and Audience

Most scholars are reluctant to read Hebrews as a Pauline epistle because it does not identify the apostle as the author. While this gives reason for pause, we should acknowledge that the letter is included in the Pauline corpus. Another objection is that the Greek style of Hebrews is more polished than that of Paul's undisputed epistles. But style differences are not enough to negate the Pauline authorship of Hebrews. Paul could have used a scribe, as he does in other epistles (Rom. 16:22). It is possible that Luke was Paul's scribe—for the Greek style of Hebrews is closest to that of Luke-Acts. This theory would account for thematic parallels between Hebrews and other Pauline epistles and stylistic similarities with Luke-Acts. An early proponent of this theory is Clement of Alexandria, who argues that Paul was the author of Hebrews and that Luke "translated it carefully and published it for the Greeks."[37]

The extensive references to the sacrificial system suggest that the letter may have been written before the destruction of the temple in AD 70. The content of the letter insinuates that the audience was composed of believers who needed instruction on how old covenant figures and institutions anticipate the superior ministry of Jesus Christ. The message of Hebrews is relevant for every generation of Christians, who must also understand how old covenant figures and institutions anticipate the greater person and work of Jesus.

SUGGESTED RESOURCES

Barclay, John M. *Paul and the Gift*. Grand Rapids: Eerdmans, 2015.

Childs, Brevard S. *The Church's Guide for Reading Paul: The Canonical Shaping of the Pauline Corpus*. Grand Rapids: Eerdmans, 2008.

Dunn, James D. G. *The New Perspective on Paul*. Grand Rapids: Eerdmans, 2005.

Gorman, Michael J. *Reading Paul*. Eugene, OR: Cascade Books, 2008.

Hays, Richard B. *Echoes of Scripture in the Letters of Paul*. New Haven: Yale University Press, 1989.

Longenecker, Bruce W., and Todd D. Still. *Thinking through Paul: A Survey of His Life, Letters, and Theology*. Grand Rapids: Zondervan, 2014.

Trobisch, David. *Paul's Letter Collection*. Bolivar, MO: Quiet Waters, 2001.

37. Eusebius, *Church History* 6.14.2.

SIX

THE CATHOLIC EPISTLES

As early as the fourth century, authors such as Eusebius grouped the seven letters following the Pauline epistles into a Catholic epistles corpus (*Church History* 1.23.25).[1] The designation "Catholic" suggests that the letters of James, Peter, John, and Jude are intended for a universal audience, whereas Paul's letters are intended for specific audiences.[2] Bruce Metzger notes, "In antiquity, the seven Catholic Epistles commonly stood in the order of James, Peter, John, and Jude—so codices Vaticanus, Sinaiticus, Alexandrinus; Synod of Laodicea (AD 363); Cyril of Jerusalem; Epiphanius; Athanasius; Gregory Nazianzus; Nicephorus."[3] The arrangement recalls the order of the pillar apostles in Galatians 2:9 (James, Peter, and John), who offered Paul the "right hand of fellowship." Jude closes the Catholic epistles corpus.

The distinct titles assigned to the letters of James, Peter, John, and Jude affirm their collection into a literary corpus. Whereas Paul's epistles designate the addressees, the Catholic epistles designate the author of the respective letters (James; 1 and 2 Peter; 1, 2, 3 John; Jude). The titles assigned to the Catholic epistles differentiate this corpus from the Gospels and the Pauline epistles.

1. D. A. Carson and Douglas J. Moo, *An Introduction to the New Testament*, 2nd ed. (Grand Rapids: Zondervan, 2005), 619.
2. See discussion in Darian R. Lockett, *Letters from the Pillar Apostles: The Formation of the Catholic Epistles as a Canonical Collection* (Eugene, OR: Pickwick, 2017), 62–64.
3. Bruce M. Metzger, *The Canon of the New Testament: Its Origin, Development, and Significance* (Oxford: Clarendon, 1997), 299.

Thematic connections are another binding feature of the Catholic epistles. Themes like inheritance (1 Pet. 1:4; James 2:5), false teachers (2 Pet. 2:1–22; 1 John 2:1–27; Jude), and the dispersion of God's people (James 1:1; 1 Pet. 1:1) are found throughout the corpus. The Catholic epistles also allude to similar Old Testament themes. For example, James 2:1–6 and 1 Peter 1:17 draw on Leviticus 19:15 to argue for impartial judgment for the poor, and James 5:1–6 and Jude 12 draw on Ezekiel 33–34 to rail against the rich and selfish shepherds, respectively.[4]

When we read the Catholic epistles after the Pauline epistles, we envision that believers should avoid false teaching and endure suffering (2 Pet. 2; Jude) to inherit the restored creation for which Paul (Rom. 4; 8) and the great cloud of witnesses longed (Heb. 11). The proximity of the Pauline epistles to the Catholic epistles suggests that the eschatological framework of the former should be carried over into the latter. The Catholic epistles include sufficient references to the return of Christ to remind readers of the eschatological framework for interpreting these letters.

James

Martin Luther questioned the canonical status of the epistle of James because it speaks so little about Christ.[5] Luther famously quipped that James is an "epistle of straw." Although Luther never went so far as to reject the canonical status of James, his comments have caused some to question the value of the epistle.

Such late opinions about James are not enough to unsettle centuries of manuscript evidence that testifies to its inclusion in the canon. As a result, we must wrestle with its contribution to the New Testament. In so doing, we see that James is not unconcerned about Jesus Christ. Quite the opposite: he cares so much about Christ that he emphasizes the importance of believers living out their faith in him. He even draws from Jesus's teachings while also drawing from the deep wells of the Old Testament.

James is positioned at the head of the Catholic epistles, underscoring that genuine believers live out their faith in Jesus. John's letters agree with this

4. See Lockett, *Letters from the Pillar Apostles*, 149–59.
5. See *Luther's Works*, vol. 35, *Word and Sacrament I* (Philadelphia: Fortress, 1960). Craig L. Blomberg and Mariam J. Kamel argue that, though Luther questioned James's canonical status, he "never rejected it and included many positive things in his writings about James alongside his concerns." *James*, Zondervan Exegetical Commentary on the New Testament 16 (Grand Rapids: Zondervan, 2008), 21.

assessment, arguing that obedience is expected of those who have been transferred from darkness to light. So do Peter's and Jude's, which contend that believers must persevere in their faith in anticipation of the return of Jesus Christ. James's canonical position functions much like Romans' placement at the front of the Pauline letter collection: it sets the tone for the remainder of the corpus.

Outline and Overview

James can be outlined in five sections. The first section is on wise living (James 1:1–27). The second is on loving one's neighbor (2:1–13). The third is on the importance of faith and works (2:14–26). The fourth contains more instruction on wise living (3:1–4:17). The fifth and final section provides final instructions, including admonishment for the rich, an admonition for patience, and guidance on the prayer of faith (5:1–20).

WISE LIVING (1:1–27)

James's address to the "twelve tribes scattered among the nations" recalls the original clans of Israel who entered Canaan and were later exiled because of their rebellion against the God who delivered them from Egypt (James 1:1; cf. Deut. 28–32). Centuries later, the prophets and other writers spoke of a time when God would regather the twelve tribes into the cosmically expanded land inheritance (Ps. 2; Isa. 11:1–12; 65–66; Jer. 31:8–14; Ezek. 37:21–22; 4 Ezra 7).[6] The promised restoration to the land coheres with James 2:5, which speaks of the inheritance of the kingdom for those "rich in faith" (cf. 1 Tim. 6:17–19). The "rich in faith" include the physical descendants of the twelve tribes as well as gentiles incorporated into the family of God.

As they await their inheritance, believers should ask God for grace to live wisely in the present age (James 1:5). God's wisdom enables believers to endure trials, resulting in the promised crown of life (1:12), and encourages them to be slow to anger, for human wrath does not hasten God's righteousness (1:19). In short, God's wisdom empowers people to be "doers of the word" (1:22, my translation of *poiētai logou*). James's emphasis on "doing" is in keeping with the obedience that has always been expected of God's covenant people and is grounded in the Torah. Obedience results in receiving an inheritance far better than what was granted to Israel's original tribes. It is the

---

6. D. A. Carson, "James," in *Commentary on the New Testament Use of the Old Testament*, ed. G. K. Beale and D. A. Carson (Grand Rapids: Baker Academic, 2007), 997.

EXILED BELIEVERS

Have you ever considered that you are an exile on the present earth? Have you ever considered that you are sojourning through the present age, just like the Israelites sojourned through the wilderness, until you inherit the new creation? Have you considered that God expects your obedience as you anticipate the reception of your inheritance?

very thing that Matthew's Jesus commissions his followers to teach people: "Make disciples of all nations . . . teaching them to obey everything I have commanded you" (Matt. 28:19–20).

Loving One's Neighbor (2:1–13)

James acknowledges the tendency to be partial toward the rich (James 2:1 7). Despite this propensity, God has chosen the poor to be "rich in faith" and to "inherit the kingdom" (2:5). James's teaching recalls the Sermon on the Mount, where Jesus promises that the "meek . . . will inherit the earth" (Matt. 5:5). James quotes the maxim "love your neighbor as yourself" from Leviticus 19:18 to argue that favoring the rich over the poor is contrary to God's will (James 2:8–10).

James expects that his readers will comply with the expectations of the law, such as not committing adultery and murder (James 2:11). James's expectations recall Jesus's interpretation of such commands in the Sermon on the Mount, where Jesus draws on Exodus and Deuteronomy to stress the obedience expected of God's people (Matt. 5:48). James even quotes the very same Torah passages as Jesus, such as the command to love one's neighbor (James 2:8; cf. Matt. 5:43), the prohibition on adultery (James 2:11; cf. Matt. 5:27), and the prohibition on murder (James 2:11; cf. Matt. 5:21). Evidently, James values the teachings of Jesus Christ, even if he does not identify them as such.

Faith and Works (2:14–26)

James stresses that faith without works is "dead" and "useless" (James 2:14–17, 20, 26). Both faith and works are necessary for righteousness (2:24). James draws on the example of Abraham to emphasize the role of faith and works in righteousness (2:23–24). James also draws on the Rahab story to show that, "when she gave lodging to spies and sent them in a different direction," her works testified to her righteousness (2:25). Both of these examples

PAUL AND JAMES

Some argue that Paul and James contradict each other—for Paul emphasizes faith and James stresses works. But this is misguided. The truth is that Paul's opponents in Romans and Galatians were relying on works for righteousness, so he emphasizes faith. James's audiences were relying on faith to the exclusion of works, so he stresses works. Both faith and works are expected of God's people. Paul and James stress the one that their audiences were in danger of forsaking.

stress the importance of obedience in the life of a believer. James is not saying that works are more important than faith. He simply stresses that faith should be exemplified through good works, confirming a person's righteous status.

MORE WISE LIVING (3:1–4:17)

Speech is powerful—it can be used to bless or curse, to bring life or death (James 3:9–12). Consequently, believers must strive to withhold the tongue (3:8). Doing so shows the maturity expected of a person who honors God (3:2) and is consistent with the wise life expected of God's people (3:13). James adds related expectations, such as being peaceful, gentle, obedient, full of mercy and good fruit, impartial, and without hypocrisy (3:15–18). Those who practice such things are "peacemakers who sow in peace" and "reap a harvest of righteousness" (3:18).

James quotes Proverbs 3:34 to stress that "God opposes the proud but shows favor to the humble" (James 4:6). Believers should live humble lives before the God who will save his people on the day of judgment (4:7–12). The proud should anticipate that the judgment will result in their condemnation (4:12). Evidence of pride and foolishness is making plans without regard for God's will (4:13–14). Wisdom compels people to entrust their plans to a sovereign God (4:15–17). Boasting of future plans is a prideful sin that God will oppose at the judgment (4:16).

FINAL INSTRUCTIONS (5:1–20)

James concludes his letter with a series of final instructions. First, he condemns the rich for living unwisely, storing up treasure for themselves, withholding wages from workers, and condemning and murdering the righteous (James 5:1–6). Second, he draws on the example of Job to encourage readers to endure suffering until the return of the Lord Jesus (5:7–11). Third, he reminds readers to keep their word so as to avoid God's judgment (5:12). Fourth, he encourages readers to offer a prayer of faith for the sick (5:13–18). The prayer of faith entrusts a person to the God who will deliver them from sickness—if not now, certainly when he returns to restore his people. Elijah offered the prayer of faith, trusting that God would provide rain for crops and water necessary for salvation (5:17–18). Last, James urges readers to prevent a believer from straying from the truth, delivering them from death (5:19–20). Such advice is in keeping with the thrust of the letter, which calls people to live out their faith, showing they are worthy of the inheritance God will bestow on his people when he returns to judge the wicked and save his people.

Canonical Function

James sets the expectations for the Catholic epistles, establishing that Jewish and gentile believers will be delivered from exile in the present age and into a cosmic inheritance. In the meantime, believers should obey the God who has brought them into the family of God and made them beneficiaries of the saving promises. Abraham and Rahab demonstrated their faith in God through their works of obedience. Such examples reveal that "faith" and "works" have always been expected of God's people. The letters of Peter, John, James, and Jude will continue to encourage readers to live faithfully in the present age, persevering through trials and sufferings and loving their neighbor, in light of the imminent return of Jesus Christ.

Authorship, Dating, and Audience

The author of the letter is James, the half brother of Jesus and one of the pillar apostles (Acts 15; Gal. 2:9; James 1:1). James eventually became the head of the Jerusalem church (Acts 21:18–19).[7] More than likely, he wrote this letter during the period of active discussion about faith and works in Paul's lifetime, making AD 45–60 a potential date range for its composition.[8] The audience of the letter would have been composed mainly of Jews in need of instruction on the importance of obedience in relation to faith.

7. See Richard Bauckham, *The Book of Acts in Its First Century Setting*, vol. 4, *Palestinian Setting* (Grand Rapids: Eerdmans, 1995), 415–80.
8. N. T. Wright and Michael F. Bird, *The New Testament in Its World: An Introduction to the History, Literature, and Theology of the First Christians* (Grand Rapids: Zondervan, 2019), 736.

1 Peter

Two canonical epistles are attributed to the apostle Peter. The first follows
on the heels of the epistle of James. In his first epistle, Peter encourages believers to live as holy exiles as they await the return of Jesus Christ and the
reception of the promised inheritance. Peter includes instructions on living
honorably before civil authorities, guidelines on Christ-honoring household
relationships, and instructions on how shepherds should oversee the flock
in view of the return of the chief shepherd. Peter draws on Old Testament
passages that point to the conduct expected of those awaiting the consummation of the eschaton.

Outline and Overview

First Peter follows a simple epistolary structure. Peter opens the letter by
exhorting God's exilic people to be holy as they await their imperishable
inheritance (1 Pet. 1:1–2:10). Peter then exhorts exiles to live out their social
relationships in a manner worthy of the Lord (2:11–4:11). Their lifestyle
should be distinguishable from that of those who do not know the true God.
Peter closes the letter by reminding readers to live exemplary lives and endure
suffering until the return of Jesus Christ (4:12–5:14).

HOLY EXILES (1:1–2:10)

Peter addresses the letter to "God's elect, exiles scattered throughout the
provinces of Pontus, Galatia, Cappadocia, Asia and Bithynia" (1 Pet. 1:1). As
in James 1:1, the notion of dispersion recalls the Jewish exile from the land
of Canaan (Neh. 1:9; Isa. 49:6; Jer. 15:7). Unlike James, Peter specifies the
gentile lands to which his readers have been scattered. The broad dispersion
of believers recalls humanity's exile from Eden (Gen. 1–3; Isa. 65–66; Rev.
20–22). As believers await the return of Christ, Peter reminds them that they
"have been chosen according to the foreknowledge of God the Father, through
the sanctifying work of the Spirit, to be obedient to Jesus Christ and sprinkled
with his blood" (1 Pet. 1:2). According to Peter, God has chosen exiled Jews
and gentiles to live obedient lives in the present age, lives that show they have
been cleansed through the blood of Christ. This expectation sets the tone for
the book: God's exiled people will live holy lives on the present earth.

The resurrection of Jesus Christ empowers a believer's rebirth into "an
inheritance that can never perish, spoil or fade" (1 Pet. 1:4). This inheritance
is analogous to "the Holy City, the new Jerusalem" that will come down from

OLD TESTAMENT PROPHETS

Peter speaks about Old Testament prophets who did not fully understand the salvation to be revealed through Jesus Christ (1 Pet. 1:10–12). From this, we gather that Christians have a better understanding of how Jesus Christ fulfills old covenant promises than authors like Isaiah, Jeremiah, and Ezekiel did. As a result, our interpretive aim is to read the Old Testament not like an Israelite but in view of the arrival of Jesus Christ. This gives us a "fuller" understanding of what Old Testament authors only "partially" understood.

the heavens (Rev. 21:2; cf. Rev. 21–22). Jesus will return to deliver his people into the lasting inheritance where they will experience "the salvation that is ready to be revealed in the last time" (1 Pet. 1:5). Believers should persevere through various trials in the present age so as to experience the future salvation about which the prophets spoke (1:6–12).

With their minds fixed on the return of Christ, believers should live as God's holy children (1 Pet. 1:13–16). Peter grounds this expectation in the central imperative of Leviticus: "Be holy, because I am holy" (1:16; cf. Lev. 11:44–45; 19:2; 20:7). Holiness, after all, is what should characterize the people redeemed through the blood of Christ (1 Pet. 1:17–21). Their redemption purifies them from the ways of the present age, leading to a sincere love for other believers (1:22–25).

As they rid themselves of all malice and slander, believers should conduct themselves as members of God's holy temple, whose lives are spiritual sacrifices to God through Jesus Christ (1 Pet. 2:1–8). Drawing on themes from the Pentateuch, Peter designates readers as a "chosen people, a royal priesthood, a holy nation, God's special possession," called to praise the God who has mercifully delivered them from the present dark age and into the light of a new creation (2:9). Their behavior shows they are fit for an eschatological inheritance.

EXILIC RELATIONSHIPS (2:11–4:6)

Peter's readers are "foreigners and exiles" who must live exemplary lives among the "pagans" (1 Pet. 2:11–12). The term "pagans" refers to those who do not worship the true God. Despite repercussions, the holy lifestyle of believers should draw unbelievers to glorify God on the day he judges the earth (2:12; cf. Isa. 10:3; Jer. 6:15).[9] Believers fulfill the prophetic vision of Isaiah

9. For a discussion of God's visitation, see Thomas R. Schreiner, *1 & 2 Peter and Jude*, Christian Standard Commentary (Nashville: Holman, 2020), 134.

of the days when God's people will be a "light" that will bring the nations out of spiritual "darkness" (Isa. 42:6–7; 49:6) and will glorify God in his holy city (60:1–14). This city is analogous to the eschatological inheritance about which Peter prophesies, where the nations will praise the living God (1 Pet. 1:3–5; cf. Isa. 65–66).

Peter addresses various ways God's people should live an exemplary existence in the present age. First, relationships between citizens and civil authorities, slaves and masters, and wives and husbands should be commendable (1 Pet. 2:13–3:7). All such relationships should be conducted in submission to the ultimate authority—the Lord Jesus (2:13, 16). Believers should disobey the expectations of immediate authorities only when they contradict those of Christ (2:11–17). In so doing, believers demonstrate their true allegiance to Christ, for whom they should be willing to suffer (3:8–4:6). The totality of their witness should give unbelievers a vision of life in the coming world, drawing them to worship the God who makes them worthy of an eschatological inheritance.

A Reminder about the Return of Christ (4:7–5:14)

The final section begins with a reminder that "the end of all things is near" (1 Pet. 4:7). As a result, the present age is giving way to the new age associated with the return of Christ, who will judge the wicked and deliver his people into an eschatological inheritance. This reminder should motivate believers to live holy lives, displaying fervent love for one another, being hospitable, and pleasing Christ with their speech (4:7–11). It should also motivate them to suffer for their faithfulness to Jesus, entrusting themselves to the God who will deliver them at his return (4:12–19).

Peter's reminder applies to overseers, who are to shepherd the flock in a manner worthy of the chief shepherd (1 Pet. 5:1–5). Their exemplary shepherding will result in their receiving the unfading crown of glory at the return of Jesus Christ (5:4). No matter their station in life or role in the church, believers must humble themselves before the God who is returning to deliver them from suffering and into a place where he will himself restore, establish, and strengthen them (5:6–10).

Canonical Function

First Peter follows in the thematic footsteps of James, urging believers to live as holy exiles in light of Christ's imminent return. The proximity of 1 Peter to

ESCHATOLOGICAL LIVING

How does the return of Jesus Christ motivate you to be holy in the present age? If you are a pastor or overseer, how does it inspire you to shepherd the people whom God has entrusted to you? What will happen to those whom Jesus finds unfaithful? What will happen to shepherds who have not cared for the flock?

SCRIBES

Greco-Roman authors commonly used scribes to compose their writings. Authors would have dictated verbatim or given scribes relative freedom in composing their letters. Before a writing was finalized, an author would have reviewed and approved of its contents. Peter would have taken a similar approach with Silas (1 Pet. 5:12). Paul would have done something similar with Tertius (Rom. 16:22) and other scribes responsible for composing his letters.

James only strengthens the call to live ethically in view of the fulfillment of the eschaton. As they await the return of Jesus, believers ought to live exemplary lives before an unbelieving world, fulfilling the vocation to draw the nations to worship the true God in a new creation. God may be so gracious as to use his people to draw the nations into his family and make them recipients of all God promised Abraham, Isaac, and Jacob.

Authorship, Dating, and Audience

Peter identifies himself as the author of his first epistle (1 Pet. 1:1). Silas, however, was the scribe who actually penned the letter (5:12). This is analogous to the way Tertius penned Romans on Paul's behalf (Rom. 16:22). Peter composed his first epistle toward the end of his life, somewhere in the range of AD 64–66, to an audience of Christians dispersed throughout the area of Asia Minor. The inclusion of 1 Peter in the Catholic epistles corpus suggests that the letter still speaks to believers scattered throughout the present age.

2 Peter

Second Peter continues the eschatological tone of the Catholic epistles. The letter uses explicitly eschatological language such as "the eternal kingdom"

(2 Pet. 1:11), the "coming of our Lord Jesus" (1:16), the "day of judgment" (2:9; 3:7), the "day of the Lord" (3:10), the "day of God" (3:12), and "a new heaven and a new earth" (3:13). The eschatological nature of 2 Peter is enhanced by allusions to prior scriptural texts and reaffirms the importance of being holy in view of the imminent return of Jesus Christ.

Second Peter introduces the theme of false teachers who will face future judgment, which is carried into the remainder of the Catholic epistles. The similar emphasis in Jude has led scholars to argue that one letter borrows from the other. Most argue that 2 Peter draws on the earlier letter of Jude. The borrowing of one book from the other results in scholars addressing 2 Peter and Jude together, without regard for their arrangement in the New Testament. A canonical approach to the New Testament requires that we follow the order of the Catholic epistles. Doing so yields results in keeping with the way the corpus has been read for centuries.

Outline and Overview

The letter of 2 Peter follows a tripart structure. The first section reminds readers that God has empowered them to live godly lives in anticipation of the return of Jesus Christ (2 Pet. 1:1–21). The second section warns readers about the future judgment of false teachers (2:1–22). The third section encourages readers to prepare themselves for the day of the Lord (3:1–18).

EMPOWERMENT FOR GODLY LIVING (1:1–21)

Peter addresses his second letter to "those who through the righteousness of our God and Savior Jesus Christ have received a faith as precious as ours" (2 Pet. 1:1). The greeting recalls the diverse peoples brought into a covenant relationship with the God who demonstrated his faithfulness—his righteousness—to save his people into a new creation through the death of Jesus Christ (cf. Rom. 3–4). God has granted all such people "divine power" to exercise the characteristics of goodness, knowledge, self-control, perseverance, godliness, and love for others (2 Pet. 1:3–7). Growth in holiness prevents God's people from being "ineffective and unproductive in your knowledge of our Lord Jesus Christ" (1:8). Those who fail to exercise godliness lose sight of the fact that they have been "cleansed from their past sins" (1:9). Believers should strive to live as those called into God's family, showing they are worthy of the "eternal kingdom of our Lord and Savior Jesus Christ" (1:11).

Peter reminds readers of his teaching and prophetic word (2 Pet. 1:12–21). His credibility is based on his witness to the transfiguration of Jesus, when the Father cried, "This is my Son, whom I love; with him I am well pleased" (1:17). Peter's recollection of the Father's words matches the same event in Matthew 17:5, Mark 9:7, and Luke 9:35. Peter draws on the tradition of Jesus's transfiguration to validate his testimony about the "coming of our Lord Jesus Christ" (2 Pet. 1:16). This should motivate readers to grow in holiness before the return of the one who will deliver his people out of the corruption of the present world (1:4) and into his "eternal kingdom" (1:11).

Future Judgment of False Teachers (2:1–22)

Peter appeals to Jude 5–10 to make a couple points about false teachers. First, he contends that there will be "false teachers among the people" just as there were among the community of Israel (2 Pet. 2:1). Those who succumb to their teaching follow in their "depraved conduct and will bring the way of truth into disrepute" (2:2). The conduct of false teachers will not go unpunished. Peter announces that "their condemnation has long been hanging over them" (2:3). Second, Peter argues that the future condemnation of the ungodly is analogous to God's judgment on wicked angels, the ancient world, and Sodom and Gomorrah (2:4–10). The future salvation of the godly is akin to God's deliverance of Noah, his family, and Lot from the sufferings of their day (2:5–8).

Peter does not mince words, calling false teachers "unreasoning animals" who "blaspheme in matters they do not understand" (2 Pet. 2:12). They will be condemned for all the harm they have caused the faithful (2:13). Moreover, false teachers have "eyes full of adultery" and are "experts in greed" (2:14). Their behavior results in the curse of being cut off from the covenant community and devoted to eschatological destruction (Deut. 27–30). Their punishment is the result of following the wicked path of Balaam, whom God rebuked through the mouth of a donkey (2 Pet. 2:15–16; cf. Num. 22:21–39). All such people have turned away from Jesus Christ and have returned to the sinful lives from which they were delivered—just like dogs return to their vomit and pigs to wallowing in the mud (2 Pet. 2:17–22; cf. Prov. 26:11; Matt. 7:6).

The Day of the Lord (3:1–18)

In the closing section, Peter reminds readers, "This is now my second letter to you" (2 Pet. 3:1). Both 1 and 2 Peter serve to recall "the words spoken in the past by the holy prophets and the command given by our Lord and Savior through your apostles" (2 Pet. 3:2). Such words serve as a testimony against those questioning the return of Christ (3:3–4). But God will return to judge all such people (3:5–7).

Believers should prepare themselves for the day the Lord judges the ungodly and renews the present earth, creating "a new heaven and a new earth," just like Isaiah foretold (2 Pet. 3:13; cf. Isa. 65–66). Drawing from a similar Jesus tradition as that of Matthew 24:43, Peter says that the return of Jesus will be "like a thief" (2 Pet. 3:10). Consequently, readers should make an effort to live holy lives and remain vigilant against all false teaching, knowing that Jesus could return at any moment to judge the world and restore the creation (3:14–18). Peter is even aware of how some distort Paul's writings to justify their godless teachings and lifestyles, "as they do the other Scriptures, to their own destruction" (3:16).

Canonical Function

The eschatological tone of 2 Peter strengthens the message of the Catholic epistles: the imminent return of Jesus should motivate believers to strive for holiness in the present age. Peter adds that living holy lives includes avoiding false teachers, who will face eschatological judgment. In so doing, believers assure themselves of entering the renewed creation. When we recall that 1 Peter is addressed to exiles in various lands, which is consistent with the similar designation in James, we envision that the Catholic epistles remind readers of their status as strangers in the present age, anticipating the day Jesus will deliver them into a renewed earth.

Authorship, Dating, and Audience

Although Peter identifies himself as the author (2 Pet. 1:1), just as he does in 1 Peter, and speaks of this being the second letter he addresses to the same audience (2 Pet. 3:1), scholars question whether he actually penned 2 Peter. They argue that the Greek of 2 Peter is better than that of 1 Peter.[10] They also contend that the letter draws on the content of Jude and appeals to Paul's writings as Scripture (2 Pet. 3:15–16). The latter suggests a date in the second century after Paul's letters had been collected into an authorized corpus. In response to the first two objections, Peter could have employed a different secretary to compose his second epistle, which draws on Jude as a source, much like Luke claims to have examined prior sources (Luke 1:1–4). In response to the final objection, Peter could have referred to earlier letters of Paul, like Galatians and 1 Corinthians, to which he and his first-century readers may have had access. None of the proposed objections provide sufficient warrant for rejecting the traditional authorship of 2 Peter.

Second Peter may be dated to just prior to Peter's martyrdom in the mid-60s AD.[11] The recipients of the letter were the same audience scattered throughout Asia Minor to which Peter addressed his first letter (1 Pet. 1:1; 2 Pet. 3:1). The inclusion of 2 Peter into the canon signifies that it continues to speak to exiles scattered throughout the present age.

▪ The Johannine Epistles

The Johannine epistles are a collection of three letters attributed to the apostle John. Witnesses such as the fourth-century codices Sinaiticus (ℵ) and Vaticanus (B) and the fifth-century codex Alexandrinus (A) testify to the common title assigned to each epistle, which always includes the name John (*Iōannou*). The Johannine epistles also share common themes, such as "truth" (1 John 1:6; 3:19; 4:6; 5:6, 20; 2 John 1; 3 John 4, 8, 12), "love" (1 John 2:10; 3:10; 5:1; 2 John 1, 5; 3 John 6), and "commandment" (1 John 2:3; 3:22; 4:21; 2 John 4, 5, 6); reminders about what readers have "seen" (1 John 1:1–2; 3:6; 4:20; 3 John 11) and "heard" (1 John 1:1; 2:7; 3:11; 2 John 6); terms for godly living like "doing" (1 John 5:2; 3 John 5:6, 10) and "walking" (1 John 1:6; 2:6; 2 John 4, 6; 3 John 3, 4); and eschatological words like "antichrist" (1 John 2:18; 4:3; 2 John 7) and "forever" (1 John 2:17; 2 John 2).[12] Such similarities justify reading 1, 2, and 3 John as a collection of letters within the Catholic epistles.

---

10. Andreas J. Köstenberger, L. Scott Kellum, and Charles L. Quarles, *The Cradle, the Cross, and the Crown: An Introduction to the New Testament*, 2nd ed. (Nashville: B&H Academic, 2016), 833.

11. Eusebius, *Church History* 2.25.5.

12. See Lockett, *Letters from the Pillar Apostles*, 182–84; Matthew Y. Emerson, *Christ and New Creation: A Canonical Approach to the Theology of the New Testament* (Eugene, OR:

The Johannine epistles are normally positioned after 1 and 2 Peter, such as in the fourth-century Codex Sinaiticus (‭א‬) and the ninth-century minuscule 1424. The proximity of the Petrine epistles to the Johannine epistles suggests that the eschatological tone of the former letters carries into the latter ones. Our expectations are only confirmed in the Johannine epistles, as we encounter themes such as the present world passing away (1 John 2:17), the last hour (2:18), the future appearance of Christ (2:28; 3:2), and the role of the Spirit (3:24; 4:13). We also encounter an emphasis on holy living (2:28–3:24; 5:1–5; 2 John 2–6; 3 John 3, 11) and being vigilant against false teaching (1 John 2:18–27; 4:1–6; 2 John 7–11). All in all, the Johannine epistles allude to the Old Testament and the Gospel of John to urge readers to live in view of the second coming of Christ.

Since 1, 2, and 3 John are grouped into a letter collection, we will examine their contents under the auspices of the Johannine epistles. The arrangement of these letters into a collection also warrants a collective treatment of their canonical function, along with matters of authorship, dating, and audience.

1 John

First John does not follow a logical pattern of argumentation. Instead, the letter repeats themes such as truth, love, and false teachers to stress the importance of living in light of the return of Jesus Christ. Campbell and Pennington argue that the best way to outline 1 John "is simply to list the contents."[13]

PROLOGUE (1:1–4)

John opens the letter with a powerful allusion to "that which was from the beginning" (1 John 1:1). John's mention of the "beginning" recalls the prologue to his Gospel, which includes the similar phrase "in the beginning" (John 1:1), which in turn evokes the same phrase in the Genesis 1 creation account. From these observations, we gather that the Christ whom John and the apostles have "seen and touched" is none other than the God who originally spoke all things into existence, whose mission is to bring "eternal life" to a world under the power of sin (1 John 1:1–2). We should not equate the

---

Wipf & Stock, 2013), 132–34; Judith M. Lieu, *I, II, & III John: A Commentary*, New Testament Library (Louisville: Westminster John Knox, 2008), 18–23.

13. Constantine R. Campbell and Jonathan T. Pennington, *Reading the New Testament as Christian Scripture: A Literary, Canonical, and Theological Survey* (Grand Rapids: Baker Academic, 2020), 348.

THE MISSION OF JESUS

What have you assumed about the mission of Jesus? Have you imagined that Jesus came to earth to deliver people into a spiritualized existence in heaven? Or have you envisioned that Jesus came to renew the entire creation? With which one of these would John agree?

phrase "eternal life" with spiritual bliss in heaven, as if John believed that Jesus Christ will destroy all he made. For John, Jesus is the creator who has returned to restore the creation. Readers should accept John's testimony so as to enjoy fellowship with the creator and redeemer of the cosmos (1:3–4).

WALKING IN THE LIGHT (1:5–10)

John bases his instruction on a central truth: "God is light; in him there is no darkness at all" (1 John 1:5). This maxim recalls how the Old Testament identifies God as light, the standard of truth and holiness, whereas darkness is associated with falsehood, evil, and sin (Job 29:3; Mic. 7:8). It also recalls how John's Gospel applies light imagery to Jesus (John 8:12; 12:35). As the one sent into the world, Jesus is the representation of the Father (8:19; 12:45). So it is through Jesus that humanity comes to know God as the "light" that is in the process of overshadowing the darkness of the present age.

Those who claim fellowship with God but live in darkness are liars (1 John 1:6). Their darkness blinds them to their need for forgiveness through Jesus Christ, showing they are ignorant of the truth (1:8–10). On the other hand, those who walk in the holiness of God's light reveal that they have fellowship with God and his people (1:7). When believers sin, God's light reveals their transgression, leading to their confession and forgiveness of sins (1:7, 9). Their forgiveness comes through the atoning work of Jesus Christ, whose death is for the sins of the world (2:1–2; cf. John 3:16).

KEEPING THE COMMANDS (2:12–14)

Those who know God "keep his commands," which is synonymous with "keeping his word" (1 John 2:3–6). John's "command" is both old and new. It is old in the sense that it is sourced in the command God gave to Moses (1 John 2:7; cf. Exod. 20; 34; Deut. 6); it is new in the sense that it is linked to the arrival of a new covenant age in Christ, when prophets like Jeremiah

---

CHRISTIANS AND SIN

Although John expects that believers will "walk in the light," he does not assume we will be without sin in the present age. He does expect that the "light" of Christ will expose the "darkness" of our sin, leading to our forgiveness through Jesus Christ. With that in mind, is there any sin for which you need forgiveness? Will you trust that the light of Christ leads you to forgiveness through his death for sins?

HILASMOS

John says that Jesus is the *hilasmos* for our sins (1 John 2:2). The word *hilasmos* may be translated as "propitiation," which signifies the appeasement of God's wrath through the death of a sacrificial victim, or "expiation," which signifies the removal of guilt.[a] While scholars normally choose one of these two translations, the reality is that *hilasmos* communicates that God's wrath has been appeased (propitiation) and humanity's guilt has been removed (expiation) through the death of Jesus Christ.

a. See Constantine R. Campbell, *1, 2, and 3 John*, Story of God Bible Commentary (Grand Rapids: Zondervan, 2017), 50.

---

and Ezekiel expected that God would empower his people to obey him from the heart (1 John 2:8; cf. Jer. 31; Ezek. 36). Those who love their neighbor show they belong to the new age of light (1 John 2:10). Those who hate their neighbor reveal they belong to the age of darkness (2:9, 11). Since believers have overcome the darkness, they should live as participants of the age of light (2:12–14).

THE LAST HOUR (2:15–27)

John's readers should not love the things associated with the present world (like lust and pride), which is in the process of passing away (1 John 2:15–17). Those who obey God will live forever in the new creation (2 John 2:17). As believers await the passing of the current age, many antichrists will come (1 John 2:18). Antichrists are those who deny that Jesus came in the flesh (2:22, 23, 26). If Jesus was not human, then he could not have been the physical descendant of David, the promised Christ and God's Son (2 Sam. 7; Ps. 2). For John, denying the humanity of Jesus is analogous to being an antichrist.

GNOSTICISM

Some argue that 1 John was written to combat the influence of Gnosticism, which taught that Jesus did not really come in the flesh. He only "appeared" to look human so as to communicate with people. Since full-blown Gnosticism did not appear until the second century, it is more likely that 1 John opposes first-century teachers influenced by Platonic ideals, which elevated the goodness of the spiritual realm over the material world, resulting in the promotion of a disembodied Jesus.

Since antichrists have rejected Jesus, John argues they have also rejected the Father, placing them outside the community of believers (1 John 2:22–23). It is of central importance that believers hold to what they have been taught about Jesus so as to have eternal life in the coming age (2:24–25). Though antichrists will attempt to deceive believers, the anointing of the Holy Spirit remains in them, just as Jesus promised (John 14–16), teaching them to reject false teaching (1 John 2:26–27).

OBEDIENT CHILDREN (2:28–3:24)

The eschatological return of Jesus Christ should motivate readers to "continue in him," which means loving God and others (1 John 2:28). Doing so shows that a person has been "born of him" (2:29). The birth metaphor alludes to John 3:1–8, where Jesus explains that a person must be "born again" to experience life in the new creation. First John 2:28 and John 3:1–8 both recall Ezekiel 36:25–27, which anticipates the day God's Spirit would cleanse his people's sins and enable them to obey his commands. John draws on birth imagery from Ezekiel 36 to explain that receiving the Spirit enables people to live as new creations, anticipating the day when they will be transformed into the glorified image of Jesus (1 John 3:1–3). Those whose lives are characterized by sin have not been "born again," showing they are unfit for life in the new creation (3:4–10).

John emphasizes his point by reminding readers to love one another (1 John 3:11). Cain is an example of someone who did not love his brother, showing he belonged to the devil (3:12). Everyone who hates their neighbor is just like Cain—a murderer with no hope of eternal life (3:15). Believers should follow the example of Jesus, who demonstrated true love by giving his life (3:16). Those who love like Jesus, which includes giving to the poor, show they have passed from the age of death to the age of life (3:14, 16–18).

The Spirit will empower such people to stand with confidence before Jesus Christ (3:19–25).

Discerning Truth and Error (4:1–6)

John instructs readers on how to differentiate the truth of God from the error of false prophets (1 John 4:1, 6). According to John, the person who acknowledges that Jesus has come in the flesh speaks from the Spirit of God (4:2). The person who does not confess that Jesus has come in the flesh speaks from the spirit of the antichrist (4:3). John assures readers that they have already overcome the age associated with all such false teachers (4:4–6).

Reemphasizing the Commands (4:7–21)

John returns to the importance of loving one another—just as God loved humanity in sending his Son to be the sacrifice for sin (1 John 4:7, 9–10, 11, 14, 19). Those who obey the love command have been born into the new age (4:7, 12) and will stand with confidence on judgment day (4:17). Those who hate others show they do not know God (4:8, 20) and have reason to fear the future judgment (4:18). Simply put, those who truly love God will love their brothers and sisters (4:21).

Confidence of Victorious Eternal Life (5:1–21)

John argues that people know they are God's children when they love God and carry out his commands (1 John 5:1–2). Such persons have overcome the world and will avoid eschatological judgment (5:3–4). Their victory is sourced in Jesus Christ, who "came by water and blood" (5:6). The water recalls Jesus's baptism in John 1:29–34. The blood recalls his atoning death on the cross in John 19:28–37. John mentions that the Spirit was present at Jesus's baptism, when the Father proclaimed Jesus as his Son (1:29–34). In this sense, the Spirit testifies to the "truth" of Jesus's identity as God's Son (1 John 5:6). The one who believes in the Spirit's testimony—that God's Son entered the waters of baptism and was the atoning sacrifice for sins—is transferred into the realm of eternal life (5:7–13).

The purpose of John's letter is the same as that of his Gospel: that his readers may believe in the Son of God to experience eternal life (1 John 5:13; cf. John 20:30–31). First John shows that eternal life is not a spiritualized existence in heaven—it is life in a new creation where the darkness has been overcome by the restorative power of God's light. As believers await their entrance into the renewed world, they should approach God with petitions that are in keeping with his "will"—those that promote love for God and neighbor—knowing that God is pleased to answer such prayers (1 John 5:14–15).

In the interim, believers ought to turn people away from a "sin that leads to death" (1 John 5:16). The context of the letter reveals that a "sin that leads to death" is failing to believe that the Spirit testifies that God's Son redeems the world through his atoning sacrifice for sins. Those who trust in Jesus should be confident that God will save them from the power of the evil one and preserve their status as those who have been born into the new age of life (5:18–20).

John closes the letter with a warning: "Keep yourselves from idols" (1 John 5:21). Idols are associated with teachers who peddle a false Jesus who did not suffer in the flesh. An immaterial Jesus is the false god of the antichrists—whom John urges readers to avoid. It is vital that believers heed John's advice not just about idols but about all he has taught in his letter.

2 John

Second John is the second shortest book in the Bible. This brief letter summarizes topics discussed in 1 John, such as loving others and avoiding false teachers. The condensed nature of the letter leads some to argue that it originally circulated as a cover letter for 1 John.

The structure of 2 John follows the organization of a traditional epistle. The letter begins with a greeting (2 John 1–3). The body encourages readers to continue living out the love command and warns them about false teachers (2 John 4–11). The letter closes with John's desire to visit his readers (2 John 12–13).

GREETING (vv. 1–3)

John identifies himself as the "elder," suggesting he holds a position of spiritual oversight (2 John 1). He writes to the "lady chosen by God" (2 John 1), recalling the way God's people are designated as a woman, mother, and bride (Isa. 54:1–8; Gal. 4:26; Eph. 5:22–32; Rev. 12:17; 21:2). John's readers are none other than the people in whom God's truth resides and to whom he extends grace, mercy, and peace (2 John 2–3).

ENCOURAGEMENT AND WARNING (vv. 4–11)

John is encouraged to find that his readers are living out the command to love one another (2 John 4–6). Although believers have always been expected to keep the love command, the arrival of the eschatological Spirit empowers God's people to live out the obedience that was so difficult under the old covenant (Ezek. 36:25–27). That is why the love command is both "old" and "new" (2 John 5).

John reminds his readers about antichrists in the present world (2 John 7–11). As in his first letter, he specifies that antichrists promote a Jesus who did not come in the flesh (2 John 7). John's readers are to avoid such people, not even welcoming them into their homes, so that they might receive their full reward when Jesus returns to judge the earth (2 John 8–11).

CLOSING (VV. 12–13)

John expresses his sincere desire to see his readers in person so that their mutual "joy may be complete" (2 John 12). John sends greetings from "the children of your sister, who is chosen by God"; these are fellow members of God's family (2 John 13).

3 John

Third John is even shorter than 2 John, having the distinction of being the shortest book in the Bible. Like the previous letter, 3 John follows the structure of a traditional epistle. The letter opens with a greeting (3 John 1–4). The body commends the behavior of a certain Gaius and condemns that of Diotrephes (3 John 5–12). The letter closes with John's desire to visit his readers (3 John 13–15).

GREETING (VV. 1–4)

As in 2 John, the author identifies himself as the "elder" (3 John 1). Unlike 2 John, the letter is addressed to a certain Gaius (3 John 1). Some speculate that this is the Gaius whom John installed as the overseer of the church of Pergamum (Acts 20:4).[14] But this is only a guess. In reality, we have no clear information about Gaius beyond what we read in 3 John. Despite his mysterious identity, it brings John great joy to know that Gaius is walking in the truth: that his whole life is characterized by faithfulness to Jesus (3 John 2–4).

---

14. Constantine R. Campbell, *1, 2, and 3 John*, Story of God Bible Commentary (Grand Rapids: Zondervan, 2017), 214; Karen H. Jobes, *1, 2, 3 John*, Zondervan Exegetical Commentary on the New Testament 18 (Grand Rapids: Zondervan, 2016), 289–90.

SUPPORTING MISSIONARIES

John's support for missionaries and other believers should cause us to reflect on our support for people whom God has sent out in his name. Are we willing to house them? Are we willing to support them financially? Are we willing to pray for them? If we are already supporting missionaries, what are some ways we can increase our assistance without overstretching ourselves?

Gaius and Diotrephes (vv. 5–12)

John commends Gaius for his faithful care of fellow believers, especially those who are strangers (3 John 5). Such people have testified to how well Gaius has loved them, sending them on their way in a manner worthy of God (3 John 6). That such people went out "for the sake of the Name" suggests that Gaius was caring for missionaries (3 John 7).

But not everyone is like Gaius. John mentions a certain Diotrephes who slanders John and his associates and refuses to welcome other believers (3 John 9–10). Although his identity is a mystery, we have sufficient information to confirm that Diotrephes was powerful enough to excommunicate those who extended hospitality to other believers (3 John 10). John encourages Gaius to continue imitating what is good rather than the evil of Diotrephes (3 John 11). After all, the one who does good belongs to God, and the one who does evil does not know him (3 John 11).

Demetrius is an example of someone believers should strive to imitate (3 John 12). John affirms that he is "well spoken of by everyone" (3 John 12). The eschatological framework of John's epistles means that believers should seriously consider John's advice, knowing that Jesus will return to judge the wicked and deliver the faithful into a new creation.

Closing (vv. 13–15)

John hopes to see Gaius in person (3 John 13–14). Until then, he prays God's peace on his child in the faith (3 John 15). He closes with greetings from "friends" in the faith.

Canonical Function

The Johannine epistles are a collection of letters within the Catholic epistles corpus. Their proximity to the Petrine epistles reinforces the eschatological nature of their message, urging readers to love God and neighbor as they await the return of Jesus Christ. We first encounter the strong emphasis on eschatological ethics in the epistle of James.

Although the Johannine epistles do not mention the exilic status of believers, unlike James and the Petrine epistles, the letter collection emphasizes that God's people belong to the new age of light rather than the old age of darkness. Their membership in the new age results in the reception of the Spirit, who empowers them to fulfill the love command and resist the teachings of antichrists. Their behavior is in stark contrast to the expectations associated with the age of darkness, which compels hate rather than love. As John's readers, we must come to grips with our status as strangers in the age of darkness, anticipating the day Jesus returns to shine his redemptive light throughout the earth.

Authorship, Dating, and Audience

The authorship of the Johannine epistles has traditionally been attributed to John the beloved disciple and brother of James.[15] Since the nineteenth century, however, scholars have raised doubts about the authorship of the Johannine epistles.[16] Some argue that John's followers wrote them. Others contend that the author chose the literary technique of anonymity.[17] Such reasons are not convincing enough to overturn the traditional authorship of the Johannine epistles. For one, manuscript titles assign authorship to John. Another reason is linked to second-century witnesses such as Papias and Polycarp, who attest that John wrote a Gospel and letters bearing his name. Last, the Muratorian Canon (ca. AD 170–215) affirms John's authorship of the letters attributed to him.

Since John wrote his epistles after composing his Gospel, the Johannine epistles may be dated somewhere in the early to mid-90s, just before he composed Revelation. His audience was situated in Asia Minor, where they would have been influenced by Platonic teachings that valued spiritual realities over the material world. Such teachings would have infiltrated the church through the presence of antichrists.

---

15. Colin G. Kruse, *Letters of John*, Pillar New Testament Commentary (Grand Rapids: Eerdmans, 2000), 14.

16. Charles E. Hill, "1–3 John," in *A Biblical-Theological Introduction to the New Testament: The Gospel Realized*, ed. Michael J. Kruger (Wheaton: Crossway, 2016), 486.

17. Lieu, *I, II, & III John*, 6–9.

◼ Jude

Jude identifies himself as a "servant of Jesus Christ and a brother of James" (Jude 1). The mention of James allows readers to envision how the letters attributed to the half brothers of Jesus bookend those of Peter and John. As bookends for the Catholic epistles, James and Jude symbolically affirm the trustworthiness of the entire corpus. Readers may therefore trust that Jesus will return to judge sinners and deliver his people into a future inheritance. Jude, in particular, urges readers to be godly and to avoid false teachers so as to receive what has been promised to them at the return of Jesus. He undergirds his argument by drawing on Jewish literature—the Old Testament and extrabiblical texts—that promises judgment for the ungodly and salvation for the faithful.

Outline and Overview

Jude's letter contains three major sections. The first describes the purpose of the letter (Jude 1–4). The second elaborates on the identity of apostates and the judgment that awaits them (Jude 5–19). The third encourages believers to persevere in the faith in order to receive eternal life at the return of Jesus Christ (Jude 20–25).

PURPOSE OF THE LETTER (vv. 1–4)

Jude greets "those who have been called, who are loved in God the Father and kept for Jesus Christ" (Jude 1). Since false teachers "have secretly slipped in among you," readers should "contend for the faith that was once for all entrusted to God's holy people" (Jude 3–4). False teachers "pervert the grace of our God into a license for immorality and deny Jesus Christ our only Sovereign and Lord" (Jude 4). But God will not allow false teachers to continue in this behavior forever—for their "condemnation was written about long ago" (Jude 4).

FALSE TEACHERS AND THEIR JUDGMENT (vv. 5–19)

Jude recalls three Jewish traditions to describe the judgment awaiting false teachers: (1) the salvation of Israel at the exodus from Egypt and the later destruction of unbelieving Israelites (Jude 5; cf. Exod. 14; Num. 14); (2) the eternal judgment awaiting evil angels (Jude 6; cf. 1 Enoch 6–19); and (3) the judgment on Sodom and Gomorrah for sexual immorality and perversion

(Jude 7; cf. Gen. 19).[18] These events serve as types of the eschatological judgment awaiting false teachers (Jude 7).

After highlighting their judgment, Jude specifies that ungodly teachers "pollute their own bodies, reject authority and heap abuse on celestial beings" (Jude 8). Jude draws on the Testament of Moses to explain the extent of their boldness, arguing that even the archangel Michael, when arguing "with the devil about the body of Moses, did not himself dare to condemn him for slander but said, 'The Lord rebuke you!'" (Jude 9). Jude compares false teachers to "irrational animals" whose deeds will result in destruction (Jude 10). He also claims they "have rushed for profit into Balaam's error; they have been destroyed in Korah's rebellion" (Jude 11). The analogy to Korah's rebellion shows that God has sealed the eschatological fate of false teachers.

Jude is not done with false teachers, labeling them blemishes at love feasts, selfish shepherds, waterless clouds, fruitless trees, wild waves foaming with shameless behavior, and wandering stars destined for the darkest existence possible (Jude 12–13). The imagery of selfish shepherds recalls the way Ezekiel 34 condemns Israel's leaders for their self-centeredness, leaving the people to fend for themselves. Jude draws on 1 Enoch to emphasize the future judgment awaiting ungodly false teachers, adding that they are discontent grumblers, living according to their own lusts, speaking arrogant words, and flattering people for personal gain (Jude 14–16). The apostles were not ignorant of such teachers, prophesying of "the last times" when scoffers would follow their "ungodly desires" and cause divisions among believers (Jude 17–19). Jude even says that false teachers do not have the Spirit, who assures people of life in the coming age (Jude 19; cf. Ezek. 36–37).

PERSEVERE IN THE FAITH (VV. 20–25)

Jude concludes with an exhortation to grow in the faith, pray in the Spirit, and remain in God's love until the return of the Lord Jesus Christ (Jude 20–21). As they await Christ's return, believers should encourage the weak in faith to avoid false teachers and shun their ungodly lifestyles (Jude 22–23). God will preserve his people until the day he returns to grant them permanent joy in a new creation (Jude 24–25).

18. Peter H. Davids, *The Letters of 2 Peter and Jude*, Pillar New Testament Commentary (Grand Rapids: Eerdmans, 2006), 49.

Canonical Function

James and Jude, written by the half brothers of Jesus, bookend the Catholic epistles corpus. Jude, in particular, encourages readers to be faithful and to avoid false teachers as they await the arrival of Jesus Christ. Jude uses language similar to that in 2 Peter, calling false teachers irrational animals, comparing them to the wicked prophet Balaam, and guaranteeing their future condemnation. The similarities between 2 Peter and Jude are the result of one author drawing from the other. Jude also uses language similar to that in 1 John, comparing those who hate others to the murderous Cain. Jude's pointed language encourages believers to grow in their faithfulness to Christ so as to avoid the harsh judgment that awaits the ungodly.

Jesus Christ, after all, is returning soon to deliver his people out of the present age of sin and deception and into the renewed place God is preparing for his people—what James 2:5 and 1 Peter 1:4 call an "inheritance," what 2 Peter 3:13 calls "a new heaven and a new earth," and what 1 John 3:15, 5:11, and Jude 21 call "eternal life." What awaits the ungodly and peddlers of false teachings, as Jude and the entirety of the Catholic epistles affirm, is final judgment. The letter of Jude prepares the reader for the conclusion of the canonical storyline in Revelation, where Jesus returns to judge the wicked and save the godly by bringing them into a new creation.

Authorship, Dating, and Audience

Jude identifies himself as the author of the letter (Jude 1). Jude is the half brother of James mentioned in Matthew 13:55 and Mark 6:3.[19] Most scholars believe that 2 Peter borrows from Jude. Thus, a date range for the letter would be anywhere from the late 50s to the early 60s. Since we know almost nothing about the audience, all we can assume is that the original readers were struggling with the influence of false teachers in the church—a matter relevant for believers until the second coming of Christ.

SUGGESTED RESOURCES

Greene, Gene L. *Vox Petri: A Theology of Peter*. Eugene, OR: Cascade Books, 2020.

Lieu, Judith. *The Theology of the Johannine Epistles*. New Testament Theology. Cambridge: Cambridge University Press, 1991.

19. The NIV translates *Ioudas* in Matt. 13:55 and Mark 6:3 as "Judas." Since the term refers to Jesus's half brother, I prefer the translation "Jude."

Lockett, Darian R. *Letters for the Church: Reading James, 1–2 Peter, 1–3 John, and Jude as Canon.* Downers Grove, IL: IVP Academic, 2021.

———. *Letters from the Pillar Apostles: The Formation of the Catholic Epistles as a Canonical Collection.* Eugene, OR: Pickwick, 2017.

Morgan, Christopher W. *A Theology of James: Wisdom for God's People.* Explorations in Biblical Theology. Phillipsburg, NJ: P&R, 2010.

Pate, C. Marvin. *The Writings of John: A Survey of the Gospels, Epistles, and Apocalypse.* Grand Rapids: Zondervan, 2015.

SEVEN

REVELATION

Most New Testament manuscripts place the book of Revelation at the conclusion of the canon of Scripture. Although some read Revelation along with John's Gospel and epistles, a canonical reading compels us to give hermeneutical priority to the placement of Revelation at the conclusion of the New Testament. Richard Bauckham argues:

> Given its character and its relation to the rest of the Christian canon of Scripture, the place which Revelation now occupies at the close of the whole canon could not be more appropriate. No other biblical book gathers up so comprehensively the whole biblical tradition in its direction towards the eschatological future. It draws out the sense in which the biblical history, not least its climax in the Christ event, points towards the universal kingdom of God, and it gives the whole canon the character of the book which enables us to live towards that future.[1]

Rightly does Bauckham contend that all Scripture anticipates the arrival of Christ's kingdom on a new earth—an event envisioned in the culminating book of Revelation.

Revelation does not provide details on the exact time of Christ's return. Nor does the book portray certain nation states as "evil" and others as "good."[2]

---

1. Richard Bauckham, *The Theology of the Book of Revelation*, New Testament Theology (Cambridge: Cambridge University Press, 2005), 146. I also cite this paragraph in my forthcoming essay "Justice in Revelation," in *Biblical Justice*, ed. Benjamin Forrest and D. A. Horton (Grand Rapids: Kregel).

2. My observations in this paragraph, with some exceptions, rely on Scot McKnight with Cody Matchett, *Revelation for the Rest of Us: A Prophetic Call to Follow Jesus as a Dissident Disciple* (Grand Rapids: Zondervan, 2023), 10–11.

INTERPRETIVE APPROACHES

There are four main positions on the interpretation of Revelation. The idealist view contends that Revelation portrays cyclical events throughout history, which consistently call believers to remain faithful to Christ. The preterist view holds that almost all the events of Revelation were fulfilled with the destruction of Jerusalem in AD 70. The futurist view contends that Revelation predicts the events related to the return of Christ at the end of human history. The historicist view argues that Revelation prophesies about events throughout history leading to Christ's second coming. Rather than choosing one view, readers should consider how elements of each perspective enable them to interpret the book of Revelation.

Readers may be familiar with the way the Left Behind series depicts the United States as a "good" nation in an eschatological tussle with "evil" nations like Russia and China. But this is not the message of Revelation. The book of Revelation announces that Christ's kingdom will topple all empires. When this occurs, people from all nations will be raised to dwell in the cosmic kingdom of Jesus Christ. It will be a "one world government" in the best sense of the phrase.

This glorious future was made known to John through an "apocalypse" (*apocalypsis*, Rev. 1:1). John's apocalypse is analogous to Jewish texts like 1 Enoch, 4 Ezra, and 2 Baruch, where God "reveals" eschatological events through a series of inspired visions. It also resembles the apocalyptic vision of Daniel 2:17–45, where God reveals to Daniel what will happen when God establishes his eternal kingdom.[3] Revelation's similarities with Jewish literature, especially Daniel 2, should persuade readers to interpret Revelation as apocalyptic literature, which "unveils" events related to the establishment of God's eternal kingdom over the earth.

The purpose of John's apocalyptic vision is not to comfort Christians facing persecution. Just the opposite: John wants to unsettle those too comfortable with life in empires that follow in the godless pattern of Babylon. He calls believers to disentangle themselves from the ways of the empire so as to have victory over the present age and receive the promised inheritance of a new creation (Rev. 21–22). Those who entangle themselves with the ways of Babylon will face eternal judgment (Rev. 16–20). After reading the

3. See the discussion in G. K. Beale, *The Book of Revelation*, New International Greek Testament Commentary (Grand Rapids: Eerdmans, 1999), 181–83.

Catholic epistles, readers should ready themselves for the canon's final call to separate themselves from all ungodliness, making themselves worthy of receiving what God promised to centuries of saints like Abraham, Moses, Isaiah, Paul, and Peter.

▓ Outline and Overview

The structure of Revelation is fairly straightforward. The letter opens with a prologue (Rev. 1:1–20) and continues with letters to the seven churches of the province of Asia (2:1–3:22) and a vision of God's throne room (4:1–5:14). The letter then includes prophecies of the progressive judgments associated with seven seals (6:1–8:5) and seven trumpets (8:6–11:19). After seven interim signs (12:1–14:20), the progression of judgments resumes with seven bowls of God's wrath (15:1–16:21). The letter moves toward its climax, envisioning Babylon's future judgment (17:1–19:21) and the final resurrection and judgment seat of Christ (20:1–15). Revelation crescendos with the arrival of the new heavens and new earth (21:1–22:5) and closes with an epilogue (22:6–21).

Prologue (1:1–20)

John addresses the prophecies of Revelation "to the seven churches in the province of Asia" (Rev. 1:4). Bauckham argues that John uses the number seven as "*representative* of *all* the churches."[4] This is confirmed at the conclusion of each message to the churches, which includes the refrain "Whoever has ears to hear, let them hear what the Spirit says to the churches."[5] This reading does not question the existence of the seven churches of the province of Asia. Rather, it views the messages to seven churches as representative of a variety of spiritual issues facing Christians throughout the Roman Empire.

John offers the seven churches "grace and peace" from God and Jesus Christ, who was the first to be raised from the dead and "the ruler of the kings of the earth" (Rev. 1:4–5). This statement draws our attention to the end of the book, when all believers are raised to dwell in the messianic kingdom established throughout the world (Rev. 21–22). John quotes a couple of Scriptures (Dan. 7:13; Zech. 12:10) to assure readers that the once-crucified-now-glorified Jesus will return to establish his cosmic reign (Rev. 1:12–18).

4. Bauckham, *Theology of the Book of Revelation*, 16.
5. Bauckham, *Theology of the Book of Revelation*, 16.

He closes the prologue with a vision of Jesus, Daniel's son of man, who holds the keys of death and Hades and exhorts him to write what he sees in his vision (1:18–20).

Letters to Seven Churches (2:1–3:22)

John composes letters to the seven churches in Ephesus (Rev. 2:1–7), Smyrna (2:8–11), Pergamum (2:12–17), Thyatira (2:18–29), Sardis (3:1–6), Philadelphia (3:7–13), and Laodicea (3:14–22). It is common for scholars to argue that these churches were under the threat of imperial persecution under the reign of Domitian or some other Roman emperor. Adela Yarbro Collins, however, argues that there is little evidence of systemic persecution against Christians in the late first century.[6] During this time, persecution was limited to localized instances of violence.[7] Although Rome did persecute believers, as John says in Revelation 17–19, it was not the result of an imperial edict or policy. As a result, John writes to churches not under the threat of Roman persecution but under the much bigger threat of complacency and compromise, of being too comfortable with life in a godless empire. This is confirmed in the stated vices of the churches, which include Ephesus forsaking "the love [they] had at first" (2:4), Pergamum and Thyatira tolerating sexual immorality (2:14, 20–22), Sardis being in spiritual slumber (3:2–4), and Laodicea being spiritually lukewarm in faith and rich in worldly wealth (3:15–17). The nature of such vices reveals that John is concerned about Christians adopting the lifestyle of an empire that persuades its citizens to love money, sex, and leisure. Only those who are "victorious" over such entanglements will dwell with the risen Christ in the new creation (21:7).

A Vision of God's Throne Room (4:1–5:14)

John is taken "in the Spirit" to the heavenly throne room (Rev. 4:2). There he receives a vision of the king of the cosmos—God himself—seated on the throne, receiving worship and praise from twenty-four elders and four living creatures (4:3–11). The twenty-four elders allude to the twenty-four divisions of priests David appointed for service in the temple (1 Chron. 24).[8] The elders will be replaced by people who will reign with God in the new cosmic temple,

---

6. Adela Yarbro Collins, *Crisis and Catharsis: The Power of the Apocalypse* (Philadelphia: Westminster, 1984), 84–107.

7. Collins, *Crisis and Catharsis*, 104.

8. Peter J. Leithart, *Revelation 1–11*, International Theological Commentary (London: Bloomsbury T&T Clark, 2018), 229.

the renewed earth (Rev. 5:13–14; 21–22).[9] The four living creatures, likened to a lion, an ox, a man, and a flying eagle, each with six wings and covered with eyes, recall the vision in Ezekiel 10:1–20 and represent all living beings who will worship God on a restored earth.

The God whom the elders and living creatures worship is the "Lion of the tribe of Judah, the Root of David," the Lamb who was slain (Rev. 5:5–6). This imagery reveals that the one on the throne is Jesus, the royal offspring of David (2 Sam. 7) and the final Passover lamb (Exod. 12; Isa. 53:7) who will lead his people out of slavery in an age marked by life in Babylon and into a kingdom on a new earth. He is the only one worthy to break the seven seals and open the scrolls that will reveal the coming judgments (Rev. 5:1–14).

Seven Seals (6:1–8:5)

John describes how the Lamb progressively opens the seven seals on the scroll, symbolizing the intensifying nature of God's wrath. The judgments linked to seals 1–4 allude to the four groups of colored horses in Zechariah 6:1–7 who are called to patrol the earth (Rev. 6:1–8).[10] The white, red, black, and pale horses will execute their respective judgments of conquest (6:1–2), slaughter (6:3–4), famine (6:5–6), and widespread death (6:7–8). The fifth seal unveils a picture of the martyrs in heaven, who await vengeance for their shed blood (6:9–11). Each was given a white robe, symbolizing how their suffering for Christ resulted in their cleansing. They were told to "wait a little longer, until the full number of their fellow servants, their brothers and sisters, were killed just as they had been" (6:11). God's people will suffer until his judgment has been entirely poured out on the wicked. The sixth seal unveils cataclysmic events that will unleash the Lamb's wrath upon the earth (6:12–17).

Before the seventh seal, John depicts 144,000 people from the tribes of Israel, who represent all the people of God throughout history (Rev. 7:1–8), and a multitude from every nation that comes out of "the great tribulation" (7:9–17). The great tribulation refers to the sufferings associated with the present age (cf. Matt. 24–25). In view of the context, the 144,000 are the people of God who will be delivered through the suffering associated with life in the fallen world (Rev. 20–22). The allusion to the tribes of Israel and the sufferings linked to the tribulation, which recall Israel's sufferings in the

---

9. Leithart, *Revelation 1–11*, 232.

10. G. K. Beale and Benjamin L. Gladd, *The Story Retold: A Biblical-Theological Introduction to the New Testament* (Downers Grove, IL: IVP Academic, 2020), 476.

wilderness, provide a glimpse into John's view of salvation—that believers will participate in a new exodus to a better place.

The undoing of the seventh seal causes "silence in heaven" (Rev. 8:1). Before the altar of God, an angel offers incense with the prayers of the saints (8:3–4). The angel then takes the incense burner and hurls it to the earth, where there is thunder, lightning, and an earthquake, symbolizing the anticipation of further judgments (8:5).

Seven Trumpets (8:6–11:19)

John envisions seven angels about to blow seven trumpets (Rev. 8:6). The first angel blows his trumpet and "there came hail and fire mixed with blood, and it was hurled down on the earth," burning up a third of the earth, trees, and green grass (8:7). The second angel blows his trumpet and a burning mountain is thrown into the sea, causing a third of the sea to turn into blood, the death of a third of the sea creatures, and the destruction of a third of the ships in the sea (8:8–9). The third angel sounds his trumpet and a blazing star falls from the sky, resulting in a third of the waters becoming deathly bitter (8:10–11). The fourth angel sounds his trumpet and a third of the sun is struck, as well as a third of the moon and the stars, resulting in a third of the day without light and also a third of the night (8:12). The fifth and sixth angels blow their trumpets and destructive locusts and a huge army arrive to torment humanity (9:1–21).

The trumpet judgments recall the exodus tradition, when God tortured the people of Egypt by turning the Nile to blood, bringing death upon animals, raining hail from the sky, releasing destructive locusts to consume plant life, bringing darkness upon the land, and killing the firstborn (Exod. 7–12). The progressive ferocity of the plagues led to Israel's deliverance from Egypt (Exod. 13–14). As the judgments on Egypt resulted in Israel's salvation from oppression, so too will the trumpet judgments turn out for the torture of the wicked and the deliverance of God's people.

There is a delay between the sixth and seventh trumpet blasts. During this interim, John sees an angel "coming down from heaven . . . robed in a cloud, with a rainbow above his head" (Rev. 10:1). The mention of the angel being "robed in a cloud" alludes to Exodus 19:9–19, when God descends on Sinai in a "dense cloud," and Daniel 7:13, when the son of man descends to the earth with the "clouds of heaven."[11] From such allusions, we envision that the

---

11. G. K. Beale and Sean M. McDonough, "Revelation," in *Commentary on the New Testament Use of the Old Testament*, ed. G. K. Beale and D. A. Carson (Grand Rapids: Baker Academic, 2007), 1116.

angel is the divine Son of Man, who is one and the same with Jesus Christ. He is the one who holds a scroll in his hands while straddling the sea and land, symbolizing his coming judgment over the entire earth (Rev. 10:1–7). John also envisions two witnesses, described as "two olive trees" and "two lampstands," who are martyred and resurrected (11:1–14). The imagery of olive trees and lampstands reveals that these figures represent the people in whom God's Spirit dwells—that is, the church (cf. Exod. 25:31–39; Jer. 11:16; Rom. 11; Heb. 9:2). Though they suffer for their witness, God will raise his people from the grave, assuring them of life in the new creation.

When the seventh angel finally blows his trumpet, we see a picture of the consummation of God's kingdom (Rev. 11:15–19). This is the time when the almighty Christ will raise the dead, judge the wicked, and reward the righteous (11:18). The seventh trumpet blast anticipates the more robust picture of judgment in Revelation 20, when those who overcome life in the present age will be raised to dwell in a new creation and the wicked will suffer eternal torment.

Seven Interim Signs (12:1–14:20)

The number seven continues its prominent significance in the book of Revelation, as John now includes seven interim signs between the trumpet and bowl judgments. The first sign is a woman who gives birth to a son who "will rule all the nations with an iron scepter," a quotation from Psalm 2:9 (Rev. 12:5). The quotation reveals that the child is God's very Son, who will rule over the nations of the earth. The second sign is a war in heaven between the archangel Michael and his angels and Satan, who is cast down to the earth (12:7–12). A loud voice from heaven announces that God's people, despite their suffering, have already conquered Satan, the ruler of the present world (12:10–11). The third sign is a battle between Satan and the woman who gave birth to a male child (12:13–17). John uses female imagery, as he does in 2 John, to symbolize the people of God (Rev. 21:2; 2 John 1, 13; cf. Isa. 54:1–8). God protects his people from the power of Satan until the time of their deliverance (Rev. 12:14).

The fourth sign is the worship of a beast that comes out of the sea (Rev. 13:1–10). The beast is the devil's agent, shouting blasphemies, exercising great power and authority over the nations, and persecuting believers (13:2–8). The beast miraculously recovers from a near fatal wound, resulting in the entire earth worshiping the beast (13:3). The entire scene mimics the way the Father gives the Son authority over the nations through his death and resurrection. But God's people must not worship the beast, no matter how miraculous his recovery. His people must patiently endure their present suffering and be faithful to the true king of the world (13:10).

The fifth sign is a beast that comes out of the earth, having "two horns like a lamb" but speaking "like a dragon" (Rev. 13:11). This second beast does miracles so as to convince those on the earth to worship the beast "whose fatal wound had been healed" (13:12–14). He has power to kill those who refuse to honor the first beast and to make people adopt a mark on their foreheads to participate in commerce (13:15–17). The sixth sign is the 144,000—a number symbolic of all the redeemed throughout history—worshiping the Lamb (14:1–5). This is the same group pictured in Revelation 7:4, who had the name of the Lamb and the Father written "on their foreheads" rather than the name of the beast (13:16; 14:1).

Before the seventh sign, Revelation 14:6–11 records a vision of three angels urging the earth's inhabitants to worship the creator God, who will soon execute judgment. The angels announce the fall of Babylon (about which John will expound in Rev. 17–18) and warn of eternal torment for those marked as worshipers of the beast (about which John expounds in Rev. 20). Believers should endure suffering and remain faithful to Jesus so as to receive a future inheritance, where they will rest from their resistance to the beast (14:13).

The seventh sign is the return of the Son of Man to harvest the earth with a sickle, which is another symbol of God's coming wrath (Rev. 14:14–20). The scene warns readers to align themselves with those who worship the Lamb rather than those who will be judged along with the beast.

Seven Bowls (15:1–16:21)

John sees "in heaven another great and marvelous sign: seven angels with the seven last plagues—last, because with them God's wrath is completed" (Rev. 15:1). Those who triumphed over the beast are praising God, singing the song of Moses and of the Lamb (15:2–4). Moses and Israel sang a similar song after having triumphed over Pharaoh and the Egyptians (Exod. 15). The allusion to Exodus 15 allows readers to envision that the victorious ones in Revelation 15 are praising God for their exodus-like victory over the beast. Soon the victorious ones will be delivered into a land far better than Canaan (Rev. 21–22).

The seven angels responsible for the bowl judgments increase the ferocity of God's wrath, pouring out sores on those who worship the beast (Rev. 16:1–2), turning the sea to blood (16:3), changing the rivers and springs to blood because of the shed blood of the saints (16:4–7), scorching people with the sun's intense heat (16:8–9), plunging people into darkness and giving them painful sores (16:10–11), drying up the Euphrates and sending unclean frogs representing unclean spirits (16:12–16), and bringing cataclysmic events that result in the destruction of Babylon (16:17–21). The bowl judgments associated with sores, the seas and rivers turning into blood, the land plunging into darkness, and the appearance of unclean frogs recall the plagues poured out on Egypt (Exod. 7–12). John creatively envisions how the judgments on Egypt serve as "types" of God's coming wrath on the earth.

While some are inclined to read the seals, trumpets, and bowl judgments as cyclical events throughout history, Revelation 16 reveals the escalating nature of the judgments at the conclusion of history.[12] The judgments will continue to intensify in Revelation 17–20.

Judgment on Babylon (17:1–19:21)

After the conclusion of the seals, trumpets, and bowls judgments, John receives a vision of God's judgment on Babylon. The term "Babylon" was not limited to the ancient empire that conquered Jerusalem in 587 BC. Over time, this term became a metaphor for nations who oppressed God's people and enticed them to worship false deities and adopt a godless lifestyle. Scot McKnight puts it well: "Babylon became for Jews and early Christians the most graphic image, metaphor, or trope for a city filled with arrogance, sin, injustice, oppression of God's people, and idolatry."[13] In John's day, the term "Babylon" applied to the Roman Empire. Since then, many nations have followed in the pattern of the ancient empire that oppressed God's people and enticed her with a lifestyle that promoted sin, oppression, luxury, and indulgence. As a result, McKnight is right to argue that "Babylon is a timeless trope."[14]

God will pour out wrath on Babylon for enticing people with evil deeds like sexual immorality and excess wealth (Rev. 18:1–8). He will also judge her for persecuting believers (17:6; 18:2). Babylon will get exactly what she deserves: "death, mourning and famine. She will be consumed by fire, for mighty is the Lord God who judges her" (18:8).

A voice from heaven urges believers, "Come out of her, my people, so that you will not share in her sins, so that you will not receive any of her plagues" (Rev. 18:4). "Coming out of Babylon" is a call to avoid being intertwined

---

12. See discussion in Thomas R. Schreiner, *The King in His Beauty: A Biblical Theology of the Old and New Testaments* (Grand Rapids: Baker Academic, 2013), 622–23.

13. McKnight, *Revelation for the Rest of Us*, 44.

14. McKnight, *Revelation for the Rest of Us*, 47.

LIVING IN BABYLON

Revelation should cause us to examine the ways we have become accustomed to the oppressions and godlessness of our own countries. We should examine how our nations look more like John's description of Babylon than the kingdom of God. We should ask ourselves how we have justified vices that John condemns, like excess luxury and slavery, which testify to our need to "come out" of Babylon. We should examine whether we have become comfortable in nations that Jesus will judge at his second coming. Then we should work to disentangle ourselves—i.e., "come out"—from ungodly practices associated with our present nations that "mark" people as members of Babylon rather than the kingdom of God.

with the oppressions and excess luxuries associated with life in an oppressive empire. John even castigates those who benefit from the slave trade, which profits from the misery exacted on "human beings" (18:13). When we recall that the messages to the seven churches were focused on awakening believers from their spiritual slumber, we understand why John urges readers to disentangle themselves from the ways of Babylon, which include vices like idolatry, sexual immorality, the accumulation of wealth, and participation in the slave trade. Those who refuse to come out of Babylon will be judged along with the beast, false prophet, and all who persecute God's people (18:9–19:21).

Final Resurrection and Judgment (20:1–15)

John's vision of judgment culminates in Revelation 20. First, Satan is bound for a thousand years and is later released for a short period of time (20:1–3). The "binding" of Satan points to his limited ability to exert power over God's people. The earlier allusions to the exodus tradition suggest that John recalls Pharaoh's limited power over Israel: as Pharaoh was not able to hold Israel captive, neither will Satan be able to.[15] Soon God's people will be free to complete the new exodus to a new creation.

John then envisions the dead in Christ rising from the grave to reign for a period of one thousand years (Rev. 20:4–6). At the conclusion of the thousand years, Satan is released to deceive the nations and gather an army for battle against God's people (20:7–9). The devil is then cast into a lake of fire, "where the beast and the false prophet had been thrown" (20:10). All the dead are

15. Beale and McDonough, "Revelation," 1146.

THE MILLENNIUM

Scholars differ on the interpretation of "a thousand years" in Revelation 20:2. Amillennialists argue that the thousand years represent the present reign of Christ over the church. Premillennialists argue that the thousand years are a literal period of Christ's reign between the tribulation and the eternal state. Postmillennialists take the period of one thousand years as a literal or figurative period before the return of Christ and the conversion of the nations.[a] Each option is well within the bounds of Christian orthodoxy.

a. See the helpful discussion in Constantine R. Campbell and Jonathan T. Pennington, *Reading the New Testament as Christian Scripture: A Literary, Canonical, and Theological Survey* (Grand Rapids: Baker Academic, 2020), 377.

raised to stand before God's throne, and "anyone whose name was not found written in the book of life was thrown into the lake of fire" (20:15). The scene recalls Daniel 12:2, where "multitudes who sleep in the dust of the earth will awake: some to everlasting life, others to shame and everlasting contempt" (cf. Ezek. 36–37). Only those "whose name is found written in the book . . . will be delivered" (Dan. 12:1) into the new heavens and earth, about which John expounds in Revelation 21. Those whose names are not recorded "in the book of life" are cast "into the lake of fire" (Rev. 20:15).

A New Heavens and Earth (21:1–22:5)

John sees a vision of "a new heaven and a new earth" (Rev. 21:1), which is the very place Isaiah envisioned centuries before John (Isa. 65–66). This is the renewed creation where God's people will dwell, after the prior heaven and earth have passed away, and is equivalent to the new Jerusalem (Rev. 21:1–5; cf. Isa. 60). All who are faithful to Jesus will inherit the new creation promised to people like Abraham, Isaac, and Jacob (Rev. 21:7). Those whose lives are entangled with the ways of Babylon, like the cowardly, the vile, murderers, and the sexually immoral, will have no portion on the new earth (21:8).

John draws on imagery from Isaiah 60 and Ezekiel 40–48 to describe the new Jerusalem, full of glory and brilliance, as the place where the Lamb will dwell with his people (Rev. 21:9–21). This is the place where God, in all his beauty and splendor, will live with the people whose names have been written in "the Lamb's book of life" (21:22–27). John uses imagery like the "river of the water of life," the "tree of life," and "crops of fruit" to portray the new

Jerusalem as an Edenic paradise (22:1–2). He even mentions that "no longer will there be any curse," meaning that people will return to life in Eden with no serpent to tempt them (22:3). Humanity will live as God intended: "They will reign forever and ever" (22:5).

Epilogue (22:6–21)

All that the Lord revealed to John is true—and is happening soon (Rev. 22:6)! Readers would do well to heed all that John has said so that they will be among those who will dwell in the place God is preparing for his people (22:14). Jesus testifies, "Yes, I am coming soon" (22:20). John responds as a true worshiper: "Amen. Come, Lord Jesus" (22:20).

■ Canonical Function

Revelation has the distinction of being the final book in the canon. Reading Revelation from this position enables readers to tie together the strings of the scriptural narrative. We see how the Jesus of the Gospels returns to establish his kingdom over a renewed earth. We see how the Spirit who arrived in Acts has completed the eschatological renewal of God's people by raising them from the grave. We see how the Jesus Paul desired to preach to the ends of the earth has delivered the nations into the cosmic inheritance promised to Abraham's offspring. We see how the Jesus of the Catholic epistles has returned, judging the wicked and saving his people for an imperishable inheritance. When we consider the entire canonical narrative, we see how Revelation promises that God's people will participate in an exodus journey far greater than the one from Egypt—a new exodus that will culminate when God's people are delivered from the power of sin and into a renewed paradise.

Revelation speaks the final canonical word, assuring believers that the exile from the garden will not last forever. The serpent will be crushed. The curse will be undone. Humanity will return to Eden. Readers should maintain their faithfulness to Jesus Christ, despite all the enticements of Babylon, so they can dwell in the place where all things will again be "good."

■ Authorship, Dating, and Audience

The author identifies himself as "John, your brother and companion in the suffering and kingdom and patient endurance that are ours in Jesus" (Rev. 1:9).

This is the same John who composed the Gospel of John and the Johannine epistles—the beloved disciple and apostle John. What he composes no longer relies on his eyewitness testimony of the historical Jesus, as do his Gospel and letters. It is based on a vision of events related to the return of the one he once saw and touched (1 John 1:1–5; Rev. 1:1). Early authors like Justin Martyr (*Dialogue with Trypho* 81) and Irenaeus (*Against Heresies* 4.20.11) argue that the apostle John is the author of Revelation.[16] There is little reason to doubt that the beloved disciple and apostle John composed Revelation.

John composed Revelation after writing his Gospel and letters, somewhere at the conclusion of the first century. An acceptable date range would be anywhere in the AD 90s, while John was on the island of Patmos (Rev. 1:9). John originally addressed the book to the seven churches in the province of Asia, an audience that had become too comfortable with life in Rome, while also intending the letter for all Christians throughout the empire (1:4). The inclusion of Revelation as the final book in the New Testament testifies to its abiding authority for all believers throughout history.

SUGGESTED RESOURCES

Bauckham, Richard. *The Theology of the Book of Revelation*. New Testament Theology. Cambridge: Cambridge University Press, 2005.

Blaising, Craig A., Kenneth L. Gentry Jr., and Robert R. Strimple. *Three Views on the Millennium and Beyond*. Counterpoints: Exploring Theology. Grand Rapids: Zondervan, 1999.

Collins, Adela Yarbro. *Crisis and Catharsis: The Power of the Apocalypse*. Philadelphia: Westminster, 1984.

Gentry, Kenneth L., Sam Hamstra Jr., C. Marvin Pate, and Robert L. Thomas. *Four Views on the Book of Revelation*. Counterpoints: Exploring Theology. Grand Rapids: Zondervan, 1998.

McKnight, Scot, with Cody Matchett. *Revelation for the Rest of Us: A Prophetic Call to Follow Jesus as a Dissident Disciple*. Grand Rapids: Zondervan, 2023.

Schreiner, Thomas R. *The Joy of Hearing: A Theology of the Book of Revelation*. Wheaton: Crossway, 2021.

16. Leon Morris, *Revelation: An Introduction and Commentary*, rev. ed., Tyndale New Testament Commentaries 20 (Grand Rapids: Eerdmans, 1987), 28.

THE RELATIONSHIP
BETWEEN THE GOSPELS

Readers of the Gospels will recognize the glaring similarities and remarkable differences among Matthew, Mark, Luke, and John. The most glaring similarities are among Matthew, Mark, and Luke. Scholars label these writings the Synoptic Gospels and argue that their similarities are due to their dependence on written sources. The attempt to discern shared sources behind the Synoptics is called the "Synoptic problem."

We will briefly survey the attempts to solve the Synoptic problem. Then we will review the relationship of the Synoptics to the Gospel of John. Before doing so, we must acknowledge that the church has preserved the final form of the Gospels, not the written sources behind them. Discussions about sources endeavor to arrive at how the Gospels were composed and do not negate the authority of the canonical Gospels of Matthew, Mark, Luke, and John.

The Synoptic Problem

Roughly 93 percent of the content in Mark's Gospel appears in Matthew and Luke. The overlap is evident in similar content, parallels in sentence and word order, and analogous words.[1] For instance, Matthew 19:13–14, Mark 10:13–14,

---

1. Gary M. Burge, *Interpreting the Gospel of John: A Practical Guide*, 2nd ed. (Grand Rapids: Baker Academic, 2013), 23.

and Luke 18:15–16 record people bringing little children to Jesus.[2] These accounts are more or less the same in content, narrative flow, and wording. One of the obvious differences is Matthew saying that "the kingdom of heaven belongs to such as these" (Matt. 19:14), whereas Mark and Luke say that "the kingdom of God belongs to such as these" (Mark 10:14; Luke 18:16). Other Synoptic Gospel accounts exhibit divergences from the Old Testament, like when Matthew 3:3, Mark 1:2–3, and Luke 3:4 quote the Septuagint version of Isaiah 40:3 and alter the last sentence from "make straight paths for our God" to "make straight paths for him." It is unlikely that this change is coincidental. It is more likely that the Gospel authors copied from a common source.

Four proposed solutions to the Synoptic problem are Matthean priority, the two-source theory, the four-source theory, and the Farrer hypothesis.

■ Matthean Priority

Matthean priority has its roots in the venerable Augustine of Hippo, who argues that Matthew was the first to compose a Gospel, followed by Mark and Luke. Augustine explains the agreements among the Synoptics by arguing that Mark used Matthew as his source, and Luke used both Mark and Matthew. Others have adopted a form of Matthean priority as an attempt to solve the Synoptic problem, even if they disagree on the dating of Mark and Luke. William Farmer was a prominent twentieth-century proponent of Matthean priority.[3] Today, very few scholars defend this solution to the Synoptic problem.

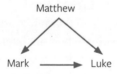

■ Two-Source Theory

Two-source theory proponents argue that Mark was the first to compose a Gospel (what scholars call Markan priority). Where Matthew and Luke

---

2. I draw the examples in this paragraph from Mark L. Strauss, *Four Portraits, One Jesus: A Survey of Jesus and the Gospels* (Grand Rapids: Zondervan, 2007), 44–63.

3. William R. Farmer, *The Synoptic Problem: A Critical Analysis* (New York: Macmillan, 1964).

agree with each other, they borrow from the earlier Gospel of Mark. Where Matthew and Luke agree with each other but not with Mark, they borrow from an early source called Q, which contained early sayings, discourses, and parables of Jesus (minus the passion narrative). The letter Q is an abbreviation of the German word *Quelle* ("source"). Most scholars prefer the two-source theory over other solutions to the Synoptic problem.

Four-Source Theory

The four-source theory elaborates on the two-source theory. B. H. Streeter initially proposed this theory to account for the unique material in Matthew and Luke.[4] While holding to the priority of Mark and the use of Q, Streeter argues that Matthew's unique material comes from document M, which contained parables like the hidden treasure and the pearl of great price, and that Luke's unique material comes from document L, which contained parables like the good Samaritan, the lost sheep, and the prodigal son. The four-source theory, which attributes all the content in the Gospels to written sources and eliminates the unique contributions of the Evangelists, has not attracted many proponents.

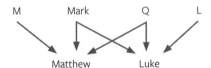

Farrer Hypothesis

The Farrer hypothesis is named after the British scholar Austin Farrer, who proposed a solution to the Synoptic problem based on Markan priority but without the existence of Q. Farrer argues that Luke borrows from the earlier

---

4. Burnett Hillman Streeter, *The Four Gospels: A Study of Origins, Treating of the Manuscript Tradition, Sources, Authorship, & Dates* (London: Macmillan, 1951).

Gospels of Matthew and Mark. Where Matthew and Luke agree with each other against Mark, Luke borrows from Matthew. In recent years, the Farrer hypothesis has increased in popularity because it explains the exclusive agreements between Matthew and Luke without requiring the reconstruction of a hypothetical source.

Likely Solutions

The two most likely solutions to the Synoptic problem are the two-source theory and the Farrer hypothesis. First, Matthew and Luke were more likely to have added material to the shorter Gospel of Mark. It is unlikely that Mark, as Matthean priority proponents assume, would have omitted accounts such as the virgin birth and resurrection appearances. Second, reliance on sources for all the content in the Gospels, as proposed by four-source proponents, eliminates the authorial creativity of Matthew and Luke.

The choice between the two-source theory and the Farrer hypothesis depends on how comfortable one is with the hypothetical source Q. If one has no trouble with Q, then the two-source theory is a viable solution to the Synoptic problem. If one would rather rely on hard evidence, then the Farrer hypothesis is the preferable solution.

John and the Synoptics

John authored his Gospel in the AD 80s, about two decades after the composition of the Synoptic Gospels. Approximately 8 percent of John's Gospel overlaps with the material in the earlier Synoptic Gospels.[5] While agreeing that they share little material in common, scholars disagree on John's relationship to the Synoptics. Some argue that John writes independently of Matthew, Mark, and Luke. Others claim that John uses the Synoptics—or is at least aware of their presentations of the historical Jesus.

5. Andreas J. Köstenberger, *A Theology of John's Gospel and Letters: The Word, the Christ, the Son of God*, Biblical Theology of the New Testament (Grand Rapids: Zondervan, 2009), 553.

John was an eyewitness to many of the events recorded in the Gospels. He would have recalled such events within the context of the narrative of the life of Jesus. John was also one of the pillar apostles in Jerusalem (Gal. 2:9). So he likely had access to the Gospels of Matthew, Mark, and Luke or, at the least, been privy to their presentations of the historical Jesus. Being an eyewitness to the life of Jesus and aware of the content of the Gospels, John composed a Gospel that did not slavishly copy the others. John's Jesus was present in the Genesis creation account. His Jesus performed seven identity-revealing signs, culminating in the resurrection of Lazarus. His Jesus spent extensive time preparing his followers for his departure, promising to send his Spirit to be with them until his return. John's Jesus also confirmed his resurrection to doubting followers like Thomas and reaffirmed the ministry of Peter. The Gospel of John even closes with an affirmation of the trustworthiness of the canonical accounts about Jesus (John 21:24–25). Composing a Gospel that complements the others would have been nearly impossible without access to the Synoptic Gospel tradition.[6]

Summary

The Synoptic Gospels and John present complementary pictures of the historical Jesus. The similar portrait of Jesus in the Synoptics depends on the one painted by the early Gospel of Mark. Matthew and Luke draw from Mark's reliable account. Where their agreements do not line up with Mark, they draw their material from a common source. While John's Gospel is different from the Synoptics, John is aware of the content of Matthew, Mark, and Luke and composes a Gospel that does not slavishly replicate their contents, presenting a Jesus whose signs reveal that he is one and the same with the creator and redeemer of the cosmos.

SUGGESTED RESOURCES

Black, David Alan, and David R. Beck, eds. *Rethinking the Synoptic Problem.* Grand Rapids: Baker Academic, 2001.

Burge, Gary M. *Interpreting the Gospel of John: A Practical Guide.* 2nd ed. Grand Rapids: Baker Academic, 2013.

6. Köstenberger, *Theology of John's Gospel and Letters*, 555–63.

Gardner-Smith, P. *Saint John and the Synoptics*. Cambridge: Cambridge University Press, 1938.

Porter, Stanley E., and Bryan R. Dyer, eds. *The Synoptic Problem: Four Views*. Grand Rapids: Baker Academic, 2016.

Stein, Robert H. *The Synoptic Problem: An Introduction*. Grand Rapids: Baker, 1987.

APPENDIX 2

THE TEXT OF THE NEW TESTAMENT

The text of the New Testament did not float down to the earth on a cushy angelic pillow. Although we do not have the original autographs, we do have a centuries' long textual tradition of manuscripts that testify to the contents of the twenty-seven books of the New Testament, which were originally written in Greek. Scholars have used textual criticism to analyze ancient manuscripts to determine the content of the original writings, resulting in various standardized editions of the Greek New Testament. We will review such matters as they relate to the establishment of the modern text.

New Testament Manuscripts

The conquests of Alexander the Great (336–326 BC) were responsible for spreading the Greek language throughout much of the known world. As the language spread, it morphed into what some scholars call Hellenistic Greek, which is the form of Greek common to the period 300 BC to AD 330. The language so permeated the ancient world that it even became the preferred language of many Jews, resulting in the need for a Greek translation of the Old Testament. "Septuagint" is the name given to the various translations and recensions of the Greek Old Testament produced between the third and first centuries BC.

During the initial centuries of Christianity, the Septuagint was the version of the Old Testament used in Christian churches. When apostles like John, Paul, and Peter composed their new covenant writings, they naturally wrote in the Greek language, for it was common to their audiences. As their writings were collected, they were eventually organized into codices—ancient books—that included both the Septuagint and the New Testament.

Some witnesses to the New Testament are papyri, many of which survive only as fragments. Some important papyri are Papyrus 46 ($\mathfrak{P}^{46}$, ca. AD 175–225), which includes ten Pauline epistles, and Papyrus 52 ($\mathfrak{P}^{52}$, ca. AD 100–150), which contains portions of John 18:31–33 and 18:37–38. Other Greek manuscripts survive as entire codices, which sometimes do not contain specific pages or entire books that have been lost over the years. Some important Greek codices are Sinaiticus (‎א) and Vaticanus (B), which are from the fourth century, and Ephraemi Rescriptus (C) and Alexandrinus (A), which are from the fifth century. Today, we have over fifty-seven hundred available Greek manuscripts.

Other important witnesses to the New Testament are (1) ancient translations in languages like Latin, Syriac, and Coptic, (2) patristic quotations from the works of early church fathers, such as Cyprian and Origen, and (3) lectionaries used in Christian worship. All in all, we have a plethora of witnesses to the text of the New Testament.

■ Textual Criticism

Textual criticism is the process of examining the abundance of witnesses to the New Testament to determine the wording of the original autographs. One traditional approach to textual criticism is reasoned eclecticism, which divides the evidence into external and internal criteria.

External criteria are the age, quantity, and family origin of the manuscripts. Manuscripts have typically been grouped into Alexandrian, Western, and Byzantine families. Priority is normally given to the Alexandrian tradition, which is viewed as having more control over the scribal production of texts.

Internal criteria focus on how well a reading fits the context of an author's writing. Shorter, more difficult readings are preferred over longer ones, since scribes were more likely to add words than to remove them. Scholars also give preference to readings that explain the origin of others.

A text critic who follows a reasoned eclecticism approach weighs the external and internal criteria to determine the original wording of the New Testament.

A more recent approach to textual criticism is called the Coherence-Based Genealogical Method (CBGM). Tommy Wasserman and Peter J. Gurry summarize the approach as a "method that (1) uses a set of computer tools (2) based on a new way of relating manuscript texts that is (3) designed to help us understand the origin and history of the New Testament text."[1] The computer tools are available online and allow critics to view "coherence" between textual witnesses to see how they are related to one another. This view dispenses with the traditional grouping of manuscripts into text-type families. The only exception is the Byzantine text type because of "the remarkable agreement one finds in our late Byzantine manuscripts."[2] The ultimate goal of the CBGM method is to "reconstruct, not the original text," but a "starting point" or an "initial text" from which others arise.[3] This approach to textual criticism has already led to changes in the text of the Catholic epistles in standard editions of the Greek New Testament.

Standard Editions of the Greek New Testament

Scholars use manuscript evidence to produce standard editions of the Greek New Testament. In 1516, Erasmus relied on only seven Greek manuscripts from the Byzantine era to produce what would come to be known as the *Textus Receptus* ("received text"), which includes readings like the longer ending of Mark and John's account of the woman caught in adultery. The King James translation was based on Erasmus's *Textus Receptus*. Compilers of later Greek New Testament editions, like Johann Albrecht Bengal (1734), Johann Jakob Griesbach (1774–75), Constantin von Tischendorf (1849), and Brooke Foss Wescott and Fenton John Anthony Hort (1881), had access to an increasingly larger number of witnesses. Modern editions like the Nestle-Aland and the United Bible Societies (UBS) versions have gone through various revisions based on a dramatic increase in the number of available manuscripts and revisions to the practice of textual criticism. The Nestle-Aland text has undergone twenty-eight revisions, and the UBS has undergone five. Our modern translations are based on standard editions of the Greek New Testament, for which translators had more access to earlier reliable witnesses like Sinaiticus (ℵ) and Vaticanus (B) than did the translators of older translations like the King James Version.

---

1. Tommy Wasserman and Peter J. Gurry, *A New Approach to Textual Criticism: An Introduction to the Coherence-Based Genealogical Method* (Atlanta: SBL Press, 2017), 3.
2. Wasserman and Gurry, *New Approach to Textual Criticism*, 9.
3. Wasserman and Gurry, *New Approach to Textual Criticism*, 11–12.

■ Summary

The modern text of the New Testament is the product of thousands of textual witnesses to the words of apostles like John, Peter, Paul, and James. By analyzing an abundance of manuscripts, ancient translations, patristic quotations, and lectionaries, scholars strive to determine the words of the New Testament text. The result is standard editions of the Greek New Testament sourced in textual evidence unavailable to earlier scholars like Erasmus and Tischendorf. From such modern editions of the Greek New Testament, scholars compose modern translations in an increasing number of languages around the world.

SUGGESTED RESOURCES

Aland, Kurt, and Barbara Aland. *The Text of the New Testament: An Introduction to the Critical Editions and to the Theory and Practice of Modern Textual Criticism.* Translated by Erroll F. Rhodes. Grand Rapids: Eerdmans, 1995.

Anderson, Amy, and Wendy Widder. *Textual Criticism of the Bible.* Bellingham, WA: Lexham, 2018.

Hixson, Elijah, and Peter J. Gurry, eds. *Myths and Mistakes in New Testament Textual Criticism.* Downers Grove, IL: InterVarsity, 2019.

Metzger, Bruce M., and Bart D. Ehrman. *The Text of the New Testament: Its Transmission, Corruption, and Restoration.* Oxford: Oxford University Press, 2005.

Porter, Stanley E. *How We Got the New Testament: Text, Transmission, and Translation.* Acadia Studies in Bible and Theology. Grand Rapids: Baker Academic, 2013.

Wasserman, Tommy, and Peter J. Gurry. *A New Approach to Textual Criticism: An Introduction to the Coherence-Based Genealogical Method.* Atlanta: SBL Press, 2017.

SCRIPTURE AND ANCIENT WRITINGS INDEX

SUBJECT INDEX

Note: Books of the Bible appear in the subject index in alphabetical order. These entries point only to substantive discussions. "OT" and "NT" refer to Old and New Testaments, respectively.